PLANNING A LIFE IN MEDICINE

DISCOVER IF A MEDICAL CAREER IS RIGHT FOR YOU AND LEARN HOW TO MAKE IT HAPPEN

The Princeton Review

PLANNING A LIFE IN MEDICINE

Discover If a Medical Career is Right for You and Learn How to Make it Happen

John Smart, M.S.

Stephen L. Nelson Jr., M.D. Ph.D.

and Julie Doherty

Illustrated By Cris Dornaus

Random House, Inc.
New York
www.PrincetonReview.com

Princeton Review Publishing, L.L.C.
2315 Broadway
New York, NY 10024
E-mail: bookeditor@review.com

ISBN: 0-375-76460-7

Editorial Director: Robert Franek
Production Editor: Christine LaRubio
Production Manager: Scott Harris
Editor: Erik Olson

Manufactured in the United States of America.

9 8 7 6 5 4 3 2

2005 Edition

This book is dedicated to my best friend and inspiration,

Beatrice Lyyli Smart, my mother.

J.S.

CONTENTS

INTRODUCTION

THE PATH OF HEART

Life is a journey, not a destination. You can choose a worthy and challenging goal, but real life happens to you in the long stretches of living between the realization of your noble plans; it happens in the hourly effort you make, the daily direction you take, and how you treat yourself and others in the process. Troy Gardner, a philosopher and friend of mine, likes to say: "How you live your seconds, is how you live your days, is how you live your life." That about sums it up.

If you believe your path is in medicine, you are committing to a lifelong climb. The ascent into the field is steep and demanding, requiring spirit, motivation, commitment, and a lot of stamina. Once you've made it through the first gate, you'll find another always ahead. Arrival at full medical practice requires at least a ten-year journey from the beginning of your premedical years. Yet the most significant thing about that destination: it marks a new beginning in your journey. You will face a long tradition of rules and proper conduct, one that pushes you to think of and act with great responsibility for the well-being of others. The medical terrain is often rocky and constantly changing, requiring you to be open-minded, confident, and talented in a number of areas.

But what heights you will reach! Your ability to help other human beings, to deeply impact their lives, will grow powerfully on your journey, both as your experience grows and as awesome and surprising new scientific advances move from the lab to the bedside at ever higher rates each year for the rest of your life. You will see a constantly expanding and partly unmapped future ahead, shaped by avalanches of new medical information that you will carefully navigate, for the benefit of the growing number of people who depend on you.

During your premedical education and initial medical training over the next ten years, you will be challenged ethically, emotionally, intellectually, and physically. You will have to work hard, think quickly, plan ahead, use skills and reasoning, and sometimes, make miracles happen. And yet, when they come, these miracles are at the heart of everything you will do as a doctor. Every year, medicine develops increasingly powerful therapies and treatments. As a physician, you will have the opportunity to deeply touch and, at times, save the lives of your patients. You will be an intimate part of many difficult, wonderful, and life-changing experiences. You will see children being born, a heart beating inside of a living body, people living with terminal illnesses, and people dying. Are you ready to take this journey? Is there a place for you in medicine? As Dr. Steve Nelson says, you must accept that you will never reach a point where your medical training ends, where you can say that you "made it." Medical school is not about making you a doctor as much as it is about developing lifelong habits of learning and hard work, which are much more important at the start of internship than any knowledge you learned from a book. Medical school is the start of a wonderful, rewarding, lifelong journey that will consume your life, demand your passion, make you want to quit at times, expose you to both the wonders and horrors that all people are capable of, and if you are willing, it will give you a greater purpose than any other occupation ever could.

Becoming a physician is, in many ways, the ultimate professional challenge in our society. By choosing to be a premedical student, you are entering the realm of the most demanding, life-changing, and for many, inspiring profession on the planet. So you are wise to approach this challenge by reading this book—it shows thoughtfulness and foresight on your part. The good news is that it is not a challenge reserved only for natural climbers, and it is not a solo effort. There will be guides and coaches aplenty who will make your life tremendously easier if you allow them to do so. Becoming a physician is about learning the skills and scaling the peaks necessary to climb with the team. If you love science and medicine, enjoy working with people, can humbly take direction and correction, and are capable of planning ahead, you can become a doctor. The most important thing is that you be willing to persist in finding your place over the long term.

You must be willing to reflect, work hard, make plans and back-up plans, and apply to medical school more than once, if necessary. You will face several years of difficult preparation to get through the first big gate, your acceptance to medical school. But if you have persistence, confidence in yourself, and the abilities listed above, you will eventually succeed. We have written this book not only to aid your success, but also to help you find a path to medical success that you love, one that you are happy to walk every day, one that has the kind of ideals you aspire to embody. Not simply a path, but your path of heart.

The path of heart is the path that will excite, ennoble, and inspire you throughout your lifetime. Students on this path are both passionate and aware of how little they really know in the great field of medicine. They aren't solely focused on being accepted to medical school. Instead, they maintain perspective and balance while approaching the many challenges that must be overcome on the way to becoming a doctor. They delight in learning and persist in studying, even when the path grows steep. They take the time to form relationships with other people in the field and to strengthen their friendships, though they may have to make sacrifices to do so, and they choose quality over quantity, particularly in the early years of their training. If it takes more than one admission cycle to get into medical school, they aren't distraught. They stay on the path, continuing to do the little things every day of their journey that will make them a better candidate and ultimately, a better physician.

The alternative to following the path of heart is to take shortcuts, to cheat, to give only the minimum necessary requirements, to lose your perspective and your spirit, to take on more than you can capably do, to succumb to excessive perfectionism and constant stress. The result will be disappointment, self-abuse, cynicism, negativity, or depression. Without a deep desire to do what you are doing and the respect for yourself to do it with dignity, feeling, and honor, it will be difficult to succeed in the long years ahead. Those who manage to simply muscle, luck, or cheat their way into medical school (and there indeed are some who do every year) end up "bummed out in wonderland," unable to enjoy the amazing opportunity they have been given.

The path of heart is focused and self-aware. It minimizes competitiveness and hurry. It perseveres, and is always seeking balance. It is engaged, not isolated. It sees the long term but works in the short term. It is patient, reflective, and compassionate. If you seek to improve yourself with every passing day, if you believe in what you are doing, and have the courage to pursue your dreams, then you will find your path of heart.

WHO SHOULD READ THIS BOOK

If you have picked up this book, you are probably considering a career in medicine. In fact, you probably already know that you want to be a doctor. Maybe you are a **high school student** preparing for college, curious about what it takes to get into medical school. Maybe you are a **premedical student,** somewhere in the medical school admissions process. Or maybe you have recently **graduated from college,** or have been in the work force and are now considering a **career change,** exploring medicine for the first time. No matter who you are or what you are doing right now, this book can help you envision your journey and scout out your own personal, successful path to medical school.

Perhaps the ideal reader is a **mature high school senior or college freshman or sophomore,** just setting out on their premedical journey and resolving to reconnoiter and prioritize the terrain ahead. Yet at the same time, within the two covers of this book we provide advice (Chapter 10) for another group very dear to our hearts, one that can really benefit from good counseling: **older and nontraditional students.** The truth is, no matter where you are on your path to becoming a physician, you will find some valuable life insights here that have come from almost a decade of our collective experience (John and Steve's) at Hyperlearning/The Princeton Review in California, assisting thousands of premedical students through a major rite of passage: getting accepted to medical school.

Looking out over the soaring mountains and breathtaking vistas of the medical field, you may be tempted to set out immediately, forging a trail with machete and headlamp, forgoing maps or compass. Yet if you want to climb far, preparation, pacing, and professional assistance are all essential to your success.

We encourage you to make notes in the margins as you read this book. Skim where familiar, but try not to skip. Be an active reader: write questions, make lists, and come back and think about them again. If you have already brought home *Planning a Life in Medicine*, you've signed us on as members of your premedical advising team. We take that job seriously, so let's begin thinking about what you need to do.

As you read this book, imagine yourself the step of the journey we describe. Picture in your mind's eye every challenging thing you must do to become a physician and try to imagine the interesting rewards and experiences that will come after you have been admitted to medical school. Let those visualizations motivate you to make the daily sacrifices today that will take you ever higher up the mountain. See the path ahead through your pre-clinical years, to your clinical rotations, to your boards, to your internship, to your residency, all the way to becoming a practicing, passionate physician. If that is your path, you can learn to climb it well, stopping frequently to smell the roses and enjoy the increasingly amazing view. Remember that getting into medical school is not an endpoint, but rather the first phase in a lifelong journey. The journey begins every day you put another foot forward. Look up. Believe in yourself. Put your heart into the climb, and nothing can stop you.

Res Firma, Mitescere Nescit

"That which is built on a strong foundation, cannot be torn down."

Video Assignments in the Path of Heart:

Some days you might crave inspiration as you travel your path. At the end of each section of this book, we have compiled an important set of movies to treat yourself with after you finish various projects in the months ahead. Consider any one of them a "reward" for a job well done, like completing each section of this book! Take the time to reward yourself regularly throughout your journey.

The first movie on each list has a medical theme, the second two are sports or achievement related. Three movies, times 15 sections, gives 45 great movies to excite and inspire you. Most are dramatizations, but a few, like MD and Survivor MD are true life stories that you should see. All are great for keeping you motivated, so be sure to watch as many of these as you can throughout your premedical career.

Video Assignments for the Introduction:

MD: The Making of a Doctor, *Breaking Away*, and *American Flyers*

CHAPTER 1
THE INWARD SPIRAL AND OTHER TOOLS FOR LIFE

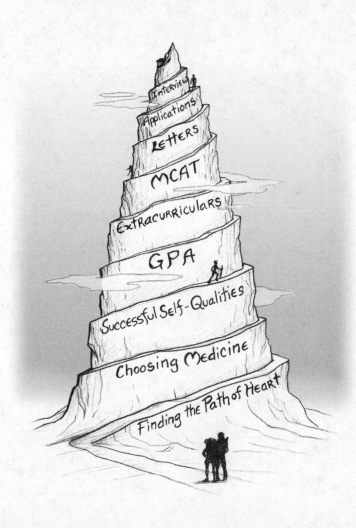

Pursuing a career in medicine takes maturity, courage, commitment, and foresight. The journey is long and arduous, and there are many obstacles along the way. As a medical student, intern, resident, and doctor, in addition to great rewards, you will face a slew of unique difficulties that will occasionally test you and your commitment to the field. What tools and skills will you need to succeed? Who will be your sources of support? How can you best prepare for a lifetime of learning and challenge?

The most important qualities come from within. To get into

medical school, you must begin with drive, determination, and a sincere desire to become a doctor. Once you have made a commitment to become a doctor, you will need some good maps of the terrain, like the ones this book provides, to manage the many tests you'll encounter in your undergraduate years. But you will also need to seek the help of an extended team, such as a few dependable premed climbing buddies, professors, advisors, and mentors, and other books and resources that speak to your heart.

Listed in this chapter are certain study skills and personal tools that will help you on the climb and to deal well with the occasional defeat that happens in this difficult, rarefied terrain, so that you can quickly pick yourself up, dust off, and try again. You will need to recover from falls quickly and fully, without self-pity, anxiety, jealousy, or any other psychological traps. You will learn to

maintain a dancer's balance and to pick paths that aren't too far outside your abilities, so that your mistakes will be small and easily remedied. You'll also need stamina throughout the ascent. Staying in motion, with brief rests as needed also helps; there's nothing like keeping active to keep your attention on the course ahead. Most importantly, you will need to find a strong sense of purpose in your preparation, education,

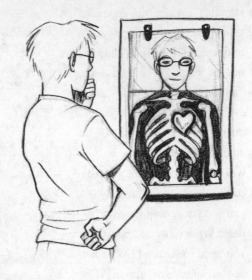

and career. Why is it important for you, particularly, to succeed at this quest? A greater purpose will help you stay focused on present challenges while maintaining an awareness of the bigger picture. When you know in your heart why medicine is right for you, and what unique contribution you intend to bring to the profession, nothing can stop you from achieving success. It is a very exciting and transforming journey that you are about to begin.

THE INWARD SPIRAL

Let's begin with one of the most basic tools necessary for any extended journey. The inward spiral is a process of observation and reflection that each of us uses, either consciously or unconsciously, either well or poorly, as we negotiate a complex world. We want you to use it consciously, to use it well, and to use it as frequently and precisely as you need to get the job done. It involves two parallel processes, both understanding your world and understanding yourself, at first in broad, general terms, and later in very deep and specific ways. **Inward spiral thinking** begins by giving yourself time, place, and permission to generate a long list of ideas and possibilities for your future, and then slowly narrowing your focus to a few options that you recognize to be strong fits with your own particular skills, sensibilities,

goals, emotions, and intellect. What is health care really like? Who are you and who do you want to be? How long will it take you to become who you want to be? Is medicine really for you? If so, what will be your unique path into medical school and your passionate and personal contribution as a doctor? The inward spiral is a tool that can help you answer these questions as you learn about medicine, understand yourself, and start the journey down your path of heart.

Specifically, we'll consider four tightening cycles: **exploring options**, **narrowing down**, **reconnaissance**, and **picking a path**. As you read each, envision yourself in that process. You can spend too little time on any cycle (a common mistake) or too much on one because you are scared to move to the next stage. But the biggest mistake is to *ignore* the cycles altogether. Ask yourself whether you've completed each of these processes at the level your own "well-lived life" demands. Remember, you are only a premedical student once. Wake up to the special nature of your time and place on this planet. You are very unlikely to get another chance to take the journey you are on today. It is sometimes said that "true freedom is knowing all your options," so get to know them well before you choose.

CYCLE ONE: EXPLORATION

The more you know about the rough layout of the terrain, the better you can plan for your particular climb. Being a doctor sounds great, but how well do you understand the field? As a premed, you will become an authority of sorts on a range of medical issues with your family and friends. It is your responsibility now to set aside regular time to research medicine and to learn about the various general and specialty practices available within health care.

Medical schools are not just looking for accomplished students, but rather students who have also made a strong, specific, heart-felt commitment to helping others in their extracurricular affairs. While understanding medicine is not a formal requirement of admission to any medical school, throughout the admissions process you will be tested in many small ways on your basic knowledge of and dedication to the field. Do you have a first-hand understanding of a physician's job? If not, you need a plan to help you get that experience, starting now.

Evaluating Medical Specialties:
THREE GOOD BOOKS

Life After Medical School: 32 Doctors Describe Their Careers, Leonard Laster, MD, © 1996

Our Medical Future: Breakthroughs in Health & Longevity by 2000 & Beyond, J. Fisher, MD, © 1993

How to Choose a Medical Specialty, 4th Ed, Anita Taylor, © 2003

More importantly, learning more about medicine will help you define your goals and enable you to envision your future as a physician. When you are cramming for a biology final or preparing for the MCAT, good grades and high scores aren't sufficient motivation for you to succeed. What are the real, deeper reasons you are doing what you are doing? If you can't answer this question yet, then you need to *find your vision*.

Countless resources are available at your local university. Schedule a fixed amount of time each week or month to take advantage of them. When you realize how little time you actually have available in your busy premedical schedule to research medicine, spending three hours to discover something truly valuable to you becomes a fascinating challenge, one that competes daily with all your other responsibilities, whether you are aware of this or not. Begin by visiting the health sciences library at the nearest university. Ask for instruction in how to use the reference resources, and learn how to locate various books, periodicals, and articles about medicine.

If your are not already skilled in the use of reference materials and research facilities (many students aren't, even after spending years and tens of thousands of dollars on tuition), most college and university libraries offer free classes on a frequent basis. Sit in on a class. Get to know the reference librarians, and bring them interesting questions to be answered. For example, what skills do admissions officers think premedical students are the most lacking in? See *Academic Medicine*. Where can you find the annual salaries of various types of physicians? See *Journal of Medical Economics*.

In the beginning, you may want to flip through general medical reference books, writing down the names of fields that catch your eye. Does something sound interesting that you don't know anything about? Jot it down and keep exploring. You can discuss curious words and phrases with an expert (medical librarian, physician, professor) later and learn a tremendous amount of information in one conversation. Skim the major newspaper indices to see which articles on medical practice or research sound interesting to you. Browse CD-ROMs, electronic databases (Medline, Digital Library, National Library of Medicine Gateway), and the Internet (Google is your friend!).

Persist in reading about topics until you have reached some tentative understanding. If you keep a **Medical Explorations Journal**, you can occasionally return to old topics to look for more ideas. The second time you look at old notes, your long-term understanding of them will be greatly improved. As you research, notice your reaction to the material. What are you most exited about? Diagnostic advances? New tools or therapies? New areas of patient care? Research programs? Ways to make medicine more efficient and accountable in society? Who are the healers that seem particularly heroic to you? Are you more interested in the inner lives of patients or the details of their treatment? Or both?

Ideally, if most of the medical fields are really still a mystery to you, choose a consistent time that you will devote to research and reflection every week. For example, you may want to go to the library for several consecutive Friday afternoons over the course of a couple of months. Respect this cycle enough to give it plenty of time, and don't expect immediate results.

Also, don't unnecessarily limit yourself at this point. Though it will be tempting to make immediate judgments about the kind of medicine you would like to practice, the less you do this now, the more opportunities you will see as you go forward. Do not let your inner critic object to anything in the medical profession before you have really considered it.

Here is a valuable exercise for the exploration cycle of the inward spiral: make a crude **concept map** of the **health care industry**, starting with the types of physicians you know about. Who are the other major forces and players in the health care sector, besides physicians? See what you can come up with from memory, and add to it as you start your research. See how many different specialties you can mentally name and define, to yourself and to your friends. Which are "specialties" and which are actually "subspecialties?" What is the difference? What are the most popular specialties, and the least popular? Which are specialties that are considered "primary care" medicine? What percentage of doctors work in primary care? What percentage work in specialties? What percentage of MD's work in research, administration, pathology, and other areas with less or even no live patient contact? What other types of allied health professionals practice patient care? A research librarian will help you with such questions, and finding the answers is like learning the geography of a complex and multifaceted new world, one that you will soon inhabit. Knowing the landscape will help you decide the best place for you within it.

Medical Specialties

Here are some of the more common medical specialties. (This is a partial list.) Several of these, such as cardiology, gastroenterology, hematology-oncology, infectious disease, endocrinology, nephrology, and pulmonology are actually <u>subspecialties</u>, accessible only after doing residencies in specialties like internal medicine or pediatrics, followed by the subspecialty fellowship.

Anesthesiology: relief of pain and administration of medication to relieve pain during surgery

Cardiology: diagnosis and non-surgical treatment of disorders of the heart

Dermatology: disorders of the skin

Emergency Medicine: diagnosis and treatment of sudden illness and traumatic injury

Endocrinology: problems with hormones

Family Practice: primary care doctors who diagnose and treat common problems in children and adults

Gastroenterology: diagnosis and treatment of problems of the gastrointestinal system, including the stomach, small intestine, large intestine, gall bladder, and bile duct

Genetics: diagnosis of inherited (genetic) disorders

Gerontology: diagnosis and treatment of ailments of senior citizens

Hematology: blood forming organs and disorders

Immunology: specializes in the reaction of the immune system

Infectious Disease: focus on diseases caused by infectious agents

Internal Medicine: primary care of adults

Nephrology: kidney disorders

Neurology: diagnosis and non-surgical treatment of problems of the nervous system, including the brain, spinal cord, and nerves

Neurosurgery: surgical treatment of disorders of the nervous system

Obstetrics/Gynecology: specializes in the female reproductive system and delivery of babies

Oncology: non-surgical treatment of people with cancer

Ophthalmology: surgical and non-surgical treatment of eye diseases and disorders

Orthopedic Surgery: surgical treatment of disorders or fractures of the skeletal system

Otolaryngology: "Ear, Nose, and Throat" doctor (or ENT for short)

Pathology: studies the causes of disease and death

Pediatrics: primary care doctors specifically for children

Plastic Surgery: surgeons who treat malformations or injuries that affect the appearance of an individual

Psychiatry: prevention, diagnosis, and treatment of mental disorders and substance abuse

Public Health/Preventive Medicine: specializes in disease prevention and health promotion at the population/community level

Pulmonology: disorders of the lungs and breathing physiology

Radiology: specializes in techniques (such as x-ray and MRI) that allow the visualization of structures inside the body

Surgery: specializes in surgical procedures

CYCLE TWO: NARROW DOWN

Once you have assembled many pages of notes about medicine (could you make such an important life decision without really doing this?), you'll start to notice that you are rediscovering a lot of the same basic material. Once you've made your concept map detailed enough, your search will begin to repeat itself. That is a signal that you've reached a good stopping point. It's time to take a closer look at the information you have compiled.

Begin to evaluate your options in the field. Make a list of every medical specialty you have researched that was mildly interesting to you. At this point, the list should be long. Much, much later in your journey, at the end of your fourth year of medical school, you will need to choose a single field (or two in a combination program) to which you can dedicate all your considerable skill and passion. For now, narrow your vision down to as many as you can easily keep in memory over time. In 1956, Harvard psychologist George Miller said this was seven different items, plus or minus two. More recent studies suggest our working memory is actually lower, perhaps only four or five unique items. Try to compare and contrast the specialties you commit to memory as you learn more about them and yourself over your premedical journey.

Eight Good Narrative Exposures to Different Medical Specialties:

My Own Country: A Doctor's Story of a Town and Its People in the Age of AIDS, Abraham Verghese, MD, © 1994 **(Family Practice)**

Emergency Doctor, Edward Ziegler and Lewis Goldfrank, MD, 1987 **(Emergency Medicine)**

Life on the Frontlines of Brain Surgery and Neurological Medicine, David Noonan, © 1989 **(Neurology/Neurosurgery)**

The Transformed Cell, Steven Rosenberg, and John M. Barry, © 1992 **(Experimental Oncology)**

Medical Detectives, Berton Roueche, MD, © 1991 **(Public Health)**

Virus Hunters of the CDC, Joseph McCormick, Susan Fisher-Hoch, Leslie Alan Horvitz © 1996 **(Epidemiology)**

Maternity Ward, Susan Stanley, © 1992 **(Obstetrics/Gynecology)**

Unnatural Death: Confessions of A Medical Examiner, Michael Baden and Judith Hennessee, © 1989 **(Pathology)**

Gifted Hands, Ben Carson, MD, © 1990 **(Surgery)**

It's easy to stop your search early, concluding that "only surgery" or "only neurology" would make you happy. Don't give in to that temptation now, even if others do. Stretch yourself to learn as much as you can about a number of future possibilities, and if one area feels particularly right, that feeling won't go away if it is genuine. The point is, you can't really know that now. There are just too many things you have to discover before you need to make that choice. You will be rotating through a full range of medical career choices during your third and fourth years of medical school. Can you see the compelling reasons that students dedicate themselves to each choice? Will you be able to use your premedical and clinical years to learn to work better with the entire health care community?

Evaluate your favorite choices not only by what your early research tells you, but by looking within yourself: What images and ideas speak most to your heart? What excites you? What would you like to begin doing right after medical school? What about in twenty years? Imagine yourself at the top of each of those fields. Do you like the view? Write a few ambitious, sweeping statements describing your future self. In your envisioned future, what will you do daily, and what will be your grand challenge in that field?

Michelangelo said that great creations are made mostly by careful subtraction. His statue *David*, he said, was patiently waiting inside the marble block, and deciding what marble to remove was the artistic part of his work. Once you have surveyed the medical marble, and carefully subtracted down to a list of fields that speak to your heart, to your vision and passion, you can begin to take more practical issues into consideration: Which types of practice would play to your strengths and which might strengthen your weaknesses? Which of the vision goals you have listed seem most realistically achievable with your precious and limited time? What resources are available to you in each field?

For me the most enjoyable part of medicine happens when a sick patient comes in through the door and nobody knows why the patient feels ill. At this moment the most powerful tool for helping this person is your brain, which you will use to diagnose and treat this person. I have always enjoyed riddles and logic puzzles, and in this puzzle your ability to solve the problem can make the difference between life and death. Emergency medicine and internal medicine offer the most opportunities to face

At first, do this inner work alone when you can. Yes, this *is* work, and for most, the real start of your medical career. As guidance counselors know, if you can't be motivated to do at least some career research on your own time, you risk being too dependent on your environment and the motivations of others to find your own true path. So take time to listen carefully to your quiet inner voice to evaluate how you feel about each idea. Once you have narrowed the list to a sizable number you can keep in memory, begin to discuss these possibilities with friends, family, and mentors. What is their opinion? Do they think you might be good in medicine? What do they see as your strengths? What subjects make your face light up when you talk about them? Answers to these questions are clues to which specialty lies on your path of heart.

CYCLE THREE: RECONNAISSANCE

Now that you have come up with a manageable, but not-too-restrictive list of four or five options, it is time to take action. Go out and learn what each of these medical fields *really* entails.

Perhaps you are interested in being a **pediatrician**. What does a pediatrician's job entail on a daily basis? How do pediatricians care for children who are ill? How do they handle children who do not have health care coverage or whose parents do not speak English? What are other challenges facing a needy child? What percentage of a pediatrician's job is spent in primary care, in surgery, or in preventive medicine? What is the setting like? Do you mind stepping over toys on your way through the waiting

room? Do crying babies instinctively make you irritable and standoffish, or do you enjoy the challenge they represent? To what extent will your nursing and support staff help you in a public clinic? In a private pediatric group? In solo practice? How much time will you spend with kids, and how much time will you spend talking to their parents?

Maybe you are considering **oncology** (cancer medicine). What is it like to work with people who have serious and terminal illnesses? How do doctors explain complicated procedures or recommend high-risk treatments? What are the effects of chemotherapy on a patient's health and psyche? How much time do oncologists spend with patients, in preventive care? In diagnosis? How quickly is medical research improving quality of life and length of life for different types of cancer?

Note that medical specialties have different work hours, different pay scales, different skill requirements, and different post-graduate education requirements. As you research medicine, consider some of the more practical aspects of each field. How much compensation do you feel you need? How many hours are you willing to work, for how long, and with how much oversight on all your decisions? Whom do you want to care for? Where do you want to live?

If you take the time to really learn about a few medical fields that appeal to you, you will learn a vast amount both about yourself and about the industry. Most people find they can quickly identify fields they like and fields they don't like as soon as they step into a real-world environment. But in your time as a premedical student, as well as in your two pre-clinical years in medical school, you will have as many as six more years of abstract academic work before you will be required to set foot in real-world medical environments. Don't wait to be told what your options are; find them out now while you have the time. You will never be told about as many as actually exist, and you will never know what they are like unless you've taken just a little time to experience them. At this point in your explorations, it is even more important to proceed than to plan. Be proactive. Get out and pound the pavement. Any experience, even unplanned, is better than none at all, or the usual one or two limited medical exposures during your undergrad years, a common situation in the premedical community.

Get to Know People in the Field

Look through **medical directories**, **faculty activities directories**, and **local newspaper indices** (under "health" or "medicine") to find interesting people in your area. Call people in the fields that you are most strongly considering. Talk to anyone who can give you insight, such as nurses, secretaries, doctors, and professors. Keep an eye out for potential mentors. Who is friendly? Who likes to talk to students? Come back again to the nicest ones, and form relationships.

Make **site visits** to as many different facilities as you can. Learn what types of skills you need to be a specialist and what it takes to be a great primary care physician. What is the work like? Can you picture yourself in this environment? Who would your patients be? Are there aspects of the job that are utterly unappealing to you? Could you live with those? Are there challenges that could keep you interested in this field over the long term? What do the practitioners tell you about their field? Would they advise you to go into their field today if they were in your position as an interested student?

Most importantly, consider the qualities it takes to excel in your areas of interest. Think about where you are lacking in your own abilities. What will you do between today and the day you submit your medical school application to improve in your weakest areas?

Find a Mentor

Developing a **mentoring relationship** with an older physician or teacher is essential to the young doctor or premedical student. Mentors provide needed advice, support, and wisdom, and serve as an important model of your life in the future. Ideally, they are a significantly older person whose life, accomplishments, and experiences are inspiring to you. Mentors can also help you approach issues that come up during the medical school admissions process. For example, your mentor can give you insight as to how doctors deal with tough ethical dilemmas in the modern health care environment, or help you whittle down the list of medical schools you plan to apply to.

Finding a good mentor can take some time and persistence, but it is worth the effort. Some schools provide lists of faculty who are willing to mentor students, especially for minorities or women, who have fewer role models currently working in the field. But even if you don't have a "cheat sheet," you can find a good mentor by asking around, consulting faculty directories, or talking to helpful people at information desks when you make site visits. Sometimes the parent of one of your friends or classmates may be working in a field that interests you and can make a great mentor. Over the course of your training and career as a doctor, you will find yourself seeking out several informal mentors who will guide and advise you through different stages of the process. So begin now! The earlier you find your first mentor, the better you will become at building a medical mentor network.

Inspiring individuals are often happy to give advice, especially to young, enthusiastic students who want to follow in their footsteps and become a great doctor. Unfortunately, inspiring people are usually surrounded by patients, secretaries, admirers, and others whose demands on their time make them difficult to reach. Don't be discouraged easily. Even if it takes a while to get an appointment with some important potential mentor, continue to persist in a friendly manner. Once you schedule an appointment, go prepared to talk. Be confident. You are on your path of heart and people will respond to your earnestness and sincerity.

Once you have found a mentor with whom you feel comfortable and who is willing to meet with you on a regular basis (often once a quarter or twice a year), try to see the relationship as an interchange between two people at different stages of their careers. When a student really takes his or her mentoring relationship seriously, it can be fulfilling and interesting for both parties involved. When you go to visit your mentor, **bring a small gift**, like flowers, a book, questions, or a copy of an interesting article you have just read, and a topic or two you would like to discuss. Ask your mentor about her life and how she chose medicine. Ask her who her mentors were. Read biographies of those people, when available.

Most importantly, **listen** to your mentor. A mentor is not just someone who will write you a medical school recommendation — though he or she can do that, too. A mentor has years of experience in the field and can help you walk your path of heart. Keep your ears and mind open.

Get Involved

A **medically related volunteer job** can be informative, rewarding, and useful to your overall admissions candidacy. Hands-on experience is the most effective way to build your understanding of a specific field and the health care industry in general. However, you should be selective in choosing how to spend your time. In Chapter Five, we will discuss the best ways to choose an internship or volunteer opportunity. As you make site visits, keep your eyes open for opportunities and ask people about what you might be able to do as a volunteer.

Get a Job

In addition to volunteer work, one of the best ways to learn about the realities of medicine is to work in the field. Jobs abound in the health care industry. Why work in a coffee shop after school when you could be working in an emergency room, gaining real-world experience and admissions points in the process?

You can get an **Emergency Medical Technician (EMT) license**, for example, through a short, simple certification process. Such programs are available at little or no charge at many community colleges. Why not do this over one of your summers as a small but important step down your path of heart? With an EMT license, you can get a job, at least as an initial experience in an emergency ward or in ambulance transport, doing real work in a patient care team. This will give you some first-hand insight into the field and demonstrate your commitment to medicine in your medical school application.

Premed Advisor

Most colleges have a premed advisor who helps students plan their premed curricula, coordinate the application process, research medical schools, and learn more about the realities of health care professions. At many colleges, the premed advisor will also serve as the point person for medical school recommendations.

At small colleges, a premed advisor may more likely take on the role of mentor or advisor; at large universities, premed advisors often have many students to help and don't have much time to devote to each individual student. No matter where you are, don't be surprised if your premed advisor has less time or energy to help than you might expect. Make an appointment to see what type of prescription or insight your advisor can give you, and follow through. If you report back that you have followed their advice in a timely manner, you may get a greater degree of help on the subsequent visit. Finally, don't neglect the small library of resources that they keep in their own office. Often these are the most useful materials available, including those published by the **NAAHP** [National Association of Advisors for the Health Professions]. If you are lucky, you'll be able to read some of those publications during your visit, and add notes to your journal.

Take Some Time Off

You simply may not have had enough time to research medicine or to volunteer in a hospital while you were racing to keep up your undergraduate GPA and to study for the MCAT. With the large number of choices and specialties available to doctors, you may feel that you have only scratched the surface during college and want more real-world experience and insight. Or, you may feel that you need to take more time to learn about yourself before heading off to medical school. Explorations in the inward spiral are as much about getting to know yourself as they are about getting to know medicine.

If you finish college, but feel like you still haven't had the time or experience you need to find your path of heart, seriously consider taking a year or even two off before applying to med school. This advice is rarely taken by those hard-driving premeds that are still not certain they've made the right career choice. It requires facing what for some is a secret fear: Will I remain motivated for medicine if I don't have structure? If not, what else would I do? But once you get to medical school, you'll find that many of the most balanced and self-directing people are those who took time off when they needed it. If you do so, use at least some of this period to work full-time or to volunteer extensively in a medical field. You could also choose to work in something that is not directly medically related, but will teach you about the world, other people or cultures, or allow you to more deeply explore your passions. For example, you could join the Peace Corps, be a teacher, coach a team, or attend language school in a foreign country. But at the same time, test your love of medicine by working at least part of this period in a hospital, clinic, or private practice office.

During your time off, maintain long-term focus on medicine with daily or weekly reading and note-taking, however brief, and continue your explorations in the inward spiral. What have you learned about yourself and the type of career you want? What type of people do you relate to and what type of career is most fulfilling? Who would you like to be and whom do you want to help? Some people take longer than others to decide what they want out of life. A few students know even in high school that they want to be a cardiologist, for example. But most such early resolutions aren't kept, and for good reason; not enough self-knowledge and career knowledge has been gained to make a deeply informed decision. Give yourself the time to make the right choices. In the end, you will be a stronger candidate and a happier doctor if you listen to your passions and find your path of heart.

CYCLE FOUR: PICKING A PATH (OF SPECIALIZATION)

College trains us to be generalists. We want to keep our options open as long as possible, building skills in a variety of areas and be able to make dinner party conversation in every genre, from Britney Spears to Immanuel Kant.

When it comes to medical school application, however, keeping your options open is not the path to success. To gain admission you must be driven, special, talented, and unique. You therefore must take the time in your premedical years to **become well-versed and talented in at least one thing**. It doesn't matter if this skill or expertise has anything to do with medicine: music, language, business, sports, science, politics, anything will do. But you should be able to see and easily explain how excelling in your specialization will make you a better physician. You might specialize in two subject areas if they are strongly complimentary. However, if you think that you can be simultaneously experienced and excellent in more than one or two things while a full-time undergraduate student, you are setting yourself up for disappointment. **Choose one field, or perhaps two if they have useful synergy,** upon which you will focus most of your spare energy and excellence during your premedical years.

If you are a freshman or sophomore following the inward spiral, we advise you to seriously consider gaining special extracurricular experience in one of the areas of medicine on your list. It doesn't matter which one, any of them will do. But once you've made a choice, study it, so that you know its benefits and drawbacks as deeply as its long-term practitioners. This knowledge will give you confidence and easy entry into that field for ongoing extracurricular work.

If you are a junior or in your application year to medical school, look back carefully over the most important specializations (skills, talents, intelligences) you have already developed in your life, and ask yourself what you can do to demonstrate your excellence in them, and how they have made you a better physician candidate. If you don't need to apply to medical school this year, perhaps taking a year off, combined with a specialized medical extracurricular experience, would be just what you need to round out your background before applying.

If you are able to choose a medical specialization early enough, you will be able to use your experience to find out if medicine is a career you can be happy with, not just live with, before you invest the time, effort, money, and heart into medical school preparation and application.

You can't get away from the immense power of specialization, so use it wisely to gain quality experiences early in your college years, in one or two fields, while carefully keeping a small number of alternative options open for your long-term future. Even if you later decide to "specialize in generalism" as a medical practitioner by choosing a career in a primary care field such as family practice, you will quickly find that there is still a special subset of skills and information that you will have to master. Specialization is a fundamental fact of life. An undergraduate medical experience where you really learn a lot about some special area of practice will give you confidence that you can do more of the same, provide a great clinical recommendation for your application, and start you on the road to being an excellent physician. Many students gain medical experience by volunteering in such tried-and-true environments as a local hospital **emergency room**, the **student health clinic**, or a local **free clinic**. Undergraduates cannot practice patient care without a license, so they are potential liabilities to any institution that lets them tag along. But the truth is, just about any physician, nurse, or medical technician, in almost any environment, whether big hospital or private practice, has the ability and authority to do limited teaching and "preceptorship" activities with interested students.

Teaching by **observation** and **apprenticeship** is one of the oldest and most time-honored traditions in medicine. There are tons of meetings going on in hospitals and universities that interested students are allowed to attend if they can find a sponsor. You will likely end up getting most of your clinical extracurricular experience in the setting of a formal volunteer program, and there is absolutely nothing wrong with that, but the reality is you can gain *any* type of medical experience you are interested in, simply by meeting the people involved, being curious, patient, respectful, volunteering to help where needed, and asking questions at the appropriate time.

Studies show that it is impossible to predict whether you will stay with the particular specialty you have chosen to learn about during your premedical years, so don't expect that your undergraduate medical experience will in any way irrevocably place you onto one future path. It is also worth repeating that you will be under no pressure to pick a medical specialty until your fourth year of medical school, so don't feel like you have to have any firm idea about that choice during your admissions process. However, having a few well-articulated possibilities in mind will show the admissions committee that you have some understanding of the profession.

Dr. Steve Nelson, for example, after receiving a PhD in radiation biology, started medical school expecting to specialize in radiology, then carefully considered psychiatry, and ended up choosing pediatrics, based on experiences he had in his third year of medical school. On his residency application, he stated he planned on doing pediatrics infectious disease, then briefly considered adolescent medicine, and ended up doing pediatric neurology, again based on valuable experiences in his second and third years of residency.

Such option-weighing is not at all uncommon, and indicates the flexibility inherent in the medical training process. Steve advises that while it is never wrong to research and gain early experience in any medical areas that interest you, he suggests that you never decide *against* something until you have spent time actually doing it, which will not happen until your third and fourth years in medical school. Moreover, you must also realize that—besides the intellectual aspects of a specialty—different specialties have different work hours and schedules, different salaries, different skills requirements, and different lengths of post-graduate training (internship and residency). You get the picture – plan ahead, but be prepared to re-evaluate your choices throughout the journey.

All this said, admissions committees are always impressed with applicants who have taken the time to **understand and become excellent** in at least one area of extracurricular activity during college, whether that area is medically related or not. How you approach your specialization challenge, the work habits, motivation, self-talk, empathy, and emotional outlook you develop are far more important than the particular challenge at this stage of your education.

Specialization is powerful because it leads to an overall simplifying of behavior. When you specialize, you consistently prioritize one thing over others (this is harder than it sounds) and can devote much of your free time and energy towards becoming really great in that area. Smart students think about the payoffs of specialization throughout their medical education. Why then do **only twenty to thirty percent** of premedical students gain significant extracurricular experience in medicine? One argument is that most students need to explore non-medical experiences to gain breadth. While there is some truth to this statement, it is also true that there is a very wide breadth of types of experience available within medicine itself. At the same time, with reasonable planning, students can do well in school, gain specialized medical experience, *and* still have free time every week for all experiences that college allows.

We have a theory: many premedical students may think that doing medical extracurriculars will require even more of an emotional investment in what is *already* admittedly a difficult and occasionally traumatic journey. They may silently ask themselves: "What if I am not accepted? At least I can say to myself that I didn't dedicate my life to the goal." If you have had such thoughts yourself, we suggest now is the time to ditch them for good. One of your main jobs at this point in life is to become excellent at something, anything, prior to application. Why not seriously consider something in the medical field? Don't worry that you must perform perfectly in a medical extracurricular, either. Just put in the time and learn.

Once you have chosen a path for some specialized work, imagine yourself at the top of the field. Study its leaders. What qualities do they have? What conferences do they attend? Will you start attending them as well? Think about what you will need to do to make a difference. What great things could you accomplish in the course of a career? In a summer? Pick the best, most achievable ideas and prioritize them. As you develop your general skills in many areas during college, bring them all to bear on your chosen area of specialized excellence and experience.

As you start the journey down your path of heart, periodically revisit the process of general exploration and reflection. You should occasionally go back to the beginning of the inward spiral and apply it to the entire arc of your life, as far as you have lived it. Look further out at the world and look deeper within yourself. As you find your interests widening, re-evaluate your choices and continue to research your options. As you proceed, ask yourself: What am I specifically doing to improve myself every day? How do I know I am improving? If you can occasionally watch yourself in this way, you will quickly guide your thoughts and behaviors toward choices that make you into the amazing, caring, and self-reparative person you've always known you can be.

OTHER TOOLS FOR LIFE: CREATING HEALTHY HABITS

With all the requirements and pressures that come along with being a premed, it is important to foster good study habits, organizational skills, and good overall balance in life and work. Assuming you've been blessed with good natural health, motivation, and reasonable intellectual and emotional intelligence, you will probably find that **balance** is the remaining key you will need to reach the pinnacle of your professional aspirations. Great athletes have great balance and flexibility, as do great thinkers, artists, and statesmen, who learn to delicately balance all the most important yet conflicting issues, constituencies, and arguments on any topic. Creating **healthy habits** is one of the most dependable ways to keep your balance.

As an infant, it took you many months to learn to walk. For species that move on two legs like us, walking is "controlled falling," requiring constant balance. Fortunately, you can get so good at this balancing act that it becomes automatic. So it is with walking your path of heart. Learning how to balance your many demands and desires is the key to success in your premedical years. Like walking, this starts with a lot of careful, conscious attention to your balance. Eventually it becomes instinctive, intuitive, and automatic.

Everyone has his own methods of working, studying, achieving, coping with stress, and relaxing.. There are, however some general healthy habits that all premedical students should seriously consider developing. Below are our top recommendations. How many of these are you already doing? Are you doing a mental status check with regard to each of these habits on a regular basis? Highlight those you are currently missing, and see if you can start adding them to your daily routine. It takes two or three repetitions to begin to set a new habit, so get started now, note any progress you make (or fail to make), and don't get discouraged!

MAINTAIN DIRECTION WITH ACTION

Preparing for medical school is a very time-consuming process, requiring a number of years to complete. Whether taking a traditional or nontraditional approach, you will need to accomplish a large number of tasks in an efficient and timely manner. With everything you are expected to do, you will want to learn pragmatism, and unlearn perfectionism. To maintain a high level of efficiency and action, keep the following points in mind:

Think Ahead

The key to good time management is achieved through the habit of frequent "status checks." Remind yourself mentally of your plans and goals. Stop briefly and often to take stock of your future. Where will you be in ten minutes? One hour? One day? One week? One year? Look at your to-do list, look at your small, portable calendar. Make quick mental adjustments, take a short break, then get right back into the flow state. Most people do this kind of future thinking only a few times a day. You need to develop the habit of doing it *several times an hour*. All productivity begins with a habit as surprisingly simple as this.

Organize Your Time

Whenever you stop to see your future, you will have to prioritize. You must learn to make hard choices at these points or you will feel perpetually rushed and overcommitted. Make daily or weekly to-do lists, but realize you will be forced to choose, each day, to do only a small handful of the things on them. Will they be good choices? Will you accomplish your tasks at the best time? Take your planner or PDA (personal digital assistant) wherever you go. Consult your schedule and lists and do your best to stick to them. In your day-to-day routine, set your sights on the short term, and focus on making and keeping commitments.

Use Tools

Nobody can remember everything they need to do and when they need to do it, especially not a premedical student with twenty different potential tasks to complete at any given moment. Your brain needs a little help! So help it out. If you aren't in the habit already, start using organizational tools to help you stay on task and keep up with your commitments. Your organizer should be small enough that you can keep it with you wherever you go, in the outside pocket of your backpack, your wallet, or clipped to your belt or purse (if it is a personal digital assistant). A wide range of organizational tools are available. Try out a variety and see which work for you.

If you are easily distracted, get an inexpensive scheduling watch (like the Casio Data Bank) to remind you of important appointments. Try using scheduling programs, like the calendar in Microsoft Outlook, and see if they help you keep up with weekly tasks. Consider investing in a personal digital assistant, or buy a paper organizer and get in the habit of consulting it often. Hang a wall calendar next to your computer, within easy writing reach. Keep a notebook by your bed, and a pad of paper in your car. Bottom line: find memory tools that work for you and get in the habit of using them now.

Be High Yield, Not Perfectionist

Don't overexert yourself in every thing you do. Focus on covering ground, rather than being the best. "Progress, not perfection" or "Completion, not perfection" should be your motto. With all the tasks you have ahead, you cannot expect to be stellar at each. What's more, medical schools aren't looking for perfection. They are looking for students who can prioritize, plan, and get things done efficiently. On a day-to-day basis, concentrate on *making and keeping planned commitments* rather than coming in first.

MAINTAIN BALANCE

We've already mentioned how important it is to maintain a sense of balance and perspective. One way to get that balance is through long-range perspective. If you have a sense of purpose, and remember who you are and why you are doing what you are doing, you can't be easily knocked off course by all the random daily problems. Seek balance in every aspect of your life, from a well-managed course load to a decent social life.

Everyone has his or her own way to maintain balance and a sense of well-being. As you prepare for medical school, don't get so caught up in achieving that you forget the bigger picture.

If you have a hard time staying on an even keel, ask yourself if you are keeping the following key habits of balance:

Love Yourself and Others

Great physicians bring not just skill, but also compassion to their work. Maintain a sense of humanity throughout your preparation. In the end, this is one of the greatest and most precious qualities you will bring to your patients. Human relationships will also give you a sense of happiness and fulfillment throughout your preparation. Believe it or not, you don't have to go it alone.

Prioritize People

No matter how rushed you feel, make it a priority to spend time with old friends and develop new relationships with peers and mentors. Though you may feel too rushed to make new friends, maintaining a positive, healthy social life will give you the resilience and joy that the premed lifestyle requires. When you go to medical school, the friends you choose to make in your entering class will be part of a vital support network.

Slow Down and Simplify Regularly

As your life speeds up and becomes complicated, try to find activities that will help you slow down and simplify. For example, take a slow walk without a Walkman® or radio and use the time to just think. Write in your journal. Clean the house to keep down clutter. Go to the beach and watch the waves. Wash the car. Call someone who is depressed and help them to feel better.

Exercise, Sleep, and Eat Right

A glaring irony of medical preparation is that so many wannabe doctors have a hard time remembering the importance of maintaining their own health. For any long-term productive lifestyle, you must sustain your physical health and energy level. Try to get enough sleep on a regular basis (even during finals), eat healthy, fresh foods (not just Mountain Dew®s and Rice Krispie®s and try to find time for cardiovascular exercise, such as a quick morning jog or swim before class. If you are overweight, start walking *everywhere*, and you'll be surprised how much new stamina you develop. After all, you are going to be a doctor, and the best leaders lead by example.

Seek Inspiration

In moments of anxiety or crisis, seek inspiration from those who have traveled this path before you. Call a friend who has always lifted you up. Inspirational people will help draw your attention back to the larger goals and lifestyle choice you have made. Copy quotes that you find uplifting and post them in your room, above your desk, or at your computer. Read a biography of a person whom you admire. If you have a religious faith, read some scripture and be open to its meaning. Listen to music.

KEEP A JOURNAL

Keeping a **journal** of your thoughts and experiences is an excellent way to contemplate and answer life's questions. Through writing, you can maintain and develop perspective on life, set goals for your education and career, appreciate things you might otherwise take for granted, and compile a meaningful record of your successes and difficulties. For many people, keeping a journal is very relaxing as well, allowing them to release all the stress and worry onto a page, rather than continuing to dwell on it, or needing to unload their negative energy onto other people, especially friends and family. Looking back over old journals, you will see just how dramatically your ideas can change and grow. In some ways, you may even cease to recognize the person you were a few years ago.

A FEW GOOD BOOKS ON JOURNALING:

Journaling from the Heart,
Eldonna Bouton, © 2000

The Many Faces of Journaling, Linda Senn and
Mindy Galiguire © 2001

At a Journal Workshop, Ira Progoff © 1975

Journal to the Self, Kathleen Adams © 1989

Practice of Process Meditation, Ira Progoff,
© 1980

Complete Idiot's Guide to Journaling, Joan
Neubauer, © 2000

If you do not already keep a journal, consider beginning one in any form that appeals to you. You may wish to write longhand in a big day planner or notebook, or to use a portable or home computer. If you already write in a journal on a regular basis, try to incorporate questions from the inward spiral and try to answer them. Use your journal to contemplate where you are going, to set goals, and to monitor your feelings and progress

Open your journal and ask yourself some tough questions. Respond truthfully and thoughtfully. You may want to ask yourself: Why medicine? If it is because you want to help people, why haven't you considered teaching, social work, or counseling? If you say you like patient care, then why are you not pursuing nursing or physical therapy? In addition to helping you narrow and define your goals, writing will help you think out clear, concise, answers that will be of use when you are interviewing for medical school.

In recent years, many doctors have begun to help their patients keep journals. Journals can be used as a compliance and educational tool, as a record of medications taken, of progress in their therapies, and for questions to ask the doctor at the next visit. By advocating journaling, some doctors have been able to facilitate long-term behavioral changes in exercise, diet, substance abuse, psychosocial issues, stress reduction, and the use of medication by their patients. These are some of the most difficult, and often overlooked, aspects of medical care. If you familiarize yourself with the process of journaling now, it will become another tool you bring to your professional career.

MEDITATION

When you are busy working and studying, it may seem counterproductive to take time out of your day to do, essentially, nothing. In fact, the opposite is true. Studies indicate that people who either briefly **meditate** or engage in **guided imagery** (visualizing what they want to do or be) every day have increased productivity, heightened focus, more energy, and a deeper overall sense of well-being. Every day, especially in times of stress, take a few minutes to step back from your life, pause to refresh, and dedicate a little time to either meditation or quiet reflection on the future.

Getting used to taking this type of down time can be difficult. Frequently, students will take breaks from their schedule by going to the movies, watching TV, going out to eat, or talking to friends on the phone. While these activities can definitely be relaxing and a welcome change of pace, they do not replace the need for reflection and meditation, nor, according to researchers, do they have the powerful and positive effects that meditation can have on your consciousness.

Guided imagery (seeing yourself as a successful medical school applicant, established doctor, etc.) is great, but don't forget meditation. Even if it is only for a few minutes each day, be sure to take the time to quiet down, observe yourself relaxing, and then briefly observe "nothing" by meditating. People who have difficulty concentrating, whose thoughts go in a hundred different directions when they are trying to study, are particularly in need of some regular practice in shutting down their busy minds. Meditation is basically a habit that trains the mind how to do *one thing at a time* (e.g., to presently think no unwanted thoughts) so that it is much easier to study hard for three hours straight when necessary. Books and tools are available to help you with this. Some physical regimens, like yoga, incorporate brief meditation as part of their routine.

REASSESS PERIODICALLY

Even after you have chosen a medical path, continue to evaluate your choices, your progress, and your commitment to your goals. Take another look at the **big picture**. Do you like what you see? Are there other paths you might want to take? Are you living up to your commitments to yourself, or are you falling short? Do you need to make some changes in your goals or priorities?

Remember you will not actually have to choose a specialty until your fourth year of medical school. That means that you have time now to explore your options. If you initially get experience in one area of medicine and find that leading you in another direction, don't fight it. Just make sure you dedicate enough time to achieve excellence in some special thing during your undergraduate years. Use these years to experience a wide range of things, now, so you can make informed choices later. Realize that you are building new skills every moment of your life, so try to choose those skills with the big picture in mind.

Video Assignments for Chapter 1:
Vital Signs, Vision Quest, and *The Karate Kid*

CHAPTER 2
REAL-LIFE MEDICINE AND TOP TRENDS IN HEALTH CARE

To be a successful medical school candidate, you should know some of the classic **positives and negatives of medicine**, as well as some major drivers, or **meta-trends** influencing the future of the profession. Although you will sacrifice a lot to become a physician, you will accrue many benefits as well. Every year brings increasingly miraculous technologies, treatments, and therapies to the field. What's more, as these technologies accelerate in effectiveness and affordability, so does the degree to which we value human life in general. The constant interplay between accelerating technology and our long-standing ethical desires is allowing us to pursue increasingly higher standards of humanitarianism and compassion. Doctors are the arbiters of this new compassion and the primary brokers of the healing power in our society.

Through your explorations in the inward spiral, you have introduced yourself to some of the fields, trends, and thought in current medical practice. Don't stop looking now. Find **medical publications** whose subject, format, and tone you like and start a habit of looking through them on a regular basis. Getting a student-rate subscription to an interesting magazine may motivate you to browse each issue. Your long-term goal is to develop an informed, comprehensive view of the therapies available to today's patients, including an understanding of the social, diagnostic, and treatment controversies in health care. You can begin learning about these issues now, even with little medical training. Just browsing an article in the morning will give you something to think about during your spare time in any typical day.

Medicine is a healthy, contentious professional field, with **difficulties, dilemmas, and controversies** that you will need to learn about. How should you advise your patients who are experimenting with alternative therapies? Should prostate cancer screening, which is expensive and takes resources away from other types of medical care, be done for your male patients who are younger than 50? Should doctors prescribe medicine for "off-label" uses if there is some research that indicates it might help a patient's medical problem? For each controversy, try to deeply understand both sides before forming your own opinion. Develop the habit of lifelong learning now, as it will be critical to your continuing success as a doctor.

REAL-LIFE MEDICINE: SOME BENEFITS AND DRAWBACKS OF DAILY PRACTICE

What is it like to be a doctor? How many hours will you work and how much money will you make? Will you be respected? Will it be stressful? What will your daily routine be like? Medicine is a unique field with requirements, responsibilities, and opportunities unlike any other profession. Here are some fundamental issues to consider as you contemplate a medical career.

ARE YOU A PEOPLE PERSON?

Being a physician is all about helping people. If you like being in almost constant contact with people, this is a major benefit. If you don't, medicine is probably not for you. No matter what your specialty, you will have to work with people. The average doctor spends most of his or her time seeing patients, and the rest writing up results, making treatment plans, and other patient-related activities. Some specialties, like pathology or radiology, involve less patient contact, but there is still a lot of contact within the health care team. Other specialties, like general practice or psychiatry, involve vast amounts of psychosocial human interaction. Doctors also spend an average of ten percent to twenty percent of their time in charitable or community activities. How does that sound to you? Even if you pursue a medical specialty that does not involve the same level of patient interaction that most do, you will still need to work well with other doctors, nurses, technicians, and allied health professionals. There is also a vast amount of paperwork (authorizations, lab results, protocols) to be handled, some by you, but even more by your staff. People skills will be very helpful in managing this flow of paperwork as well.

Furthermore, you will be dealing with **people who are sick or injured,** and who come to you with major concerns and questions about their health. Health issues make many people scared and anxious, and they will expect you to calm them down, to give them hope and an understanding of what is going on in their bodies. You may have to explain complex concepts to people who have little medical knowledge, or break difficult news to a patient whose condition is severe, irreparable, or terminal. Needless to say, this type of work requires above-average emotional intelligence, empathy, and desire to help.

This is not to say that all doctors must be some version of Patch Adams. There are plenty of successful doctors who would be uncomfortable appearing on a talk show. At the most basic level, however, being a doctor is about helping other people. Bottom line: if you don't feel comfortable or happy working with people, you may be looking into the wrong field. Even academic or research medicine requires a greater desire to help and work with people than many other technical paths one could take in the world.

Most people you encounter in medicine are ill, and the sickness often makes them needy, depressed, anxious, demented, and otherwise unpleasant to be around. Although most of my classmates see this as an opportunity to help, some med students dislike sick people. These students are mostly unhappy in medical school. You should find out if you want to be around sick people before you start going through the trouble to complete your premed requirements.

–Rob, Albert Einstein College of Medicine

LONG HOURS

Medical school is a pressure cooker, during which students must complete a vast quantity of work. "Like trying to drink water from a fire hose," is a common description of a medical school education. After that, new MDs go straight into a residency program, where they work just as infamously long hours for low wages. Unfortunately, the sleep deprivation doesn't end as soon as you finish your internship. Physicians also work long hours building their practice, even more than in other professions. On average during their career, physicians work about 58 hours per week. As this number is an average, physicians in some specialties work fewer hours, while others will work more, particularly in the early years of their career. Medicine is not a 9 to 5 job.

Although the increasing prevalence of women in medicine is making the profession steadily more family friendly, doctors are still required to spend long hours at work, and they must put most other life priorities on hold. For some people, the desire to start a family, expand one's circle of non-medical friends, and maintain a more open-ended personal life are ultimately more important than being a doctor. If you want to be a doctor, realize that it will become your number one priority for many, many years, to the exclusion of other things. That's just the way it works.

SALARY AND COMPENSATION

Even with the changes caused by managed care, the rising costs of malpractice insurance and increased regulation, doctors still maintain a high standard of living. The average physician still makes over **$160,000 annually**, a decent living by any standards. Although their salaries have seen a slight drop over the past several years, physicians remain the highest paid professionals in the United States. Powerful lobbies protect the physicians' status in this regard. At the same time, only 16,000 new physician trainees are accepted to medical school each year, a number that has stayed the same for the last twenty years, even as the U.S. population has steadily increased over that time period. Whether you consider this helpful or not, the fact remains that no such control on the number of new entering students exists in other major professions, such as law or accounting. This means that you do not have to worry about physician oversupply in the future, regardless of what you may hear in the media on this issue.

Here is a sample of physician salaries in a number of specialties, after expenses but before taxes:

Medical Specialty	Annual Salary
Anesthesiology	$220,000
Internal Medicine	$150,000
Pathology	$175,000
Pediatrics	$120,000
Psychiatry	$130,000
Radiology	$260,000
Surgery	$217,000

Of course, you will have to pay your dues for a long time before attaining these earning levels. After you finish medical school, you will likely have a considerable debt to repay (the average medical student graduates with about $60,000 in loans). Don't expect to pay it back during your residency, however. Residents are notoriously overworked and underpaid, with a median salary of $35,000 annually.

In short, though doctors make a good living once they have finished their extensive education, you should not be looking into medicine primarily for its income-generating potential. If you calculate the salary you receive for the hours you will actually work over the course of your lifetime, you would probably be better off in overall earnings, and in free time to spend those earnings, by going to business school or becoming a plumber. If you choose medicine, go because it is the primary challenge you want to take on in your professional life, because you are rewarded by the act of healing people, and because it is something you would do even if you were not paid as well. If you can find your path of heart, whether in medicine or not, you'll be able to deal less stressfully with the inevitable fluctuations in your salary and other material compensations that occur in the natural ups and downs of economic cycles in society.

INTELLECTUAL STIMULATION

As a doctor, your education never ends. Even in your day-to-day routine, being a responsible physician will test your knowledge and expertise. On top of that, your friends and colleagues will be intelligent, talented, and motivated health care professionals. The ability and drive of many of these individuals will inspire you, and you will meet several true geniuses over the course of your career. If you like the constant challenge of **interpreting torrents of new information quickly, cleverly, and responsibly**, for immediate and powerful human benefit, there is probably no better career in the world than medicine.

POWER AND RESPECT

Doctors are at the top of the medical pyramid, leading teams of nurses and other health professionals. As a doctor, you will be in charge. Some people consider this a privilege to be earned, but at the same time it can be a burden. After you have received appropriate training, you will be expected to make the **final call**

on difficult and ethically challenging situations. You will make diagnoses that will change people's lives. Most of your patients will look to you as the ultimate authority on their case. Fortunately, you can find a range of levels of assistance in your leadership duties, varying both by specialty and by practice environment, whether small clinic or large medical team.

Outside the hospital, doctors generally are given a lot of respect. People tend to view doctors as intelligent, educated, and highly accomplished individuals—and rightly so. It is no secret how difficult it is to get into medical school, and everyone knows that medical training itself is a long, grueling process. Nevertheless, having a prestigious career, if you are motivated by this benefit, may not be worth the many years of medical preparation and training and the considerable costs of a medical education. If you are looking for other prestigious careers in which you can help people, there are other health care professions, such as nurse practitioner, and other fields, such as business, law, education, or social work, where you may quickly rise to a leadership role with sustained effort, talent, and desire.

Only you can make the final call for or against becoming a doctor, but the more you know about the benefits and drawbacks, the more quickly you'll be able to decide whether you can love the field of medicine—warts and all. No profession is perfect, and if you can love medicine given both its pros and cons, that love is likely to last the length of your career and beyond.

HEALTH CARE META-TRENDS: CONSIDERING THE FUTURE OF MEDICINE

Medicine is constantly changing. Yet the more some things change, the more others stay just the same. The special status of the medical profession won't go away. A physician's ability to profoundly influence his patients' lives will only increase. But while some of today's problems will remain, others will diminish greatly in coming years. In general, doctors will probably worry about very different things twenty years from now.

Back in the 1900s, physicians worried about infection, sanitation, and getting adequate basic resources. In the 2000s, they worry about oversight by insurance agents, increasing regulation, and lack of time for patients in a managed care setting. In 2020, they are probably going to be worrying about a different set of issues yet again, such as managing an incredible number of **therapeutic alternatives**, astonishing quantities of **patient data** (some of it collected in realtime, through wireless sensors), and using their accelerating **medical networks**, **databases**, and early **artificial intelligence systems** for maximum benefit with each unique patient, who will receive more **personalized and preventive care** than ever before.

They will probably *not* be worrying as much about today's oversight and insurance issues, as those issues will have become a lot more legislated and standardized, and will be handled less and less by physicians, and more and more by the various institutions and practice agencies that the doctors join.

Many other permanent changes will occur. In the United States and other industrialized societies, solo practice outside of a network is about as likely to return as the building of automobiles in garages. Both of these are rare in the United States today, and are very likely to stay rarities. This is because such work (medical care, automobile production, and many other socially important fields) becomes increasingly complex with each passing year, and is held to higher and higher community standards. That isn't to say we won't see the continued existence of rural practitioners, such as our beloved country docs and intrepid developing-world physicians. It's just that these practitioners will be vastly more connected to their peers and supported by their digital networks and social and technological infrastructure than ever before. Technological networks are spreading across this planet much faster than all other aspects of culture in the industrialized world. The country doctors of 2020 will have very strong connections to their practice group, to the laws of the country in which they operate, and to the world. We are building a far more information-rich and computation-rich future than many of us can even imagine.

If you were first attracted to medicine because a parent or grandparent was a doctor, consider how much the field has changed over his or her practice career. Ask the following question of any MDs you know: how is health care different today than when you first started practicing? Ask your mentor the same question. Where is health care going and what should I expect?

Many recent trends in medicine seem to signal difficulties for physicians. With rising insurance premiums and the introduction of managed care systems, declining government support for medical care, the rising costs of health care, and limited funds for basic research, health care is a battleground among physicians, patients, insurance companies, government groups, and pharmaceutical companies. Deciding to pursue a career in medicine will demand that you will walk into this battleground.

But another, more positive way of seeing these trends is to realize that **good health is increasingly a subject worth fighting for**, perhaps the most fundamental subject that all human beings care about. For the first time, physicians are witnessing other segments of society care deeply about health issues, so they now have to share power with other groups in the battle. That should not be seen as a problem in itself, as increased democracy, transparency, and accountability can only improve the quality of care in the long run. It seems a safe bet that physicians will continue to gain power in coming years. Some of this will be social power, but even more will be accelerating therapeutic power due to the exponential advances of science and technology, and the informational networks in which they operate. Physicians will remain the leading authority on health care issues, even as these issues become increasingly important to all members of society.

ACCELERATING TECHNOLOGICAL ADVANCES

Perhaps the most important and easily predictable trend we can envision for the future is that computing technology is very likely to continue to advance at a breathtaking rate. For at least the last one hundred years, the amount of **computing power** that each of us can buy for $1,000 has *doubled every eighteen months, on average*. As researchers like Ray Kurzweil have shown, this doubling has continued even while computers have switched their structure (from mechanical, to electromechanical, to vacuum tube, to transistor, and now to integrated circuit) five different times over the last century.

This accelerating rate has continued regardless of economic slowdown, world wars, or any other short-term factors. A number of scientists have proposed that this acceleration of information-processing ability will continue as far into the future as we can envision, as long as new types of computer architectures are constantly being invented. If this is true, this means that while our social systems and institutions may continue to be much the same from year to year, our computing systems, and the scientific discoveries that they are able to help us make, will continue to accelerate into the foreseeable future.

What does this mean for medicine? It means we will continue to see **increasingly miraculous drugs, treatments, diagnostic tools, and computer and information-related services** become available to patients, making health and healing more powerful than ever. Accelerating data storage technology will eventually allow patients to come to their physician with their entire medical history only a mouse-click away. Telemedicine is allowing doctors who are physically in separate locations to share research or discuss cases with one other, helping doctors reach patients who are in remote or rural locations, and to more frequently touch base with any patient in a time-efficient manner.

Technology is also helping to eliminate some of the costly red tape associated with health care. Doctors use computerized database systems to bill patients and store their records, as well as software programs to send prescription requests over the Internet. In addition, technology is helping the general patient base get access to information about their health and health care issues. With resources like the Internet at their disposal, patients now know more about maintaining good health, and can conduct independent research about their medical conditions and treatment options. All of this is great news, but there are even more changes just around the corner.

How will we use computers in medicine once health care professionals and their patients can operate and retrieve information from them through voice-recognition systems? How quickly will the intelligence and usefulness of our computer systems improve once we are all talking to them through a common interface? These are open questions, but it remains clear that **computers will play a key and accelerating role in improving our health in coming years**. If you want to have a good understanding of the future of medicine, take time to build your information-processing skills, to look at the way computers are being used today in medicine, and to consider how fast and in what ways computer hardware and software is improving every year.

ACCELERATING BIOMEDICAL RESEARCH

We are living at the very beginning of an era of incredible advancement in cellular and molecular medicine, biotechnology, and biomedicine. For doctors, this is wonderful news. Every year, doctors can make increasingly powerful therapies available to their patients. Life can be preserved and saved as never before.

The "golden age" of biomedical research has only recently dawned. Back in 1986, most biomedical research was conducted by the government, with industry funding only 36 percent of the total. But by 1997, U.S. private spending on medical research had finally grown to a majority, or 52 percent of the total ($36 billion in that year). In the early eras of scientific research in a certain sector, public funding usually dominates. But once it has developed enough valuable advances that truly benefit large groups of people, private funding inevitably increases. This corner has only very recently turned for medicine, and it suggests that after many years of "innovation equilibrium," during which many medical innovations did *not* substantially improve therapeutic outcomes, we will now start to see accelerating perceived usefulness of our biomedical and therapeutic applications, as well as accelerating private funding of basic biomedical research.

In some ways, this increasing private industrial research will drive medicine forward faster than traditional public academic research. Pharmaceutical and biotech companies are going after large and lucrative new markets with their innovative and increasingly well-funded research ideas. Yet one downside is that market forces, as opposed to patient need, are driving the industry. Therefore, certain types of important research, such as research conducted with substances that cannot be patented, or research on orphan diseases (diseases that affect only small percentages of the population) are neglected early on by private industry because they have less profit-generating potential. This provides opportunities for the public sector (government, university, nonprofit) to lead research efforts into drugs and treatments for these conditions.

Regardless of the type of health care research or health care delivery systems we choose to support, there are great and irreversible accelerating benefits that come from the *tools* presently being developed through for-profit ventures. For example, for-profit industry is primarily driving today's advances in such cutting-edge areas as combinatorial chemistry, rational drug design, and genomics. Once these new tools are invented, they can then be used by both public and private sector institutions for deeper and wider research into these spheres.

Advances in medicine continue by leaps and bounds. Over the next several decades, doctors will gain the ability to provide therapies that are steadily more powerful and increasingly targeted to the individual patient (e.g., pharmacogenomics). This increasing "intelligence" in all medical therapies will improve their power and decrease their side effects. The power of medicine both to cure disease and to maintain health will be increasingly impressive.

RISING COSTS OF HEALTH CARE

As health care technologies become more effective, society invariably begins to use the health care system much more extensively, and the total cost of health management, as a percentage of national productivity, continues to rise. While our economy has its cyclic ups and downs, our total expenditure on health care and pharmaceuticals has steadily increased in recent decades, driven more by the new usefulness of the therapies, and the increasing social value of a long, healthy life, than by any other economic factors. Every year, an increasing amount of the U.S. gross domestic product (GDP) is spent on health care-related goods and services, more than in any other industrialized nation. In 1960, 6 percent of U.S. GDP was spent on health care. By 2000, 20 percent of GDP was spent on health care-related goods and services. It is very likely that this fraction will continue to increase in coming decades, even as politicians seek ways to slow this advance.

As a result of this inflation, physicians are under increasing pressure to keep costs down. Doctors are encouraged to cut back on personal time spent with patients, to minimize referrals to specialists, and to order expensive tests only when absolutely necessary. But pushing from the other side are an increasingly informed patient population, who are motivated to get access to an ever more useful set of therapies. Consider the example of Viagra®, one of the first simple and effective therapies for male sexual dysfunction. Once this advance came along, it was not possible to keep large numbers of informed patients from getting access to it. Further complicating the picture, patients informed about a drug or therapy that they believe to be effective can create a surge of demand that drives up its cost, particularly in the short run, before competition sets in and patents expire.

New Health Care Delivery Systems

Managed care systems were introduced in the last decade to counteract the skyrocketing price of health care, and many are very poorly designed, as they are still in the early stages of their development. Until rather recently, medicine was very much an open frontier; physicians had a great deal of autonomy and could recommend treatments or therapies according to their own judgment about what a patient needed or wanted, as opposed to what was the most cost-effective or most clinically proven option. Since the advent of managed care, with its **health maintenance organizations (HMOs), preferred provider organizations (PPOs),** and other oversight systems, doctors have been forced to bow to major cost controls, to adhere to pre-approved medication schedules, to cut back their time for examination procedures, and to suffer heavy-handed restrictions on the way they conduct their primary and follow-up care.

Health Management Organizations

Health management organizations tend to control costs by allowing the insured to only visit doctors in their provider network. These doctors either receive a yearly salary from a particular HMO, or charge all their participating HMOs reduced fees (a small fraction of what they used to charge health insurance agencies and fee-for-service patients) for their services. The doctors are also given onerous and constantly changing management guidelines about costs and expenditures, limiting, as already stated, the use of expensive tests and treatments unless absolutely necessary. Health management organizations also try to limit patient access to pricey specialists. Patients in an HMO who need specialty care must go first to a primary care doctor, who then recommends from a list of specialists who are part of the provider network. In the past, if you developed a rash from poison ivy, for example, you would have had the choice to visit either your general practitioner or a dermatologist. Today, you must visit your primary care doctor first, who will only very selectively refer you to a dermatologist for care.

For doctors trained during the good old days of medicine, the new managed care systems can be extremely frustrating. Many feel that the level of care has decreased noticeably since the introduction of these systems. They dislike the close scrutiny of their expenditures, the greatly increased paperwork, and the inability to run tests or refer patients to specialists as often as they would like. In addition to the problems created for doctors, a near-term effect of managed care has been increased patient frustration. Patients feel they no longer receive the quality of care they received in the past and are aggravated by long waits, short office visits, and the inability to choose their own doctors.

Downsizing and Restructuring of Hospitals

The growth of managed care has seen an increased emphasis on cutting costs by promoting outpatient care and reducing hospital stays and clinical activities in the large medical institutions. As a result, many hospitals have begun to lose money and have subsequently merged and downsized, cutting staff in the process. Meanwhile, some of the new and smaller emergent care centers and networks are growing. Much of this can be understood as a natural and healthy resizing and downsizing, part of the normal cycle of any industry as it undergoes a restructuring in the way funding flows and oversight systems operate. Nevertheless, it can cause a lot of strain on health care networks in the process.

Changes to Medical Education

In a traditional medical curriculum, students spend their second two years of school doing clinical rotations in an affiliated teaching hospital, giving them exposure to a variety of different clinical settings and access to the latest technologies and therapeutic approaches. Overall, this system is widely considered the best way for medical students to finish their education with a strong, modern, comprehensive understanding of health care. Unfortunately, it is even harder for teaching hospitals to cover their costs than for traditional hospitals, since many of their doctors are involved in academic work as well as patient care. In addition, many teaching hospitals care for the lowest-paying, state-insured, underinsured, and uninsured patients. As steep as the typical medical school tuition is, it still doesn't cover the full cost of an actual medical education, given the price tag for most health care related goods and services.

Therefore, as managed care has encouraged large-scale cutbacks in spending, many academic medical centers have restructured, closed, and merged with other hospitals.

As a result of these systemic changes, some medical school programs have changed their curricula to include greater focus on health economics and health care management, more training in outpatient medicine, and less lecture time. Medical education will continue to adjust to these new realities. Medicine will remain an area of tremendous opportunity in the years ahead, and it will maintain its essential stability, as with any system that is central to modern society.

The Bright Side of Managed Care

While managed care has put strain on doctors, hospitals, and medical school programs, there have also been some positive outgrowths of the system. Managed care doctors are usually salaried, which gives them greater security and financial stability regardless of the number of clients or the fluctuating work levels they handle. Managed care doctors also tend to work fewer hours than those in a fee-for-service system, a sign that more balance is irreversibly creeping into the profession.

In addition, many new doctors entering medicine today do not mind the billing restrictions, authorizations, and increased oversight imposed by managed care, since they have never worked in the previous system that existed in a simpler and less medically costly era. There is no other professional field in which millions of dollars are sometimes spent with little oversight, approval, or validation, and many new doctors feel that the increasing restrictions on medical spending can be justified.

If you feel that you would not be happy practicing in a managed care environment, other options are available. Military medicine, for example, gives doctors greater autonomy and authority than managed care systems. In addition, the increasing popularity of PPOs strongly suggests that the managed care system will be modified in the future to include more patient choice and flexibility. Managed care is still in the early stages of its development, and there is strong reason to believe that the rules and restrictions, both on doctors and on patients, will become increasingly fairer, more balanced, and more "fine-grained" with time. This means we are likely to see more people employed in an oversight capacity, many more computer resources, and somewhat more bureaucracy. But, at the same time, physicians are likely to have increasingly more focused sets of tasks they must be responsible for, less unnecessary busywork, and many more institutional and technological resources to help them accomplish their work in the years ahead.

Older & More Informed Patients

With every passing year, the patient base in the United States becomes older, slightly larger, and more discriminating. There is an increasing health consciousness in the United States, and people value their lives as never before. Americans expect high-quality, comprehensive health care and they are dissatisfied when they receive less than that. They want access to high-quality doctors, and they appreciate superior skill and knowledge.

Increasing patient demands will most likely be the genesis of large-scale, positive changes in the health care industry. Managed care, for example, will be forced to change as competition continues and therapies improve. In the past several years, PPOs have become more and more desirable as patients demand more freedom of choice and better access to treatments and specialists.

As the baby boom generation reaches their 60s, and as life expectancy increases in general, a larger percentage of older patients will bring their special, more complex health concerns into the system. As a result, there will be a greater need for doctors who can treat chronic disease, prevent degenerative disease, and provide palliative care. Fields such as **geriatrics, internal medicine, cardiovascular medicine, neurology, and psychiatry,** as well as elective fields, such as **cosmetic surgery**, will expand to meet the needs of aging patients. There will also be an increased interest in funding research on conditions that affect the elderly.

In 1993, only $45 million dollars of the U.S. National Institute of Aging budget was targeted to basic biomedical research on the process of aging. As Leonard Hayflick observed, that was roughly equivalent to the money our society spent on Superbowl commercials in that year. Fortunately, that situation has changed significantly over the last ten years, as increasingly better understanding of biochemistry, genetics, and molecular biology has opened up promising new research opportunities. Funding for aging-related research will only continue to increase in the years ahead.

UNDERINSURED AND INDIGENT CARE

Today, an estimated **forty-five million people** living in America do not have any form of health insurance. This remains **one of our most significant outstanding social problems**. People without health coverage usually do not have the money to see doctors on a regular basis or pay for expensive medications. Therefore, to receive medical attention, they must resort to emergency room care, usually after a problem has become serious. This causes significant financial stress to the modern medical system, since late intervention is almost always pricier than preventive measures. At the same time, significant numbers of uninsured Americans, thinking they cannot afford the cost of care, often suffer or die from treatable medical conditions.

This problem is multifaceted, and not likely to be solved in the immediate future. Who pays for the people who can't pay for themselves? Until recently, systems like Medicare and Medicaid helped the elderly and indigent cover the costs of health care. Now, governmental contributions to these systems are so sparse, in some cases, that it is not possible for doctors to treat patients under these forms of coverage at the accepted standard of care, without losing a significant amount of money in the process. With the cost of health care steadily increasing, the government is failing its responsibility to compensate the health care industry for indigent care. Doctors and hospitals have been left to care for the elderly and indigent without financial compensation.

Creating adequate state or national public health programs will be a very controversial and difficult issue. At present, the responsibility and costs for uninsured care fall primarily on the shoulders of **hospitals**, which are already struggling from the financial fallout of restructuring. It has gotten to the point that some doctors simply cannot afford to treat patients on Medicare or Medicaid. As a result, many American hospitals have struggled on the verge of bankruptcy for many years. Fortunately, the gloom and doom predictions of catastrophic failure that were made by several health care futurists in the 1990s have not come to fruition. Our nation's health care system is much more stable and resilient than many originally expected. Nevertheless, there are still major cost concerns facing the medical profession.

If you are entering medicine with a noble desire to help the old, indigent, and underrepresented, be forewarned that you will face a daily struggle between your own interests, your patients' needs, and the minimal funding available to the task. This situation is likely to continue for at least the next few decades of your career, as such social issues are complex and slow to change. Fortunately, technological development is not subject to the whims of political debate, and history shows that it has always occurred at an accelerating rate regardless of the party in office in any given year. It is reasonable to expect that some increasingly powerful and inexpensive therapies will become available to even the uninsured over the span of your medical career, regardless of whether public health care reform is able to provide significantly more governmental aid to all Americans.

INCREASING DIVERSITY IN THE HEALTH CARE PROFESSIONS

Every year, medical schools see an increasing diversity in their entering classes. As the patient base in the United States becomes larger and more multicultural, the population of our physicians and health professionals is becoming increasingly reflective of the larger population, adding a deeper dimension to the care and service available.

Women, for example, comprised only seven percent of medical students in 1960. In 1993, women still only comprised thirty percent of medical students. But by the **2001–2002 academic year, women represented forty-nine percent of entering medical students**. This is an auspicious development, as it will advance many more **family, relationship, and other social issues** within the medical community, making medical training and practice more responsive to the needs of the whole and balanced human being.

The medical profession is also becoming more ethnically diverse. Many minority recruitment and mentoring programs are encouraging underrepresented students to consider medicine. In the 2000–2001 academic year, sixty-three percent of accepted applicants were white/Caucasian and 19.7 percent were Asian/Pacific Islander. Underrepresented minorities (**URMs**), including African American, American Indian/Native Hawaiian or Alaskan, Mexican American/Chicano, and Mainland Puerto Rican students, comprised about **11.4 percent of matriculating medical students**, up 1.6 percent from the previous year.

These trends portend optimism about a more humanizing, more socially integrated role for physicians in our twenty-first century community.

Your Video Assignments for Chapter 2:
Lorenzo's Oil, Hoosiers, and *Hoop Dreams*

CHAPTER 3
APPROACHING ADMISSIONS

You are now entering admissions terrain. There are seven key challenges (we like to call them Great Peaks) in medical school admissions, and we will address each of them in detail over the next six chapters. Chapter Eight covers two of these Great Peaks together (primary and secondary applications). Because we are using the inward spiral, we will first survey the admissions geography in this "base camp" chapter in preparation for the ascent of the other seven peaks.

THE SEVEN GREAT PEAKS
OF MEDICAL ADMISSIONS

The seven main challenges of medical school admissions are:
1. GPA and academic performance in college
2. MCAT scores
3. Extracurricular preparation
4. Letters of recommendation
5. Primary applications (American Medical College Application Service [AMCAS] and others)
6. Secondary applications
7. The interview

All are worth separate and special consideration, as your performance on every one of these climbs will be carefully assessed by medical school admissions committees.

Medical schools share a common candidate-application process, but they can vary significantly in the way they evaluate candidates. First, the commonalities: every admissions committee does an initial evaluation by way of some type of admissions index. This is a semi-formal system that assigns an initial set of points or category ranking to each applicant based on his or her performance, mainly on GPA and MCAT scores, plus a few objectively quantifiable elements from the primary application. For example, a certain number of points might be assigned to a candidate who has to work more than twenty hours a week to pay his or her way through college. This index is most commonly used in the first round to eliminate low-performing students from further consideration. It may also be consulted in later rounds for decisions between close candidates, but this is less common.

If a student's application achieves the initial minimum index or category value, the admissions committee then reviews his or her subjective criteria— the extracurricular preparation, letters of recommendation, and the essays submitted with the primary and secondary applications. Most of the top schools also consider subjective aspects of a student's academic record in this phase, such as the type and difficulty of courses taken, GPA trends, special academic projects undertaken, and reputation of the major or school attended. Students who pass this more subjective evaluation are then offered interview spaces. After the interview, the interviewers' impressions are prepared for the student's file, final admissions decisions are made, either on a case-by-case basis or with groups of applications being ranked by committee vote.

To be offered a spot, usually a minimum of **three different members** of the admissions committee must agree on recommending your candidacy, and committee decisions usually must be further approved by the dean of the medical school. Admissions committees are generally large, around **fifteen to thirty members**. A 2000 study found that they typically include fifteen percent **medical students**, twenty percent PhDs, and the rest MDs. They are almost all **volunteer**, there are nearly **twice as many men as women**, and about sixteen percent are **underrepresented minorities**.[1]

When admission committees vote, only occasionally—about twenty percent of the time—will individual members change their initial opinions of a candidate's qualifications for admission after deliberation within the group. An interesting recent study listed the specific reasons why these vote changes occurred at one U.S. medical school (University of Kentucky) in decreasing order of frequency: MCAT scores, medical experience, comparison with other applicants, grades, letters of evaluation, interviews, individual attributes, state residency status, service experience, expressed desire of committee members

1 Doulgas G. Kondo, MD, and Victoria E. Judd, MD, "Demographic Characteristics of US Medical School Admission Committees," *The Journal of the American Medical Association* 2000, 284: 1111-1113.

to discuss the applicant at the meeting, AMCAS personal statement, and diversity.[2] This seems to suggest that after outstanding MCAT scores, outstanding undergraduate medical experience is probably the next most important factor in getting yourself recognized as a uniquely desirable applicant. Bottom line: medical school admissions is a collaborative activity, and each committee will bring its own background, biases, and beliefs to the process.

Depending on who you are and what your preparation has been to this point, the trek up some of these admissions peaks will be easy, while others will be unexpectedly difficult. One often-cited motto, both for keeping balance and minimizing procrastination is: **"Plan and do first those things which scare you."** If any one of these challenges gives you anxiety just thinking about it, then you need to plan ahead and act most regularly on that one, beginning now. If you are anxious about maintaining your undergraduate GPA, you can find courses, majors, and universities more appropriate to your abilities. If letters of recommendation scare you, you can start planning them now. If it is the MCAT, you can start taking sample tests. If it is the interview, you can begin conducting mock interviews at your career services center, and taking the humanities courses that will improve your verbal communications skills.

Though you may often feel pressure to be perfect on each of your climbs, don't get caught up in competitiveness, and keep any self-doubt brief and focused on your own path. There are multiple trails up every one of these Great Peaks, so celebrate your individuality. Your unique

---

Other Medical School Admissions Books

(Skim these in the Careers/Medicine Section of your local university bookstore)

Becoming a Physician, Jennifer Danek © 1997

The Insider's Guide to Medical School Admissions, R. Stephen Toyos © 1997

The Definitive Guide to Medical School Admission, Mark Goldstein and Myrna Goldstein © 1998

The High School Doctor, Nagendra Sai Koneru, Omar Wang and Vineet Arora © 2002

A Boring But Necessary Reference Book:

Medical School Admission Requirements (MSAR), Meredith T. Moller (Ed.), © New Each Year

---

2 C.L. Elam, et al, "Review, Deliberation, and Voting: A Study of Selection Decisions in a Medical School Admission Committee," *Teaching and Learning in Medicine* 2002, 14: 98–103.

path and style of climbing will inevitably get you there, so try to stay focused and balanced, and be kind to yourself and others on the way.

Remember: You don't have to scale any of these peaks alone. In addition to climbing partners, there are crampons, ropes, and many other useful tools you can pick up along the way, so look around for them. There are maps written by those who have traveled in this country before, such as this book. If you reach out to well-chosen classmates, mentors, and friends, you can build a small team of fellow climbers, and motivate and support each other on your way.

Before tackling the individual parts of the application, you should know about two additional topics of importance to your quest for acceptance to medical school. The first is a brief summary of trends in medical school admissions. This is worth skimming to understand the nature of the challenge ahead. The second describes key characteristics of the successful physician candidate, as described in the admissions publications of the 127 U.S. allopathic medical schools. These are the characteristics that medical schools say they are looking for, in their own words. You should ponder them carefully, and ask yourself how you can address each on your own premedical path of heart.

TRENDS IN MEDICAL SCHOOL ADMISSIONS

Some years it is merely difficult to get into medical school. Others years it is significantly more competitive. In the "easiest" years, two out of three candidates who apply are accepted, in other years one out of two, and in the most difficult years, only one out of three medical school candidates are admitted. Of course, the dropout

ratios during undergraduate years are easily five times higher than these, particularly in the toughest years, where some studies indicate that only **one out of twenty** students who originally declared their written intention to attend medical school as freshmen actually end up doing so. Fulfilling a premedical requirement is already one of the hardest things to do during one's undergraduate studies, so it is no wonder the dropout level is so high.

In tougher application years, the level of negative talk and self-doubt goes up a lot, and you need be prepared for that. Dropout rates from premedical programs are *particularly* high for those with poor high school science backgrounds who are unaware of the high level of premedical competition at major universities, for those transferring to big universities from less rigorous junior colleges, and for many of those coming from an underrepresented or disadvantaged background. Understanding these challenges will prepare you to see a number of your friends change their focus on their undergraduate journey, and to respectfully support them in their own life choices.

If you are on your path of heart, remember that the rationalizations and stories told by those who leave the medical path along the way, for their own unique reasons, or by the seniors who were not accepted to medical school that year, are of little importance to your own personal path. How many of your premedical friends end up choosing other careers is of little importance. Even whether you are accepted to medical school on your first application is of very little importance, if you have been walking your path well and growing your skills daily. As the Zen masters say, "First you wash your bowl." First you walk, later you learn to fly.

USEFUL ADMISSIONS STATISTICS

The following admissions statistics, most available at the helpful **Association of American Medical Colleges (AAMC) website (www.aamc.org/),** can give you an idea of where you need to be in order to get into medical school. But please do some brief research on the unique admissions standards at the particular schools you plan to apply to as well. Most importantly, the **medical school admissions statistics (MSAS)** for past years' applicants from your university, available at your campus career center, and secondarily, the **medical school admissions requirements (MSAR)** book published by the AAMC are two good places to start. (We'll have more to say on these publications in Chapter Eight.)

As you look over the GPA and MCAT statistics below, bear in mind that these numbers are averages. For example, the average MCAT score of accepted applicants at all medical schools is **30P**, but only a few students actually attain this number; most are above or below it. Also, the averages will be different for first-tier, second-tier, and third-tier medical schools, as we will discuss later.

The most competitive first-tier medical schools may use national averages as performance cutoffs for initial selection. But at most medical schools, successful candidates can still score *below* these national averages, if they are *above* average in any of the other components of their applications. Remember also that GPA averages do not show the occasional C in Sociology 101 or the failed biology midterm, real-life situations that *every* premed invariably encounters on the way to becoming a physician. These numbers are particularly helpful for telling you when you are way ahead of the curve, allowing you to spend less energy on that particular climb and devote more to scaling the other, non-academic peaks at an above-average level.

Let's begin with some good news from the student's perspective. As of 2002, we have seen a **six-year downtrend in the number of applicants to medical school,** so the admission rate has been getting better each year over this entire time period. This is a trend that balances the first half of the 1990s, which saw a steady increase in medical school applicants every year for four years. In 1992, there were 37,402 applicants for just 16,289 first year spots. But by 1996, there were 46,965 applicants for 16,201 positions. Fortunately, it has been easier every year since 1996. In the 2002 application year, 33,625 students vied for 16,488 first year places, a reasonable **acceptance rate of 49 percent**. Nevertheless, applying to medical school is still a very difficult and socially stressful process of selection, especially when you consider how talented, accomplished, and driven premeds usually are. Given past trends it is very likely that right now, or some time in the next five years, will be the best time—at least for several years to come—to apply to medical school, in percentage admissions terms. That's encouraging.

Application Year	No. of Applicants
1996	46,965
1997	43,016
1998	40,996
1999	38,443
2000	37,089
2001	34,860
2002	33,625

Finally, remember that the acceptance rates to *top-tier* medical schools will of course be much lower than 49 percent. Fortunately, as we will discuss later, the way modern medical education is organized, **you have a fair chance at gaining a top residency after attending *any* medical school in the country.** It is your residency and post-graduate training experience, much more than the particular medical school you attend, that most strongly influences your initial practice options as a physician. *So just get in!* Further, for *most* physicians, the connections you will make during your career are much more important than your medical school network. Therefore, unlike college, getting into a top medical school is much less important than just getting into a medical school, period. Medical school status is quite overrated within the premedical community at many universities.

Now for a little bad news, at least from the view of the prospective medical student. While the number of applicants is declining, the caliber of the applicant pool continues to increase steadily from year to year.

Science GPAs Inching Up
The mean science GPA for all premed applicants is slowly increasing annually. If the trend follows the same trajectory, premeds should aim for science GPAs that are about a hundredth of a point higher (3.37) in the next year or two.

Application Year	Mean Science GPA
1992	3.13
1993	3.15
1994	3.18
1995	3.22
1996	3.26
1997	3.30
1998	3.32
1999	3.34
2000	3.35
2001	3.36
2002	3.36

Non-Science GPAs Also Inching Up

Premeds continue to steadily improve in non-science subjects as well. Note also that mean **non-science GPAs** tend to be **two-tenths of a GPA point higher**, on average, than science GPAs for most medical school applicants. Remember this. It means that when you take non-science courses, committees expect you to perform measurably better in those courses, on average, than in your science courses

Application Year	Mean Non-science GPA
1992	3.39
1993	3.40
1994	3.40
1995	3.43
1996	3.46
1997	3.50
1998	3.52
1999	3.55
2000	3.56
2001	3.58
2002	3.59

MCAT Science Scores Continue to Rise

Mean MCAT scores for the general applicant pool climbed steadily throughout the 1990s, but have fortunately appear to have stabilized in the last three years.. Whereas the mean score on Biological Sciences section in 1992 was 8.2, a decade later the mean score was *more than a full point higher, at 9.3.*

MCAT Science Scores, All Applicants:

Application Year	Biological Sciences (mean score)	Physical Sciences (mean score)
1992	8.2	8.1
1993	8.3	8.2
1994	8.5	8.3
1995	8.7	8.6
1996	8.9	8.7
1997	9.1	8.7
1998	9.2	8.9
1999	9.3	9.0
2000	9.3	8.9
2001	9.2	9.0
2002	9.3	9.1

For **matriculants** (entering medical students) mean science MCAT scores are a full point higher than they are for the general applicant pool, hovering around **10.2 for Biological Sciences,** and **10.0 for Physical Sciences.**

MCAT Science Scores, Matriculants:

Application Year	Biological Sciences (mean score)	Physical Sciences (mean score)
1992	9.3	9.2
1993	9.5	9.3
1994	9.6	9.4
1995	9.8	9.7
1996	10.0	9.8
1997	10.1	9.8
1998	10.2	9.9
1999	10.2	10.0
2000	10.2	10.0
2001	10.1	10.0
2002	10.2	10.0

Also note that both applicant and matriculant averages are generally two-tenths of a point higher on the Biological Sciences section than the Physical Sciences section. As soon as you have covered all of the material that appears on the MCAT, take a sample MCAT test and see if this is true for yourself as well. You want to know early the areas where you fall short of the average accepted applicant so that you can begin to address them, as we will discuss in Chapter Six.

MCAT Verbal Scores Nearly Flat

Scores for the MCAT Verbal Reasoning and Writing Sample sections have been very slowly rising for all medical school applicants:

Application Year	Verbal Reasoning	Writing Sample
1992	8.3	O
1993	8.3	O
1994	8.3	O
1995	8.5	O
1996	8.5	O
1997	8.6	O
1998	8.6	O
1999	8.7	P
2000	8.7	P
2001	8.6	P
2002	8.7	P

. . . but they have long leveled off at 9.5 and P respectively for matriculants:

Application Year	Verbal Reasoning	Writing Sample
1992	9.2	O
1993	9.4	P
1994	9.4	P
1995	9.5	P
1996	9.6	P
1997	9.6	P
1998	9.5	P
1999	9.5	P
2000	9.5	P
2001	9.5	P
2002	9.5	P

MCAT STATS source: AAMC: Data Warehouse: Applicant Matriculant File as of 11/4/2002

Application and Acceptance Rates by Gender

As you can see, the medical school admissions is finally gender-balanced. Now let's hope this occurs not only at the practice level, but also within positions of power in the medical hierarchy in coming years.

	Women	Men
Applicants	16,556 (49.2% of total)	17,069 (50.8% of total)
Acceptees	8,630 (49.1%)	8,962 (50.9% of total)
Matriculants	8,133 (49.2%)	8,375 (50.8% of total)

Application and Acceptance Rates for Underrepresented Minorities

Students who identify as African American, American Indian/Native Alaskan, Native Hawaiian, Mexican American, or Puerto Rican mainland are considered underrepresented minorities (URM) in the medical school admissions process. In 2002, 4,294 students who applied to medical school identified as an underrepresented minority. Their numbers dropped off slightly between application and acceptance.

Underrepresented Minority Applicants and Matriculants, 2001:

	URM	Non URM
Applicants	4,296 (12.8% of total)	29,331 (87.2% of total)
Acceptees	2,013 (11.4% of total)	15,579 (88.6% of total)
Matriculants	1,906 (11.6% of total)	14,582 (88.4% of total)

It should be noted that Asian/Pacific Islanders are also classified as minorities by AMCAS, but as they comprise roughly 19 percent of medical school matriculants, they are not considered underrepresented within the medical profession.

Despite the ongoing efforts of minority recruitment and mentoring programs, the number of URM students entering medical school has been essentially flat, even slightly down over the past decade. We can and must do more to fix this disparity and be aware of a cycle of constraint; presently, too few role models can be found in the profession for URM students who are considering the possibility of medical practice.

Application Year	No. of Acceptees	No. of URM Acceptees	URM % of total
1992	17,465	1,928	11.0%
1993	17,361	1,991	11.4%
1994	17,318	2,134	12.3%
1995	17,357	2,142	12.3%
1996	17,385	2,041	11.7%
1997	17,313	1,888	10.9%
1998	17,373	1,982	11.4%
1999	17,421	1,856	10.7%
2000	17,536	1,851	10.6%
2001	17,456	1,881	10.8%

Age and the Applicant

While there is an increasing acceptance of both older (or nontraditional) medical students in the past decades, as well as increasing numbers of BS/MD students entering medicine at a younger age, the mean age for medical school remains "traditional," meaning that most students begin American medical schools within a year of graduation from undergraduate school. Currently, the mean age for entering U.S. medical students is roughly **24.5**. The following table shows the age of applicants at expected date of matriculation:

Application Year	Mean Age
1992	24.5
1993	24.6
1994	24.7
1995	24.7
1996	24.8
1997	24.6
1998	24.6
1999	24.5
2000	24.4
2001	24.4

If you are an older applicant wondering just how the application process treats nontraditional students, keep in mind that medical schools today admit a wide variety of applicants with special talents and backgrounds, bringing true diversity to the average modern entering class of medical school students, and making the world "nontraditional" less relevant. Students often take a year or two off from academics for other pursuits, stay an extra year at their undergraduate university to obtain more education, or work a while before applying. Some even take extended time off to raise a family, or switch careers after trying other professions.

At the same time, if you analyze the MSAR statistics on acceptance of older applicants, you will discover **an increasing bias against applicants older than 27**, as well as those who have **applied to medical school more than twice**. If you do not wish to fight this bias, you may decide to apply to a foreign medical school simultaneously with your U.S. applications. Foreign medical schools, for all of their drawbacks (and there are several) are much more willing to give applicants in their thirties, and occasionally even older, a chance to find their place in medicine as a physician. We will discuss these issues further in the Chapter Ten.

ANATOMY OF THE SUCCESSFUL PHYSICIAN CANDIDATE

Since most medical school applicants have a strong **academic record** (Great Peak One) and **MCAT scores** (Great Peak Two), schools need additional ways to distinguish among candidates, hence the remaining five peaks. Through the applications process, medical schools strive to select students whose applications suggest not just the intelligence but the **personality and character** necessary to make a great physician. Maximizing your chance of acceptance to medical school is not just about getting good grades and beating the average MCAT scores. It also requires convincing a committee of professionals that you have the personal qualities and work ethic that would make you both happy and productive in medicine. Medical schools will carefully scrutinize your application for signs that you will or won't be a good doctor. Keep in mind that as you are preparing for medical school, you are preparing the whole package. Seek to improve yourself as a person, not just your grades and test scores.

SEVEN KEY CHARACTERISTICS OF A MEDICAL SCHOOL CANDIDATE

At some of our test prep centers, we have assembled a 25-foot-long admissions wall. This wall contains the catalogs of all 127 U.S. allopathic medical schools displayed in Plexiglas holders suitable for student browsing. Because these schools write their admissions literature with an eye toward attracting you to apply, you can glean much about the kind of student that the medical profession is seeking. In the following pages, we outline **seven hallmark qualities** shared by successful medical school matriculants in the opinion of the schools, as well as **ten additional qualities** stressed by some schools, but not others.

Medical schools are looking for passionate, humane, and interesting individuals who can add diversity of thought and distinctive experiences to the incoming class. Despite this predilection for **"useful uniqueness,"** there are at least seven broad generalizations that can be made about the type of candidates medical schools favor. As you look over the following characteristics, ask how you are presently improving yourself in each of these areas.

1. Academic Ability

Medical school is a lengthy, grueling, and stressful process, followed by many years of notoriously difficult clinical training. If your academic background and MCAT scores do not indicate that you can handle the workload and pressure of medical education, you will not be considered at most institutions. Therefore, you must have a record that indicates academic competence and MCAT scores that reflect an ability to think critically and logically under time pressure.

Generally speaking, your undergraduate performance is the most important aspect of your medical school application. That said, many premeds prioritize their GPA to a fault. **Getting good grades is the most time-consuming aspect of medical school preparation**, but that does not mean that this process should take up all your free time. As the statistics clearly show, the average accepted student does not have a 4.0 GPA and a 36T on the MCAT. If you are already maintaining your overall GPA (science and non-science) above the national accepted average of approximately **3.45**, you should dedicate time to improving in other areas important to your application.

Further, medical schools are not expecting perfection from their candidates. Medical schools will admit students who fall short of the average acceptance criteria in a few areas, as long as they can account for the discrepancy or otherwise prove that they have the ability to do the work. While you should develop good study habits and take your undergraduate education very seriously, don't waste your precious free time trying to get perfect grades from a terrible professor, or use the "grades excuse" to neglect any of the other challenging aspects of your personal growth and development listed below.

2. Non-Academic Competence/Skills

When it comes to the undergraduate college experience, it is often said that **half your education comes from your peers**. In the dining halls and the dorm rooms, the people you meet in college have at least as much potential to open your mind and teach you about the world as your professors do. It is exactly for this reason that the top undergraduate colleges try to recruit students who are **leaders** in many different areas or who can contribute to the school **community** through unique talents or experience.

Similarly, medical schools want to enhance the overall educational environment by recruiting individuals who will bring a **wide range of skills and real-life experience** to the classroom. Medical schools try to examine many aspects of a student's life and imagine what they could contribute to the class and to the profession beyond an ability to do the work. Again, most applicants to medical school have strong undergraduate grades and MCAT scores. Medical schools need other ways to determine who has the skills and sensitivity necessary to be a great doctor.

For example, perhaps you have studied biology in school, but have also played in the orchestra, or been an Olympic swimmer. Or maybe you are an English major who has written a prize-winning thesis, or been published in a magazine. Like undergraduate colleges, medical school admissions committees are impressed by achievement in art, the ability to speak a foreign language, athletic prowess, service to the community, or other competence in any non-academic skill. So think about how you can differentiate yourself outside of your grades and coursework.

3. Contribution to the Welfare of Others

The best doctors have a profound desire to improve the lives of other people in the most fundamental ways. Medical schools look for students who show potential to make a contribution to society. They know that if an applicant doesn't seem to care deeply about helping other people *through* medicine, they are probably pursuing the wrong profession. Without an intrinsic satisfaction and love of the work, the time and money it takes to become a doctor will overshadow the benefits.

There is no single way to demonstrate compassion or commitment to service. Generally, the strength (and secondarily, the breadth) of your extracurricular activities can provide a good sense of your **commitment to helping others**. Med schools favor extracurricular activities that demonstrate compassion, benevolence, and a desire to give back to the community, whether it is through medicine, teaching, or any other community-oriented activity.

Admissions committees also look for qualities of compassion and empathy during the interview, in letters of recommendation, and in your essays. Compassion is a quality that comes from deep within and is intrinsic to thinking and feeling habits that you have developed. If you do not feel it, it *can* be learned through time and appropriate experience, like any emotional intelligence. Classic medical autobiographies like Albert Schweitzer's *Out of My Life and Thought*, or Florence Nightingale's *Notes on Nursing*, as well as contemporary books like the Dalai Lama's *An Open Heart*, Marshall Rosenberg's *Speaking Peace: Connecting with Others through Non-Violent Communication*, and Scott Hunt's *The Future of Peace* are all valuable places to observe compassion in action. Committees can usually see through a student who attempts to fake these qualities on an application and in an interview, so work on developing them for real.

4. Commitment and Follow Through

Medical school is the very beginning of your life's journey as a doctor. Once you have your MD, the challenges don't stop. As your career progresses you will have more time to enjoy your position and benefits, but that will be secondary to the main tempo of your life, your professional career. **Even family priorities, for all their importance, must often times be put on hold to allow you to follow through with professional duties, and community activities, for all their value, take a distant third.** You will continue to work hard, continue to learn, and improve yourself every day for the rest of your career.

Medical schools do not want to spend time and resources educating students who will not go on to practice medicine. The challenges of medical education are endless, and sometimes quite significant. When there is an obstacle in your path, do you persevere, or do you get frustrated easily? Do you overcome adversity or give in to defeat?

The first evidence of your potential to take on challenges and follow through with them is committing to and finishing your premedical curriculum with an acceptable GPA. Another is obtaining a respectable score on the MCAT. Other commitments, such as graduating from college, are actually not required by most medical schools but may be important to your own personal path. For some, such as students from economically disadvantaged families or first-generation college students, completing college can be a significantly greater challenge than it is for others. Medical schools give special consideration to these factors when evaluating your undergraduate performance.

Where else have you demonstrated this type of commitment and follow through? Maybe you have participated in and completed a long-term project, learned a language, acquired a difficult skill (like learning an instrument), or published a paper in a refereed journal. Sustained long-term commitment to an extracurricular activity (two years or more) while you are in college will also make a positive impression on admissions committees.

5. Emotional Intelligence

No matter what their specialty, the best doctors are those who have taken the time to develop an **inherent understanding of people**. Having a basic level of this quality is so important to the profession that medical schools take the time to *personally interview* each and every candidate they are considering for admission.

Are you able to identify with or feel for people in need? Can you communicate with them on their terms? Do you work well on team projects? Do you like meeting new people and making new friends? Can you cheer people up when they are feeling down? Can you relate to kids or teenagers? Can you get people to listen to your opinion or speak as a figure of authority when necessary? Are you a good listener?

As a doctor, you will need to make a basic, human connection with your patients so that you can earn their respect and trust. You will need to explain new and complex concepts to people who may have no understanding of medicine or the human body. You will have to recommend treatments and persuade reluctant, scared patients to follow your advice. Occasionally you will have to deliver difficult, life-changing news. All of these situations require good emotional intelligence.

While some medical fields (like general practice or psychiatry) require more patient interaction than others (like surgery, pathology, or radiology), every doctor must, at some point, communicate with patients. In fact, the average doctor (across all specialties) spends the large majority of his time with patients. On top of that, doctors direct and advise teams of nurses, technicians, and other professionals. You will not have a good working relationship with your colleagues if you are abrasive, nervous, or uncomfortable. It is natural to be shy. However, if you are regularly uncomfortable in social environments or meeting new people, you will be at a real disadvantage applying to medical school.

The best way to improve your emotional intelligence is to engage regularly in close human-to-human interaction in ways that really benefit another person. We will discuss this further in Chapters Five and Nine. You may naturally be a little nervous on interview day, but if your extracurricular activities include three years as a supervised youth tutor or in health education, or some similar demonstration of your interest in people, admissions committees are much more likely to trust that you have the necessary emotional maturity that the profession requires.

6. Verbal Skills

Medical schools expect candidates to develop strong verbal communication skills, both oral and written, during their undergraduate years. Admissions committees view verbal ability as an essential aspect of a well-rounded, well-educated individual. No matter what your future specialty, you must be able to **read, understand, and interpret complex medical subject matter, have good speaking abilities, and written talent**. The committee will pay close attention to the quality of your personal statement, your performance in English or other humanities-based courses, and your performance on the verbal reasoning section of the MCAT.

It helps to remember that 50 percent of applicants are eliminated during the interview. Though it is difficult to be certain, analysis suggests that after the simple fact of an **oversupply of good candidates**, the second most common reason applicants are eliminated is because they show **substandard verbal communication skills**, including emotional intelligence, in comparison to their peers. If you do not presently have strong verbal skills, it will take several years, not months, of dedicated effort to build them. This is particularly true if English is not your native language. If you are serious about getting into medical school, you will need at least average reading and writing skills. Ignoring this requirement may take you as far as the final Great Peak, but it is not likely to get you past the interview. In Chapter Four, we will give an in-depth overview of how to improve your verbal ability.

7. Fitness for the Profession

The hard truth is that medical schools are on the lookout for things about your past or your character that suggest that you would not make a good doctor. Health care is a demanding, prestigious, and trust-based field, and medical schools seek to admit students who are **physically, emotionally, and ethically fit** for a job within it. If you had disciplinary action as an undergrad, including the breaking of academic or other codes of conduct, medical schools will seriously question whether you are ethically fit for the profession. Is there evidence of psychiatric issues in your evaluations? Fiscal mismanagement on your record? Medical schools do not yet and may legally never be able to require credit reports, but it helps to act as if they do. Have you had repeated trouble completing your undergraduate coursework in a timely manner? The more fitness questions you bring to the table, the more explanation will be necessary.

Medical schools also have clinical skills requirements that make it harder, if not impossible, for students with certain physical disabilities to enter medical school. In recent years, however, disability activist groups have made great strides in getting spots for disabled students. For more information about the special challenges for disabled medical students, visit the **American Medical Student Association (AMSA)** website, which has detailed information on this issue (www.amsa.org/adv/cod/disres.cfm).

TEN OTHER QUALITIES TO STRIVE FOR

While the seven preceding qualities tend to be desirable at all medical schools, each school has its own additional set of values and educational focus. Some schools will have a vision and mission that is better suited to your unique background than others. The University of Chicago, for example, stresses applicant leadership abilities, whereas Washington University stresses analytical mastery and critical thinking skills.

When you are applying you should seek to find those schools whose mission best matches your background and personality. If you want to know the qualities of interest to a specific medical school, carefully read its website, catalog, and other admissions materials, paying close attention to what they say, and almost as importantly, to what they don't say. Getting feedback from the students who are actually attending a school is also a good secondary source of information, and your **career counseling office** may have feedback forms that have been filled out by alumni of the medical schools you are considering attending.

Again, while each school has its own focus, some qualities are more generally desirable than others. In our review of medical schools' written materials and websites, the following **ten secondary qualities** of successful applicants were the most commonly mentioned.

Leadership and Initiative

As a physician, you will very often be the **highest-ranking member in the medical chain of command**, leading teams of nurses, techs, and allied health professionals and generally serving as the ultimate authority to all your patients. A demonstrated quality of leadership, ingenuity, and initiative can make the difference between being Dr. Generic and a great physician. Medical schools want to admit students who will later become distinguished alumni, bringing prestige and passion to the field and to their alma mater. Will you go on to achieve distinction in your career or settle into a routine position?

To determine your potential for leadership and initiative, medical schools that are interested in this characteristic will evaluate your academic and extracurricular record. They will look for evidence of leadership roles in the past, such as in student government or as an editor of the student newspaper. They may also look for personal initiative and passion, like a self-designed major or an independent study program with a celebrated professor.

Maturity

Surviving medical school is more a test of the character you have built to date than it is an opportunity to build a new, tougher character. There just isn't much time for character-building in medical school; "character testing" is a more apt description of the process you go through. As a medical student and resident, you will be exposed to **frequent stress, time pressure, and high expectations**. With the overwhelming demands of a medical education, your social life will be put on hold for a few years, giving you much less time to volunteer, travel, hang out with friends, or engage in other life-enriching experiences. Later in your education and career, you will have more character-building opportunities, but some medical schools consciously seek out students who are already obviously mature, collected, and prepared to handle the challenges of health education. Students who display wisdom, who show balance under stress in their academic and extracurricular record, who show maturity on their interviews, or who enter medical school at a slightly older age are at an advantage in this category.

Self-Confidence

There is a minor but persistent stereotype that some urban doctors are cocky, insular, self-obsessed, sports-car-loving egoists, having too much self-confidence for their own good. In reality, however, very few practitioners are truly obnoxious in any profession. If you look around, you will discover that medicine attracts no more of this abrasive type than other top professional fields, such as law.

In the premedical world however, if there is a self-confidence problem it may be at the other extreme. Many medical school applicants appear humble to a fault, timidly outlining their positive points in their personal statement and answering interview questions with a quiet, self-deprecating humility. While overconfidence is definitely unappealing, the opposite—lack of confidence— is also something to avoid. Without being arrogant or overbearing, be confident of who you are and who you are continuously becoming.

Informed self-confidence is essential to the successful physician. As a physician, you will need to make important decisions with clarity and resolve. While you will often find yourself the final word on ethically complicated and tricky situations, you will never have perfect information at your disposal. Instead, you will have to make decisions competently with the information you do have. You will also second guess some of your more important decisions regularly, but you will need to learn to do this in a way that does not promote anxiety and lack of trust in your patients, as they will be watching your every move as well as they can. Indecisive, vacillating, and insecure people can be at a serious disadvantage as a doctor, where others will continually look to them for their leadership and decision-making abilities.

Genuine Interest in Medicine and Learning

Considering the vast body of knowledge about medicine and health care that is available today, it will take a lifetime of interest and learning for you to make any headway. What's more, the field will continue to expand at an accelerating rate for the rest of your career, creating an ever-increasing volume of knowledge, therapies, treatments, issues, and news for you to remain on top of. Fortunately, much of the information you do manage to learn will have a deeper positive impact on the average person's life than in just about any other field.

However, many professions give you the opportunity to help people, from education, to nonprofit work, to politics. **Why is medicine right for you?** While a desire to help people is essential, admissions committees also look for students who have a natural, deep interest and joy in science and medicine. You will spend your life immersed in these topics. Did you view the premedical prerequisites as just simply an obligation to fulfill? Will you run out of patience for biological detail? At the other extreme, will you get lost in the details of learning and forget their application to medicine? Whenever possible, medical schools would like to admit students who deeply and genuinely enjoy scientific understanding, the study of health, and the daily application of this knowledge for human benefit.

Diversity of Experience

Doctors are entrusted with the health and vitality of the public, yet they generally come from a small, self-selected subset of society. Medical schools understand that applicants with **unique or diverse backgrounds** will bring a broader level of understanding to the job, add depth to the class, and be an asset to any health care team. They are always looking for ways to add diversity without sacrificing applicant excellence.

There are many ways that your background could be unique in a medical school class. For example, if you grew up in a small, midwestern town with a population of 300 and then attended a big state university, you would have a strong understanding of various living environments, possibly including the special needs of rural populations. Perhaps when you were a child, you and your family immigrated to the United States from a foreign country, making you intimately familiar with a foreign culture as well as with the experience of immigrants in America. As a premed, you should take the opportunity to expand your worldview, diversify your experience, and understand new cultures when possible.

Enthusiasm and Attitude

There are times, both in life and in your medical education, when the only thing you have real control over is your **attitude**. For this reason, it has often been stated that the attitude we choose to express each day is our own "truest self." Students who inspire others with their enthusiasm, love of learning and practice, and positive outlook are an asset to any class. In medical school, where the pressures can be overwhelming, students with a positive attitude are most likely to stay afloat and get things done, rather than getting bogged down in less significant details, stress, or perfectionism. Your attitude is easily reflected in the words you choose in your application, and it is also very strongly transmitted during your medical school interview. You can cultivate an optimistic but pragmatic attitude now, while you walk your premedical path. If you develop it well, it will stay with you through a lifetime of challenges.

Open-Mindedness

Flexibility and tolerance are important qualities in the modern medical climate. Schools wish to produce doctors who can learn new technologies without needless adherence to old ways of practice, who also know when to hold on to tradition, who can improve along with the therapies, and who can **incorporate new ideas** into their worldview. In addition, physicians are often at the center of ethically challenging decisions. As a doctor, you may have patients who want to do something or have beliefs that deviate from your own moral sensibilities. **How will you approach patients whose ethical choices differ from your own?** Can you see other sides of a situation? Can you eloquently communicate your understanding of their perspective and empathy with their position, even if you have a different opinion? Can you work alongside colleagues whose opinions do not match yours? Do you treat all people with decency and respect? In your application, essay, and interview, try to exemplify open-mindedness and an ability to compassionately understand situations. At the very least, try not to be needlessly defensive, critical, or sharply opinionated in any case.

Critical Thinking Skills

Can you solve problems, see hidden patterns, or put unrelated information together in a logical way? To be a doctor, you will need a constant ability to use your brain at the best level you can muster. Despite accelerating technological developments and advancements in the field, the doctor's individual ability to evaluate information and diagnose problems remains one of the most important and powerful forces in health care.

Most medical schools evaluate a student's critical thinking skills through their performance on the MCAT, but others look closely at the entire applications record to discover your critical thinking ability. How difficult were your undergraduate courses? What other challenges did you set for yourself?

Fortunately, with systematic practice and a good test preparation strategy such as The Princeton Review's, you can dramatically improve your MCAT scores. It's just a matter of time, dedication, and a smart program of study.

Sacrifice

Some students who are applying to medical school don't realize the level of sacrifice they will be making in the process of becoming a respected physician. If your premedical curriculum wasn't stressful enough, you still have four more years of medical school, at least three additional years of residency and internship (perhaps more), then another ten years of paying down your hefty student loans and building a clinical experience base before you may begin to feel that you aren't sacrificing other aspects of your life. Even then, you will continue to put in long hours, often working much harder than any other type of professional.

Some students have to make lots of sacrifices or overcome adversity to study medicine. Other students have had to sacrifice excellence in other pursuits. This quality is extremely impressive to certain medical schools because it demonstrates that the student has already made a deep commitment to the field and will persevere through the upcoming challenges.

Career Vision or Long-Term Objectives

Some students enter medicine with a unique area of focus or career plan in mind. Many of these students will change that focus during the hectic, information-rich years of medical school, and such changing of vision is a natural and healthy process. Nevertheless, those few who have developed skills in a particular area and who continue that focus throughout medical school and residency can find it particularly easy to become leaders in their chosen field and outstanding alumni. A strong, preexisting motivation for entering medical school, for those few who cultivate this, will make your application stand out amongst the thousands and strengthen your overall candidacy. Try to develop a vision of your medical future, and run with that vision as far as your legs will take you!

Your Video Assignments for Chapter 3:

Gross Anatomy, Without Limits, and *Prefontaine*

CHAPTER 4
UNASSAILABLE UNDERGRADUATE GPA: STUDY SKILLS AND THE PREMEDICAL TIMELINE

> *"Learn the rules well so that you can break them properly."*
>
> – The Dalai Lama

It's not easy to build an unassailable grade point average during your undergraduate years. Several factors work against the premedical student. To apply to medical school on the typical four-year plan, you will have to successfully complete two full years of prerequisites while simultaneously meeting university graduation and major requirements. Since most universities don't offer a premedical major, the average premed **simply does more work** than most other college students, with no assurance that their effort will be rewarded with admission to medical school.

As if that weren't enough, premeds know that they must strive to keep their grades between a challenging B+ and an A- average, or they will probably not even be considered for a place in medical school. Even worse, the lower-level courses at many large universities function as "weeder" environments. Such classes are intended to **eliminate scores of students** from pursuing the dream of medicine simply by creating a series of fast-paced, brutal initial challenges, with little personal assistance available for those students who are slow to learn how to study science coursework. What's more, premeds are in the majority in many of these classes, and they are often not graded on absolute performance, but instead on a curve, conveniently ensuring that a significant percentage of students must get below the B+/A- average sought by the serious student.

Given these constraints, it is no surprise that most undergrads give up on their interest in medicine before they even get halfway through their premedical curricular requirements. For those who manage to stay in the game to the end, college can feel like a pressure cooker, requiring blood, sweat, and tears all the way through. Though you may feel like a hamster on a treadmill, the bottom line is this: your premedical courses are necessary steps toward your dream. Your undergraduate years are a great time to hone the skills needed for medical school, as well as an opportunity to try many new and exciting things that, as a medical school student or doctor, you will not have the time for or access to.

If you learn to plan, build strong study skills, and keep a positive attitude, your college years will be an exciting, liberating, life-enriching passage. Don't let unreasonable schedules, poor planning, lack of focus and balance, stress, perfectionism, cynicism, negativity, and self-doubt ruin the experience for you. You can enjoy college—and still get into medical school!

THE TOP TEN PAYOFFS OF AN UNDERGRADUATE EDUCATION

Though academic demands are at the forefront of any premed's college experience, you should still make time for other aspects of university life. College is an excellent time to work on developing some of the key personal characteristics we discussed in the previous chapter. Further, college is a time to experiment, try new things, and challenge your ideas and opinions.

After coaching thousands of students through the premedical process, the following is our proposed list of the **top ten practical payoffs** of a college degree. Will you acquire all ten of these payoffs during your time in college, or only a few? The choice is yours. If you skip or skimp on any of them now, you'll probably find each becomes twice as hard to develop in the future. Think seriously before forgoing any one of them, as they all could be very useful to your path of heart.

1. A WORLDVIEW AND CRITICAL THINKING MINDSET

It is often said the most important payoff of your undergraduate education isn't what particular things you study, but that you learn a **big picture** of the world, and how to **think deeply for yourself**. Each of these is an important life challenge, and each is occasionally missed by overly myopic or overly passive undergraduate students.

You've probably heard the adage that which undergraduate degree you choose is nearly irrelevant to the larger world. So, the big question is, who exactly *is* your degree most relevant to? I'm sure you know that answer by now: you and only you. Your degree is a tool that keeps you balanced and focused on your future. You will want to pick courses and a degree that first, give you a useful worldview, second, improve your thinking ability, and lastly, advance you along some chosen path.

During your freshman and sophomore years, pick general education requirements that allow you to build a broad, big picture. *College will undoubtedly be your last easy time to do so.* At the same time, improve your critical thinking skills by taking challenging courses.

There's also the question of the type of critical thinking skills that you feel you need most. Some courses and majors offer a lot of practical utility, helping you master a set of specific skills (math, science, computer programming) that you might use professionally later in life. Other degrees (psychology, sociology, history) can give deeper insight into human nature, improving your ability to appreciate and interact with people of all types, which are general skills you will use professionally later in life, no matter what you do.

Unlike your extracurricular activities, which can benefit from early specialization, many advisors suggest that seeking **balance** is usually the wisest course in your **undergraduate** curriculum. If you are *already* strong in people skills and life experience, technical courses could provide a valuable balance to your life education. They will give you the ability and confidence to better understand medical science and technology in several very useful, specific ways. If you aren't yet a people person, then a humanities major or minor could be very helpful. With humanities, you have the opportunity to learn a broad set of interpersonal critical thinking skills that you will use incessantly throughout your career.

Many college and university professors delight in drawing out their students' opinions, in broadening their minds, and causing them to re-examine their views and perceptions. Seek classes with professors who will challenge you to think in new ways. Ask your senior friends: **Who are the great professors here?** Which class changed your life the most?

College is the last easy time to really open your mind to new ideas, expand your worldview, and expose yourself to totally unfamiliar academic territory. Granted, your premedical courses and major requirements don't leave a lot of time for electives. But if you've been particularly sheltered or disadvantaged prior to starting college, perhaps a **double major**, or an **additional year** of undergraduate study would help you gain both the worldview and the critical thinking ability you ought to leave college with. One thing is certain: once you are in medical school you will be deeply focused on medicine and will not have much opportunity to learn about other topics, except through their medical dimensions. Take advantage of the unique opportunity you have now to take classes that will teach you about the world and give you a comprehensive, well-rounded education.

2. DISCIPLINE

Let's begin with a reminder from Dr. Nelson, "The amount of studying you will do in medical school, and the number of hours you will work in residency will far surpass anything that you will ever do as an undergraduate; therefore, it is important to realize that getting into medical school is only the beginning of a long but worthwhile road that demands **time, energy, determination, dedication, and incredible discipline.** If you lack these skills when you enter medical school, the chance of future success is greatly diminished."

As a premed, it may be difficult to accept that your lot in life is just harder than it is for most other students. Discipline is, however, a matter of having enough **respect for yourself and your goals** to make some sacrifices to achieve them. Maybe you stayed home to study bio when your roommates went to fraternity parties, or had to skip a great weekend ski trip to finish studying for the MCAT. Maybe you pushed through an extra hour of very focused and necessary studying for your chemistry final, even though you were ready to go to bed. Though it can be hard to make sacrifices—especially when you compare yourself to other undergraduates who are often taking easier paths—realize that making successful tough choices now builds discipline and character. This will serve you well, both now and down the road.

3. SUPERLATIVE COMMUNICATIONS SKILLS

We've said before, but it's worth repeating: to be considered for medical school, it is imperative that you develop excellent oral and written communication skills. Dr. Nelson observes: "Probably the most important skill in medicine is the **art of effective communication**—with patients concerning their medical care, with other physicians when reporting on a patient, with families about sick loved ones." As a result, medical schools view verbal skills as a fundamental part of the educated and well-rounded physician. Without them, you will be a below-average candidate, no matter what your science GPA.

College is the typical person's "last ideal environment" to build strong verbal skills. Through consistent practice in writing-based humanities courses, you will be able to build these skills more effectively than in any other way. If you were lucky enough to start college with good verbal skills, don't let them lie dormant. Continue to hone them during your undergraduate career. Think of all those patient write-ups, research reports, treatment plans, and letters you will write during your medical education, all the oral reports you will give, all the conversations you will have with patients and fellow professionals. If you do not have strong verbal skills, you must take the time now to build them, even if you fear that this may negatively affect your GPA. Later in this chapter, we will review strategies for improving your verbal abilities through writing-based humanities coursework.

4. A NETWORK OF TRUE FRIENDS

College is one of those rare times in life when you are closely surrounded by a group of peers on a common testing ground. Your fellow students share your age, your classroom and, if you live in the dorms, your home. Like you, they are facing the same challenging, life-defining questions. They are struggling through college courses and trying to define themselves and their long-term life goals.

Many students form long-lasting friendships during late-night conversations in the hallways of their freshman dorm or over slices of pizza in the dining hall. **For most people, college is one of the most socially rich, exciting, and fun times in their lives.** Sadly, some premeds feel so much pressure to perform in their classes that they don't take much time to meet new people, outside of the occasional study group. While some people have no problem balancing an intense workload with an active social life, many have a hard time finding equilibrium between recreation and responsibility. While a medical calling can often mean prioritizing work over your social life, that doesn't eliminate socializing from the picture.

Having friends and relationships is a fundamental part of the human experience and is necessary for a happy, balanced lifestyle. The key is to

prioritize the important relationships in your life. While you may not be able to stay long at the party, nothing is stopping you from putting in a brief appearance at the highlight, and talking with those few people you really care to interact with most. Make time for coffee or a weekend getaway with your freshman roommate, or try study sessions with your most serious, least distracting friends. People are an important part of your personal, emotional, ethical, and educational development. Your best college friends will help you take breaks when you need them, and help you stay on track when the going gets tough. They will keep you grounded, humane, and happy, even as you spend most of your time with your nose in a book. Furthermore, they will provide an invaluable support network during the trials of applying to and going through medical school.

5. COMPUTER AND INFORMATICS FLUENCY

Medicine is quickly modernizing, becoming increasingly reliant on **computers, the Internet, and other technological tools.** As a doctor, you will need fluency, not just familiarity, with the world of computers. You don't have to be an expert programmer, nor do you need to name and dissect a machine's internal organs; however, you must strive to become a **power user** of an increasingly complicated number of programs. Dr. Nelson's advice: "As a bare beginning, take the time to become proficient at doing **electronic literature searches** for articles, creating **presentations** with PowerPoint, and writing papers with **MS Word** (in my experience, most hospitals are PC/Microsoft based). Even more fundamentally, take a typing course or use training software if you aren't a **fast typist** already!"

A strong background in computers and technology will help you throughout your education and career. Computer skills can be particularly advantageous during your residency and internship, when you will be working with older, more clinically experienced doctors. In many cases, older doctors do not have the time to learn all the newest technology. If you are good with computers, you will come in knowing something special that you can contribute to the medical team. Today's handheld and laptop computers are particularly valuable, as they can be easily used in any clinical environment.

6. Familiarity with a Foreign Language

In most parts of the United States, you will treat patients from a variety of backgrounds and cultures. If you have some extra time, consider taking **conversational classes in a foreign language**. Future physicians practicing in the southern or western states, for example, should seriously consider learning Spanish. If you do not know this already, college is the last easy time to become conversationally fluent in a foreign language. Two or three years of collegiate coursework is sufficient to achieve fluency, combined with continued occasional exposure afterward.

If you have the opportunity, you might also choose to spend a summer or semester abroad. This would be an excellent way to continue your studies while becoming more familiar with your foreign language of choice. For **Spanish**, trips to places like Mexico, Latin America, or Spain, periodic practice in a Spanish-speaking clinical environment, perhaps a free clinic in an inner city, and watching movies in Spanish will keep your language skills polished over a lifetime.

At the same time, keep in mind that all hospitals have translators, and that electronic translation systems will rapidly improve over the course of your career. If you are an undergraduate today, it is possible, but hard to predict, that an inexpensive universal translator service may become available by the time you have completed your residency.

7. Access to Unique Work Experiences

Many companies, governmental agencies, and nonprofit organizations will hire college students to work as an intern for a semester or for the summer during college, giving them the opportunity to help out while they gain real-world experience. The benefit of internships is that they allow students the opportunity to be exposed to the inner workings and power dynamics of a functioning organization. In exchange for this opportunity, an intern usually works for low wages, a small stipend, or no wages at all. Monetary rewards, however, are not the primary draw of an internship. Interning is an outstanding way to build experience in a career field of interest, get directly involved in a prestigious research project, or do creative work at a big, reputable company.

There are many, well-established internship programs throughout the United States as well as internationally. While you are in college, visit your **career center** early and often, not simply during the final weeks of school, as the typical student does. College career centers keep lists of internship opportunities. We also have two books, *The Internship Bible* and *The Best 109 Internships*, and a career center on our website, www.PrincetonReview.com, that can help you in your search for a rewarding internship. You can also check newspapers or talk with older premeds who may have had a particularly interesting internship. In the next chapter, we will discuss ways to look for and choose an extracurricular activity or internship.

8. Specialization (Medical or Otherwise)

During college, take the opportunity to become particularly talented in some subject, no matter what it is. We suggest classes that will give you in-depth knowledge about some aspect of **health care**, but you might also find a specialization in **any other discipline**, such as political science, psychology, or education. Often undergraduates are allowed to take medical school elective classes, nursing college classes, or staff education classes in local hospitals. Any of these courses will put you in early contact with an entirely different community than that of your undergraduate peers. Friendships made here will start you thinking about the kinds of skills you will want to build on your way to becoming a physician.

When you find an academic topic that interests you, look for **mentors** on your school's faculty. Also get to know non-academic leaders in the local community in your new field of interest. Find a great internship or volunteer opportunity in this area. Take advantage of the many resources available at your college and bring them to bear on this one (or perhaps two) area(s). Again, even as you focus, that specialty will help you to better understand medicine by example. It will also help your medical school application stand out in the crowd.

Keep in mind, however, that most entering medical students do not end up choosing the specialty they originally thought they would pursue. As Dr. Nelson relates, if you are unfamiliar with medicine, it is much more important to first learn a little about **all** the areas of medical practice rather than one specific area. Start with the outer arm of the inward spiral, "specializing in medicine in general," at first. Try to pick a particular subject (or two) for more in-depth extracurricular experience during college, but only after you are satisfied that you've really surveyed the field.

9. SELF-KNOWLEDGE

During high school, you aren't offered many choices. You don't decide which school you attend, where your classes are, who teaches them, or what's taught. You don't decide what time classes start or end. You don't decide if you need to do homework or not. In high school, almost everything is already decided for you.

College is typically the first time that you are free to make these and other decisions for yourself. While most colleges maintain some basic graduation requirements (and your parents might also have some influence), undergraduates have a great deal of freedom—and responsibility. Industrious undergrads might design their own majors, classes, or special projects in a subject of specific interest to them, while more passive undergrads might only choose Tuesday/Thursday classes that start after noon. No matter what you decide, no one will be hovering over you, monitoring your choices, and making sure that you are keeping up with work. From here on out, your life is up to you.

For this reason alone, college is a very exciting period of life. For the first time, you will be able to really explore. It's your opportunity to try what you've always dreamed about, and to create new dreams if the earlier ones don't hold up to the test of time. What will you do?

Delve into college and "discover" yourself through class work, journaling, reflection, and experience. **What makes your heart beat faster?** Have you long wanted to learn more about Eastern religions? Why not take a class on Buddhism? Do you wonder how suspension bridges are built? Why not try a class in mechanical engineering?

While college may be the first time you experience true academic freedom, for traditional premeds, it may also be the last time for quite a while. Once you are in medical school, you will not be taking many, if any, ceramics classes, water polo clinics, or linguistics seminars (though we have known determined medical students who were able to fit in a few such excursions every year). Take advantage of college as an amazing opportunity to experiment, learn, and explore yourself and your passions. You can do this at the same time that you satisfy premedical requirements, and you can compartmentalize both perspectives on your life, slipping into each as the occasion allows.

10. A PRACTICE RUN ON LIFE

Though it may seem like the beginning and end of the world, college is actually a testing ground for life. Don't be afraid to take on challenges for fear of making mistakes. Medical schools are not looking for perfect people. In fact, **you can only be perfect on paper if you don't adequately challenge yourself.** If you want to go far in life, you need to be confident enough to dive into new things, regardless of the risk. Have fun and don't be too afraid of making mistakes. You can correct them quickly and easily in college, learning from them with far fewer consequences than when you enter the real world after graduation.

Try something scary that you've never done before. During one of your summers, try starting a business, or a student group around one of your interests, or work in a nonprofit organization on some longshot political initiative. Or perhaps try out for that seemingly impossible goal or vision. You may fall short of your expectations, but you'll learn something excellent in the process. Who knows, you might even succeed, or at least surprise yourself with your hidden abilities. *Carpe Diem. Carpe Medicum.*

PREMED COURSE REQUIREMENTS

While premed course requirements vary by medical school, most require students to complete **one year of biology, one year of general chemistry, one year of organic chemistry**, and **one year of non-calculus physics** before entering the program. About **half of** the U.S. medical schools also require **calculus,** and some require **English** classes.

To verify each medical school's prerequisites, the best source of information is the *Medical School Admissions Requirements* (**MSAR**). This annual publication of the Association of American Medical Colleges has official requirements for allopathic medical schools. The *College Information Booklet* has the latest requirements for osteopathic programs. Our guide, *The Best Medical Schools*, also contains up-to-date information about each school's admissions requirements and prerequisites.

Help from High School
In a few cases, **AP Credits** from advanced high school coursework can be used to fill prerequisites, though it varies by medical school. Remember, the coursework is the requirement. A college degree is not even required for entrance to most U.S. medical schools, though almost all entering students do have one. Check with the school you are applying to or ask your premed advisor.

PREMED TIMELINE:
TRADITIONAL APPLICANTS

The traditional medical student is one who prepares for and applies to medical school during college, entering a program directly upon graduation from his or her undergraduate institution. For these students, there is a rough timeline for completing prerequisites and applying to medical school. It is worth understanding and comparing this timeline to your own plan. Bear in mind that there is no prescribed order in which premeds must complete their prerequisites, and many students do not follow this traditional timeline. You can arrange your premed courses in any form that accommodates your schedule or will best ensure strong performance. If you feel that your academic record will suffer if you follow the standard timetable, then don't adhere to it! Think creatively and find your own path to the top.

That said, the following is an outline of a **typical** premedical curriculum for traditional, full-time undergraduate students:

FRESHMAN YEAR
Academic:
- ✔ One year of general chemistry
- ✔ One semester of math
- ✔ One semester of biology
- ✔ One semester of English
- ✔ Introductory major requirements (optional)
- ✔ Relationship-building with professors who can later serve as mentors, offer you the opportunity to participate in research, or write recommendations on your behalf.

Extracurricular:
- ✔ Explore all the various specialties of medical practice, on your own time.
- ✔ Begin a health care related volunteer job or internship.
- ✔ Research academic societies, premed clubs, and other student organizations and consider joining one.

Other:
- ✔ Visit your premed advisor, review course requirements, and create a premedical game plan.
- ✔ Continue investigating medicine. Develop personal and academic goals. Write them down.

SOPHOMORE YEAR
Academic:
- ✔ Full year of organic chemistry
- ✔ Second semester of biology
- ✔ Other introductory major requirements

Extracurricular:

- ✔ If you had a positive experience in your freshman year, continue with the same extracurricular activity in your sophomore year; if you didn't enjoy it or were not sufficiently challenged, begin a new one immediately.

Applications:

- ✔ Toward the end of the year, begin researching medical school programs.
- ✔ Continue seeking relationships with professors and begin a list of those who might write your recommendations.

JUNIOR YEAR

Academic:

- ✔ One year of physics
- ✔ Upper division major coursework

Applications:

- ✔ Begin drafting your personal statement (early spring).
- ✔ Request applications from non-AMCAS medical schools (April).
- ✔ Collect letters of recommendation (to send starting in September).

MCAT:

- ✔ April MCAT. This is the best month to take the test, if you have a choice.

Summer Before Senior Year

Applications:

- ✔ Complete primary medical school applications. You may start this process as early as April and ideally should complete it by **June or July** ("in the J's"). If you want to be considered seriously for a position, you'll want to submit all application material no later than September. Your chances of acceptance go down *steadily* after the J's and *rapidly* after September.
- ✔ Research financial aid options.

MCAT:

- ✔ August MCAT, for premeds who did not take the MCAT in April, or who are retaking the exam.

Senior Year

Academic:

- ✔ Finish remaining premed requirements.
- ✔ Finish remaining major/university requirements.
- ✔ Take upper-division or graduate-level classes in medically related subjects such as physiology, histology, pharmacology, and anatomy, if you have time. This will allow some breathing space during the first two years of medical school.

Applications:

- ✔ Do more comprehensive research about the medical schools to which you applied.
- ✔ Complete secondary applications, sending in letters of recommendation (September – January).
- ✔ Submit FAFSA [Free Application for Student Assistance].

✔ Prepare for interviews, wait for invitations to interview (fall, winter, and early spring at some schools).

✔ Interview and wait for letters!

CHOOSING A MAJOR

Generally speaking, medical schools have no preference as to major. Admissions committees measure students' undergraduate performance by their GPA, GPA trends, class selection, and quality of the undergraduate institution attended. Admissions committees prefer students who appear to have a well-rounded educational background, show

> **Who gets in?**
> In recent years, biology majors make up the largest majority of admits (about 60 percent), followed by chemistry majors. Humanities majors make up a smaller percentage of applicants but their acceptance rates are almost always equal or greater than physical science majors. Medical schools are quite impressed with the music major who takes premedical prerequisites on the side and does very well in them.

promise in science coursework, have strong verbal skills, and possess other key characteristics that we mentioned in Chapter Three.

Under any circumstance, **your GPA is more important than your choice of major**. Therefore, you are best off choosing a major for which you have a natural aptitude and that you will truly enjoy. You will most likely perform well in classes that you like attending. In addition, if you decide you don't want to go to medical school after all, you will at least have general experience in something that you enjoy and value.

Nevertheless, a choice of major can in some cases positively affect your overall admissions candidacy. For example, you may be considering a **science major that is nationally recognized as being difficult**, such as molecular biology, engineering, or computer science. Combined with a high GPA in premed requirements and good performance on the MCAT, a tough science major can give you a small advantage, both at top-tier and at research-oriented medical schools. But this doesn't seem to be the case at primary care-oriented schools, or at second- and third-tier medical schools, so there is no pressing reason to go the technical route, if that is not your passion. Medical schools also seem to slightly favor humanities majors who have a high GPA in science courses and a good MCAT performance. While a tough major can give your application a boost, it will be outweighed by the negative effects of a lower GPA. Choose balance, in addition to finding your passion. If you are passionate about either science or humanities but currently have no strong skills in those areas, you will do well to **ramp up slowly**, perhaps with tutoring, an additional year of introductory-level courses, or switching to a less demanding major.

BS/MD Programs

A few U.S. universities offer early admission BS/MD programs, which allow talented high school students who apply for admission to them to automatically enter medical school upon graduation from college, as long as they maintain a certain GPA throughout their college years. These programs are an excellent opportunity for motivated high school students applying to college who are already certain that they want to be a doctor.

In most cases, BS/MD programs allow you to apply to other medical schools during your junior year of college. Further, some offer more academic support resources during college than the typical premedical curriculum, and you always have the opportunity to change your path entirely in your under-graduate years. Therefore, BS/MD programs can reduce the stress of applying to medical school in your junior and senior years, without limiting your options.

The following medical schools are affiliated with BS/MD programs:

Baylor College of Medicine

Boston University School of Medicine

Case Western Reserve U. School of Medicine

Columbia U. Coll. of Physicians and Surgeons

Eastern Virginia Medical School

Emory University School of Medicine

Indiana University School of Medicine

Louisiana State U. Schl of Med. in New Orleans

Mayo Medical School

New York Medical College

Temple University School of Medicine

Tulane University School of Medicine

UMDNJ/Robert Wood Johnson Medical Program

University of Alabama School of Medicine

University of Arizona College of Medicine

University of Arkansas College of Medicine

University of CA, Davis School of Medicine

University of CA, San Francisco School of Med.

University of Illinois Coll. of Med. at Peoria

University of Illinois Coll. of Med. at Rockford

University of Iowa Carver College of Medicine

University of Kansas School of Medicine

University of Miami School of Medicine

University of Michigan Medical School

University of Minn. Medical School—Twin Cities

University of Nebraska School of Medicine

University of New Mexico School of Medicine

University of NC at Chapel Hill School of Med.

University of Oklahoma School of Medicine

University of Pittsburgh School of Medicine

University of South Florida School of Medicine

University of South Carolina School of Medicine

University of Texas Medical Branch at Galveston

University of Texas Medical School at Houston

University of Utah School of Medicine

Vanderbilt University School of Medicine

Virginia Commonwealth U. School of Medicine

There are several books, such as *Medical School from High School* (2002), A. Ilyas; *High School Doctor* (2002), by Nagendra Sai Koneru, Omar Wang and Vineet Arora; and *From High School to Med School* (2000), Jason Yanofski and Ashish Raju, which offer detailed information on the types of early admission BS/MD programs. If you are or know any high school students already interested in medicine, be sure to check them out.

GPA AND STUDY SKILLS

How Are GPAs Evaluated?

Keep it in perspective
Even though your GPA is very important to medical schools, you do not need straight A's to get in. Don't focus on undergraduate classes to the exclusion of other aspects of personal development.

Bottom line, your undergraduate academic performance is the most important factor in any admissions decision. In 2002, the average GPA for accepted medical school students was **3.45.**

Since GPA is an average of all your grades, you don't need to perform at a B+/A- (3.3/3.5) level in *all* your classes, though that would be ideal. If your average GPA in the science subjects of **biology, chemistry, physics, and math** (what AMCAS calls BCPM) is around **3.35**, you can still be accepted into medical school. However, chances are that you will need the GPA from all your other coursework to compensate, at 3.55 or higher as necessary.

Most medical schools will evaluate an applicant's GPA in the context of his or her entire academic history. Medical schools look favorably on students who have overcome adversity to achieve, or who come from disadvantaged or minority backgrounds. A demanding work schedule of more than twenty hours per week during college may receive special consideration. Also of importance, particularly for top-tier medical schools, is the quality of the college or university attended. Some allowance may be made for receiving lower grades at top public, Ivy League, and technical universities. Yet most impressive, regardless of the university attended, are **sustained periods of high, though not perfect, GPA** (3.5 or above) on your transcript. Think of your premedical curriculum as a **marathon**, not a series of sprints followed by walking. Try to achieve a consistent strong performance in all your academic work.

Achieving in Science and Math

When it comes to academics, strive for excellence and balance, not excess. Admissions committees aren't expecting you to prove you can take 24 units of science coursework at once. They just want to see an academic record that strongly suggests you have the ability, consistency, and drive to satisfactorily complete the work that will be assigned in medical school. In fact, students have been known to gain acceptance into **Medical Scientist Training Programs** (fully funded M.D./Ph.D. programs), one of the most difficult paths in the medical world, while taking **only 12 units a quarter** and producing **unremarkable (but consistent!) research papers every year** of their undergraduate career. Again, consistency is more important than brilliance to most medical schools.

If you are struggling with your academics at first, take heart: excelling in science is a learned skill. Few practicing physicians were born with a natural aptitude for chemistry, physics, or mathematics. You may need to drop some courses more than once before you can properly assess what you can handle at the B+/A- level. Nevertheless, a drop followed by a new game plan and redoubled effort is *much* better than completing a year of science coursework with a low B or C average. With careful planning, hard work, and perseverance you will achieve the science coursework grades you need to get into medical school.

Below are some general tips for approaching science and math classes. They have been compiled during ten years of teaching science and math supplementary programs at our Hyperlearning centers. If you are just starting college, or if think you might need additional help building strong study skills, please also read **Appendix One: The Basic Study System** at the back of this book. Many premedical students have thanked us for this advice over the years, since Hyperlearning first opened its doors in 1988.

Mastering Calculus, Physics, General and Organic Chemistry, and Genetics

Choose the Right Classes
Don't take on more than you can comfortably control. You will definitely be a stronger candidate if you have great grades in the standard hard science prerequisites, rather than mediocre grades in more challenging science courses. We are not saying that you should avoid difficult courses. Medical schools want to see that you went beyond the basics in at least some subject area. Therefore,

you should aim to challenge yourself, either in your major or in some advanced science courses. However, do not take advanced level classes, such as science courses for chemistry/physics/engineering majors (unless you are one yourself) or tough upper division courses for which you have questionable preparation if there is a significant risk that you will not perform satisfactorily. To reduce your risk, preview the work required, and find tutorial help in advance.

Don't Read the Book...

...just **do the problems!** In all your math, chemistry, and physics courses, and in some biology courses like genetics, your grade will depend mostly upon on your performance on a small number of exams. It would be great to have a deep, conceptual understanding of the theoretical material for the course, but in many undergraduate science classes you will not have that luxury. There just isn't enough time. What really matters in these courses is that you are able to execute classic problems quickly on the exam. **The kinds of problems you are asked to do should guide *all* of your studying in your textbook**. Multiple-choice questions that test concepts, or short essays that test holistic understanding will require that you actually read the book. But professors assign very few such problems in typical lower-division science classes. In general, you'll be asked primarily to know how to set up and grind through **simple systems of equations** (physics and math), churn out **quick quantitative response**s (general chemistry, genetics), or set up **electron flow or other diagrams** for classic structures (organic chemistry, genetics). In such circumstances, you will need to have as much problem-solving experience as possible before the exams. That usually means skimming, not reading, the textbook.

The primary benefit of a textbook in these courses is threefold: it gives you an outline of the material, an index for quick access to concepts and their brief descriptions, and lots of classic problems at chapter endings, ideally with clear step-by-step explanations for solving them. If your assigned textbook doesn't satisfy these requirements (many don't), you should either obtain another from the library or buy a second one as a supplement.

Sometimes the greatest benefit of lectures in undergraduate hard science courses, besides motivating you to do sample problems at home, is noting where the instructor deviates from the normally assigned set of problems. Such deviation is rare in introductory science courses, and often you can find out about it much faster by skimming class notes taken by a professional service, rather than actually attending class. This can be particularly true when an instructor is poorly skilled at explaining how to do test problems, as opposed to theory. **Remember, you won't generally be tested on theory, but on your ability to do a standard set of classic problems.** The sooner you prioritize, tackle, and master those problems, the sooner you will have mastery over the course.

Again, when prepping for math, physics, chemistry, and genetics courses, don't prioritize rereading chapters or reviewing class notes. Instead, do practice problems over and over again. If you have any time left after mastering the problem sets, you can quickly read the book. But you will understand the book far better after you have consulted it only as needed to finish your assigned and supplementary problems.

Practice With Old or Sample Exams

You will typically be graded in calculus, chemistry, physics, and genetics classes based on your performance on **just a few hours' worth of timed exams** over the entire course. To do particularly well on the exams, you will want to seek out and do many practice problems beforehand. The fewer such problems you have solved under time constraints, the greater the risks you take on each exam, regardless of how much reading and thinking you have done. Needless to say, the best kind of practice problems are those that were once test questions. Ask professors or teaching assistants (TAs) if they have copies of old exams, or ask friends who have already been through the course if they have any (though you should make sure the professor okays the use of old exams as well). Review the exams early and, if needed, take them to your TAs for help.

Get TA Office Hours for All Courses

TAs are a great resource. Many are well acquainted with the professor and have foresight into what material will be covered in class and tested on the exams. Like professors, however, TAs vary widely in competency. Some enjoy working with students; others do it out of an obligation to fulfill graduation requirements. Some are very good at working through problems and others quite poor. For many of the above science classes, going to a number of great TA sessions in the same day and **seeing the same problems worked through quickly several times in a row may be the fastest way to understand the course material.** This can be the best way to learn the language of problem solving. The more you see it, and the more you do it, the more you internalize it. If you have never been to your TA's office hours, you may surprised how much time (and how many hints) he or she is willing to give a friendly and dedicated student.

Though you will be assigned a certain TA in your course, there is nothing stopping you from listening to, approaching, or working with other TAs. For example, if you are taking a physics course, go to the physics department for a list of **all** the TAs teaching **all** physics courses that quarter or semester at your university, both lower and upper division. Many TAs are willing to work with students from other sections or other classes if they aren't too busy, and especially if no one else shows up during their office hours, a situation that occurs with upper division courses particularly often. When you meet with them, bring specific problems you find challenging, and ask them if they will help you work through them, until you understand how to do them yourself. For the hard science courses we have discussed, all of this is far more useful to your grade than reading and rereading the book.

Use the Tutorial Service, and Consider Hiring a Private Tutor
If you want to achieve outstanding performance in particularly important or challenging math and science prerequisites, such as calculus, physics or organic chemistry, use your **free campus tutorial service** to go over problems with you. If the service limits your access (and many do), **consider hiring a great private tutor**. When you meet with your tutor, have him or her occasionally **watch** you do sample problems and give you tips on what you are consistently doing wrong or where you could be more efficient. Try to meet for an average of **two hours each session**, and make it a fast-paced and productive two hours. If you are not already gifted in the sciences, you will find some of these courses so difficult you might need **two or three of these two-hour sessions each week** just to stay on top of the most challenging material. There's absolutely nothing wrong with that, and coming up with funds for that expense

might be a very high priority, if the free tutorial sources are not sufficient. Do what it takes to become proficient at solving problems, over the short time you have been given to complete these courses.

One of us (John) used this strategy for organic chemistry. The instructor was famous for giving book-length tests: forty-page midterms and sixty-page finals. Students only needed to finish about a third of the problems to get As in the course. Just imagine: during exams one would hear pages flipping the entire time. This was the instructor's way of discovering students who were particularly good at the material, to whom he offered invitations to do lab research each summer. With only four hours per week of tutoring with sample problems, by the time of the first quarter final exam he was able to score *almost twice as many points* as the next closest student in the room, all with very little reading of the textbook during those ten weeks. This is a powerful demonstration of the value of this simple strategy.

If you cannot afford to pay for a private tutor, **undergraduates** will often tutor fellow students for a lower hourly price. Every major university has a number of different free tutoring centers, and some of the outstanding tutors at these centers may do freelance tutoring as well, if you need the extra help. If you are still stuck finding talented, affordable instruction, ask the professor for names of students who did very well the previous year to see if you can work with one of them.

Acing Biology

Use Your Textbook!
For most biology courses, aside from genetics, conceptual understanding is more important than the ability to solve problems. Unlike other science courses, reading the **textbook**, reviewing **class notes**, and making your own **cribsheet notes** are the best way to prepare for **biology** exams. Be an active reader: underlining, highlighting, using tape flags, and notes in the margins will help you to more quickly access useful information later. If you have time, summarize key points from your textbook, lectures, and problem sets on a set of condensed cribsheets that you can commit to memory. Some find it best to

write those sheets in pencil, or on a laptop with a good graphics tablet, so that you can easily erase and restate information and diagrams more clearly as the course progresses.

Get a Second Source

Even the best textbooks will invariably fall short in certain sections, inadequately or poorly explaining difficult concepts. When studying for a test, your textbook can quickly turn from your best friend to your worst enemy, confusing you rather than clarifying a topic. To counterbalance these inevitable shortcomings, consider investing in **at least two textbooks** for every biology course you take, or checking out an alternate textbook from the library for the semester. Use your second textbook as a backup resource and turn to it automatically whenever you need another explanation. Consider buying prop-up stands that allow you to keep both textbooks open on a small desk while studying or doing homework. An open textbook is always easier to flip through for reference than a closed one on the shelf.

> **Tip**
> Always check the index when considering buying a used reference book. If it has a poor index, as many do, you won't want to use it regularly!

Ideally, you might eventually build an arsenal of excellent textbooks in your home library that contains at least one copy each of the Big Eight in undergraduate biology: biochemistry, molecular biology, genetics, cellular biology, microbiology, general biology, physiology, and immunology. All of these are great background subjects for a medical career. Place the texts next to each other on the shelf, along with a good dictionary and thesaurus. Refer to them throughout your undergrad years. An illustrated medical dictionary, such as Mosby's, would also be a nice (though unnecessary) addition, allowing you to satisfy your medical curiosity while studying biology. To save a lot of cash compiling this library, buy last year's edition, or used textbooks at a student-run or co-op bookstore, or check the Internet.

Take Great In-Class Notes

Since biology survey courses tend to cover a lot of varied information, professors must focus on a limited subset of information during lectures and exams. Unfortunately, there is no shortcut into the professor's brain to see what he or she thinks is important. The best way to find out what will be on the test is to go to class, pay attention, and **take great notes**.

Make sure to get enough sleep before these lectures. If they are at 8:00 a.m., wake up an hour earlier and do at least twenty minutes of at-home preview before class. This, rather than coffee, is the best way to wake up your brain before (rather than during) class.

Review Your Notes Within 24 Hours of Class

Your brain will prioritize and retain items that you think about *several times* while they are in your short-term memory register. To let information from your lectures really sink in, you will want to return to it before you forget it entirely. Though it may sometimes seem like a waste of time, **reviewing**, expanding, and occasionally rewriting your class notes **within 24 hours** of the lecture will greatly increase your retention for exams. At the very least, try to quickly skim your class notes within 24 hours (48 also works, but is less ideal), filling in subjects that you didn't adequately make note of in class.

It helps to remember the **"daydreaming rule"**: When you find yourself recalling some science concept while daydreaming or while falling asleep, simply because you've seen it more than once over the course of the day, that's when you know your review plan is working the way it should. Those are the classes you'll really ace, too.

Use Tutors or TA Office Hours

Just as in calculus, physics, and chemistry, get a list of all the TAs and go to their office hours! But with biology, grasping and being able to quickly outline the concept is usually more important than the problems. Use your time accordingly.

Extra Measures to Boost your Science GPA

Is Your Science Course Load Too Difficult? Remember, you will need to ensure a GPA of **3.45** to be considered for medical school. If you have your heart set on medical school but can't make the grade, here are some power tools that can help you succeed.

Balance Your Course Load

If you are struggling to keep your grades up, limit your science units to eight per semester, maximum. Take another four units of classes that will not be too demanding and will not take much time away from your science coursework. Ask around to see which courses are significantly easier than others. Most students, particularly seniors and social group leaders, can recommend one or two **mick** (Mickey Mouse, filler, fluff, air sandwich) **classes**. Build up your emergency reserve mick list, as there will probably be semesters when you will need to use it. Also **beware of** taking too many science courses with **labs** at the same time. Lab work can be *extremely* time-consuming, requires lots of tedious work and energy, and usually gives you very few units to show for it.

Summer School

Consider taking your science classes during the summer, even if they are out of sequence. Summer school classes, with their non-standard professors and their more laid back students, are **often much easier** than classes during the regular school year. However, summer classes are taught over a shorter period of time and are therefore more intensive in daily study commitment. Check the summer catalog at your school, or at other local colleges and universities that are known to be academically easier than your school. If this summer's catalog isn't out yet and you want to plan ahead, check the catalog from the previous summer.

Drive Off the Track

At many schools—especially schools that have a lot of premed students—competition in the main-track prerequisite courses can be scathing, making standards for achievement unacceptably high. Don't expect the typical university to care about that, however: they are usually looking for ways to reduce the number of premeds, not to graduate all the students who want to go to medical school. The university, in such cases, is not your friend. If this is the case at your university, consider taking courses out of sequence, such as General Chemistry I starting in the *spring* rather than the fall. Science series classes taught out of sequence, because there are more non-major students in them, are **always easier** than the main-sequence series.

Medical school literature and most undergraduate advisors will try to scare you into taking courses in sequence. Don't be afraid. We've seen many successfully admitted students who have taken the third quarter general (non-calculus) physics course, before taking the first and second courses, because this was the only way they could fit everything into their graduation timeline. By the third quarter of physics, most premeds are much less competitive than they were during the first. Medical schools do not generally care about this one way or another, and even college curricula differ about what subjects to teach first. Take courses out of sequence to save your GPA, if necessary. An A in an out-of-sequence class will always reflect better on the applicant than a B in an in-sequence class.

Play "Good Professor/Bad Professor"

Do you attend a big, competitive university? Here is another way to work the curve to your advantage: If two (or more) professors are teaching different sections of the same basic science class, like General Chemistry, go to both classes on the first day. If one is a good lecturer and the other is a poor lecturer, **sign up for the class with the poor lecturer but attend the classes taught by the good lecturer** (if you even attend your problem-based science lectures at all, that is). You will take tests and be graded on the curve in the poor lecturer's class, but you will enter each test with an advantage, having learned the material from a good lecturer (or on your own).

To cover your bases, subscribe to lecture notes for the poor lecturer's class or borrow them from a friend. Review the notes from the poor lecturer's class early enough before exams to see what special topics are emphasized. Finally, be sure to complain to the university about the poor lecturer on your evaluation forms. On rare occasions, this feedback actually results in their hiring a better instructor in the future.

Additionally, remember that some professors write more difficult tests, and they may also have a unique grading philosophy. Ask around and find out what students think about different teachers. When one of us (Dr. Nelson) was an undergraduate, there were two teachers available in organic chemistry. One almost never gave A's but rarely gave less than a B, while the other gave more A's but nearly failed about half the class. Steve chose the latter instructor, since he knew he would study enough to be in the top percentage of the class, and he wanted to ensure that his hard work would earn him an A, which it did in all three quarters.

When All Else Fails
Is your school too difficult for your current science ability? Don't let your ego get in the way of your dreams! If you cannot meet the premedical GPA requirements after several attempts at your current school, consider changing your enrollment to a less demanding local university, state, or junior college. Science classes there might be much more your speed. Students apply and are accepted to medical school from state universities all the time. Alternatively, if you downshift to a local junior college, you can almost always transfer back to the big university later (many universities even have **"transfer admission guarantee"** programs, in fact). Almost anyone can learn to excel in science with hard work, but you may need to start at a level realistic for your abilities, challenging yourself in step with the natural slope of your learning curve.

BOOSTING VERBAL GPA
We can not emphasize this point enough: medical schools want to admit students who have strong verbal and communication skills. If your verbal skills need work at the time of application, you may make it through the initial screening of MCAT scores and GPA but will likely be knocked out in the final stages. Don't spend all those years working toward a goal just to be disqualified at the very end. You owe it

You must speak up!
Fifty percent of the prospective medical students who get an interview are not accepted. Why? Schools report that the number one reason for rejection is substandard communication skills.

to yourself to build strong communication skills now, before becoming a physician.

Building Superlative Verbal Skills: The Three-Year Plan

Unfortunately, there **aren't any shortcuts** to honing your verbal skills. Studies indicate that communication skills may take as long as **three years** to show significant improvement. Therefore, if you know you need better verbal ability as an incoming freshman, the single best strategy is to take a course in English, writing, speech, drama, or another writing-based humanities class every quarter/semester for **at least three years** during your undergraduate career. If you have the time, taking four years of humanities courses is ideal.

What Type of Humanities Courses Should You Take?

To substantially improve your verbal skills, take humanities courses that require you to **write a paper every one, two, or three weeks**. Ideally, try to enroll in small seminar classes in which your written work will receive detailed, personalized feedback. If you take a larger lecture class, be sure that you will be writing papers at least every couple of weeks and that those paper are individually graded by the professor or TAs.

Resist the temptation to sign up for humanities courses that have one long paper at the end of the semester. You will not improve your verbal skills unless you consistently write and receive feedback. One long paper will not sufficiently improve the quality of your written work. Similarly, don't take courses with a lot of reading and only a few papers. In the end, you will probably end up slacking on the reading and never fully challenging your verbal skills. Before you sign up for a class, check with the professor to be sure that the course is **writing intensive.**

Bottom line: you will need to take courses in which you must express yourself, then receive line-by-line "red ink" critique from a professor. This can be very irritating, writing and taking criticism one paper at a time, but collectively it will be some of the most useful feedback you'll ever receive in college. It will help you develop a life skill, verbal communication and reasoning, that you will use no matter where your path of heart takes you.

How to Take Writing Classes Without Sacrificing Your GPA

Many premeds rightfully worry that humanities courses are **graded more subjectively** than their science coursework, and they understandably fear that a lower-than-average mark in an English class will tarnish their sparkling science GPA. This fear often perpetuates a classic vicious cycle, where they avoid verbal classes and become increasingly one-dimensional science nerds, protecting their GPA at the expense of their well-roundedness and verbal fluency. The cycle can become particularly severe with students for whom English is a second language.

Unfortunately, taking this route will hurt your chances of getting into medical school. Again, med schools feel that good verbal ability is essential to the successful future physician. If you fear that humanities classes will be a serious detriment to your grades, here are two good ways around this problem:

1) Take Humanities Courses with "Premed-Friendly" Professors

Not all English professors are created equal. Before you sign up for a humanities class, do some research into the professor and the class. To begin with, you may want to ask senior premeds which humanities classes they took and which professors are the most likely to welcome non-humanities majors. Remember, you are not looking for the easiest classes. You are looking for friendly professors who will welcome premeds in their class and grade generously while not sparing critique. Seek a professor willing to work with a premedical student who is simultaneously taking challenging science coursework, does not have a strong verbal background, and is seeking a high humanities GPA that reflects the effort put into the course.

Again, make sure that the class you sign up for has ample writing work. Before the class begins, stop by the professor's office hours and introduce yourself. Tell him or her that you are preparing for medical school and would like to improve your verbal skills. Say that you will be **striving very hard to get at least a B+ in the course**. Bring a sample of your better past writings and ask if they merit a B+, given your background. If the professor is at all doubtful, arrogant, or doesn't seem to welcome to your presence in the class, forget that course and find another. There are plenty of undergraduate professors who enjoy working with students of every skill level. Take the time to find these professors.

If English is your second language, it is possible you may need to take three or more years of lower- division, entry-level humanities courses, particularly in the English department (or ESL department, if one exists), until you feel your skills are strong enough to "risk" taking upper-division humanities coursework.

2) Take Humanities at a Local Junior College

If the above strategy isn't enough and you are still worried that humanities classes will ruin your GPA, take one humanities course per semester at a **local junior college**, concurrent with your daytime classes at the university. If you want, you can even take humanities classes just for credit—not a grade—until you have improved sufficiently to take them at your regular university.

Technically, some colleges and universities don't allow concurrent enrollment at a junior college, but you can usually ignore these bureaucratic regulations without penalty (check to be sure), especially if you are taking community college courses only for credit, on a Pass/Not Pass basis. Do note, however, that if you want to fulfill any general education or university requirements while at a junior college, you will need to check in advance to see if your classes will transfer toward your degree. Even if you can't get general education credit, don't use that as an excuse. **Three years of writing-based humanities classes is the minimum prescription for acquiring strong verbal skills, if you did not have them prior to starting college.**

In conclusion, if you need a lot of help either learning to master your science coursework or gaining sophisticated verbal skills, don't worry about this. Just put in the time, and don't try to rush things by applying to medical school too early. An extra year or two (or more!) of preparation will not be a penalty in the larger scheme of your life. If you are building necessary skills and noticing your improvement in the process, you are exactly where you need to be on your path of heart.

Video Assignments for Chapter 4:

The Doctor, American Anthem, and *The Princess Bride*

Chapter 5
Exemplary Extracurricular Activities

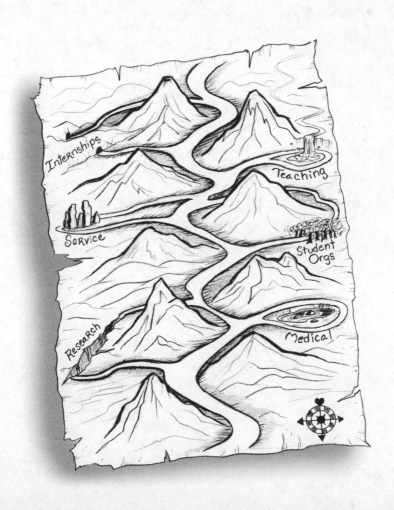

In the great task of preparing for medical school, extracurricular activities are definitely the fun part. For students with a passion for medicine and for exploring an aspect of health care during their undergraduate years, extracurricular activities can be particularly rewarding, interesting, life enhancing, and exemplary. Whether it's volunteering in a free clinic or teaching CPR in a local high school, extracurriculars give you the chance to be out in the real world and to find out what medical care is all about. In fact, so many extracurricular options await you that it may be hard to choose among them.

Through your extracurriculars, you will a gain deeper insight into various medical fields, learn about daily life in clinical settings, get important primary care experience, and meet talented health care professionals who may later become mentors and friends. Depending on how well you walk your premedical path of heart, you may be treated like a medical professional yourself, almost from the start.

THE BASICS

Extracurriculars are a key component of a medical school application. Although a few medical schools do not consider extracurricular or volunteer experience in an admissions decision, most do carefully review a student's postsecondary non-academic experiences to learn more about his or her personality and interests. Qualities that cannot be measured by GPA and MCAT scores—such as **humanity, maturity**, and **leadership**—are often measured by one's prolonged involvement in an extracurricular activity.

Most medical schools will award up to **four years' worth of admissions index points** for participation in extracurricular activities. Since you will want to get the maximum number of points, you should begin looking for a good extracurricular activity as soon as you start college. If you find a position you like, consider following through with it for your entire undergraduate career.

How Much Time Do I Need to Put In?

Though essential to your application, extracurricular activities are not necessarily time-consuming. On average, the time commitment is **four hours a**

week. You shouldn't have too much trouble fitting a few extracurricular activities into your schedule, no matter how busy you are.

To get the maximum number of admissions points, strive to participate in a minimum of four years' worth of extracurricular activities, four hours a week. (These maximum expectations are easily remembered as "**4 x 4,**" your "off-road" college experience.) If you are applying to medical schools at the end of your junior year, you will ideally want to have accrued four years of experience by the time you submit your application. If you are a typical premedical student, you'll have only spent three years in college by that time. This means you will ideally participate in more than one such activity during at least one of your college years. Alternatively, you might continue with an extracurricular that you were involved in during high school, and you would likely achieve credit for that at most schools, particularly if it was medically related.

When it comes to admissions, probably the best extracurricular history would be a combination of two different activities, each of which you participated in for two or more years. You may, however, also receive the maximum credit for a single extracurricular activity continued over three years (freshman through junior year) plus one further junior year activity. You could also submit four activities, done for one year each. Any of these combinations will maximize the extracurricular requirement—at least in terms of hours. If you have questions about how much a certain extracurricular program might be valued on your application, such as a summer internship, consult your premed advisor.

Generally speaking, you should try to follow through with any extracurricular commitment for a minimum of one year. It will take at least a year to become familiar with the work and acquire a decent amount of responsibility. On top of that, hopping around to different volunteer jobs will not display the commitment and follow-through that medical schools generally look for in an applicant. In addition, supervisors at an extracurricular activity are an excellent source of recommendation letters, adding a deeper dimension to the standard academic references. A job you kept for two years or more can produce an impressive personal letter.

If your extracurricular is a formal, longstanding volunteer position, you can talk with previous volunteers to explore the management climate and to make sure that an average of four hours a week, or something similar, is the norm. If there is no history, discuss your time commitment needs with your supervisor. It will be helpful to discuss your hourly commitment at the very beginning, to prevent any unrealistic expectations developing. If appropriate, let them know that four hours per week is your ideal. Be willing to put in eight or ten hours one week, if needed, but make sure you can subsequently put in no or very few hours in the following week. Most fundamentally, you need a supervisor who understands and will support your own premedical work needs.

CHOOSING AN EXTRACURRICULAR ACTIVITY

There are many ways that you could spend your free time. In fact, most undergraduate colleges offer so many clubs, committees, social activities, service groups, and sports leagues, that just reading through all their descriptions in the student directory is a bit overwhelming. But if you manage your time well, you will be able to participate in a number of different activities. Your premed coursework will not leave you anywhere near as much time as the typical student has. But if you are willing to explore, you can end up **learning about and sampling far more extracurricular activities than the average student.** To keep from spreading yourself too thin, set firm time limits in advance for your explorations, and be very picky about where you ultimately commit.

Qualities of a Good Extracurricular Activity

What type of extracurricular activity is favored by admissions committees? Luckily, they are usually the activities that students find the most enjoyable and fulfilling. The best extracurriculars achieve the following:

Help You Grow as A Person

Extracurricular and volunteer activities are an excellent way to broaden your real-world knowledge, face your fears, strengthen your weaknesses, and build meaningful experiences in many areas, including medicine and patient care. The best extracurriculars will challenge, strengthen, and teach you about yourself and others. Don't take a volunteer job that consists simply of licking envelopes for the American Heart Association from your home. While it may be tempting to fill up your precious extracurricular hours with fluff work, instead, use this opportunity to become a stronger medical school candidate and a better person.

Participate in something that requires **human interaction**, such as staffing the reception area of a free clinic or making public health presentations in a high school. If you find speaking to new people difficulty, let your supervisor know that one of your primary goals is to improve your public speaking skills. It may be scary at first, but this is a perfect low-risk, no-grade opportunity to grow.

When you start work as a volunteer, no one will expect you to be an expert in the field. In fact, your supervisors will most likely assume you are inexperienced, and most of them will just be happy to have your help. Look for volunteer positions that offer some responsibility from the start and supervisors who are willing to teach you the ropes.

Provide Good Role Models

When you are sampling various on-campus clubs and opportunities and trying to differentiate between them, realize that **you will learn as much from great people as from great causes.** Wherever you can find people, either fellow students or mentors, who seem like genuine role models (not just people with good images), you can learn a lot just by interacting in that environment, no matter the subject of the extracurricular.

Ask yourself about the kind of person you want to become, the qualities that will balance and complement your existing strengths, and look beyond your surface image to the key characteristics discussed in Chapter Three. Seek out both peers and mentors who are smarter, kinder, more learning-oriented, more even-keeled, more quietly self-confident, mature, or otherwise usefully differentiated from you. Such qualities will seep in to you by osmosis over the course of two or more years of extracurricular involvement.

Broaden Your Worldview

Once you are doctor, who will your patients be? Do you have a specific interest in treating children, the elderly, women, athletes, cancer patients, AIDS patients, drug and alcohol rehab patients, obesity clinic patients, or some other specialty group? Ask yourself how well you understand that group and their special needs. For example, if you want to be a pediatrician, do you know the greatest at-home, educational, or social challenges facing a low-income child? Do you understand the range of cultural differences, risks, and difficulties facing low-income families in the United States? In the world? Maybe you should consider an extracurricular activity in social work, or teaching an after-school program in an inner city, or helping in a summer advancement program for youth.

Perhaps you expect to work with a wide cross-section of the public, as an internist or surgeon, for example. If so, try to find an extracurricular activity that is usefully complementary to your previous experience and background. Did you grow up in a suburb? Look into volunteer opportunities in an urban free clinic or the emergency ward of an inner city hospital. Did you grow up in the southwestern United States? Why not learn Spanish so that you can better communicate with all the people in your community?

Similarly, working as a volunteer or intern in another country will teach you about a new culture and give you the opportunity to learn a foreign language in the process. Admissions committees are particularly dazzled by volunteer work in a developing country, in which you had the chance to work with the medically indigent or other underserved communities.

Bottom line: When you are looking for a volunteer job, **think outside your current realm of experience**. Look for activities that will expose you to new experiences, cultures, or environments. You don't have to be like the successful premed we met who traveled to Bosnia to help the medics in refugee camps during his sophomore summer, but keep his story in mind. There was a one-year waiting list for the only formal program available, so he simply went and volunteered on site, showing great personal initiative. Going to places in great need, places very different from your familiar environment, is just one of many examples of the personal broadening process. Extracurriculars can be life-changing experiences.

Help People in Need

Your volunteer time can be spent anywhere, but you will have the greatest personal impact in neighborhoods or communities that are specifically underserved or in need. Such work will be more rewarding than in a traditional setting, because you know that you are providing an **otherwise unavailable service**, no matter how small your contribution. In addition, you are likely to be given more responsibility in an underserved community, rather than simply filing paperwork for a hurried physician, who could hire any temp worker to do the job. Most importantly, working with the medically indigent or underserved, in difficult and somewhat unpleasant environments, will teach you compassion, resilience, and cultural awareness—qualities that will make you a much better physician as well as a stronger medical school candidate.

Teach You About the Realities of Health Care

How many types of health care environments can you name? Do you know the differences between a private hospital and a public hospital? Between home care, elder care, and preventive medicine? Between a small clinic and a large, multi-physician practice group?

You can read and study all you want, but until you work directly in health care, you will have little idea of how the system works in the real world. If you choose wisely, your extracurricular activity and your discussions with those who practice in the field can provide a **window to the health care industry**. You can gain insight into how recent changes in medical administration have affected the practice environment, how teams of doctors and nurses work together, and the wide range of ways patients interact with (and sometimes ignore) their health care team.

Though there are many types of extracurricular activities, you will want to find the time to participate in *at least one* activity in which you work directly in a medical environment–ideally a clinical environment. Generally, medical schools expect that applicants have at least some small measure of medical experience and know-how before they enter a medical program; otherwise, you could just as well be applying to business or law school. There is a real risk, from their perspective, that you might not understand the kind of commitment you are making.

Extracurricular Options

Now that you know what qualities to look for in a volunteer job, let's be more specific about the kinds of opportunities that exist and how to find them.

Primary Care Experience

Primary care medical experience, because it fills all the above-mentioned requirements, is the most desirable extracurricular activity for many premeds, as well as among the most impressive to medical schools. Jobs in primary care give you a chance to grow personally, interact with many patients, and learn more about the realities of medicine. No matter what field you eventually want to practice in, primary care experiences are always desirable early on because they develop your general patient-handling skills.

What Is Primary Care Medicine?

The five areas in primary care are

- Family and Community Medicine
- Internal Medicine
- Pediatrics
- Geriatrics
- Obstetrics/Gynecology

Where Do You Find a Primary Care Experience?

The best way to find a primary care position is to get in touch with local organizations and request information about volunteer opportunities. Start with lists of local clinics, emergency rooms, preceptorships, hospices, or volunteer-based organizations like the Red Cross. Ask them what volunteers do, if they are trained, and if there is a minimum and average weekly time commitment. Your premed advisor may also have a list of organizations that like to use student volunteers, as may your campus career services center. Some places, like your student health clinic, can be a useful and easy place to start but should not be the end of your search. Survey first, choose later.

For the most rewarding, life-changing, and valuable experience, try to find something that will afford a decent amount of responsibility in a field that interests you. Many premeds choose to volunteer in an emergency room.

Emergency rooms can be a good choice because they serve a broad cross-section of the population, and they are often looking for an extra set of hands. They also give you a great look into one of the most dramatic, life-and-death health care environments. Sometimes you can even follow the care of patients who are transferred to various inpatient treatment environments within the hospital. You can also get exposure to the wide range of outpatient treatment protocols.

On the other hand, emergency rooms can also be too busy or formal to provide you with much real medical exposure, leaving you to file paperwork while everyone else rushes around doing the real work. Therefore, before you start working in an emergency room, you may want to consider getting an **emergency medical technician (EMT)** license, a simple certification process which will allow you to work directly in patient care. There are even summer programs in some locations that will get you half way to becoming a paramedic, a significant advance in your scope of experience beyond the EMT credential. Don't forget nursing experience as well, which offers valuable exposure and training.

You can get primary care experience in other ways. For example, you might consider working in a hospital or clinic that serves people with chronic illness or disability. These fields allow you to build long-term relationships with patients and staff, without the frenzied pace of an emergency room. Most likely, you will be granted a fair amount of responsibility and will be able to work directly in patient care, even without a certification.

When you are choosing a primary care volunteer job, think about whom you would like to help. What moves you? Where could you make a difference? Do you want to work with HIV/AIDS or Alzheimer's patients, battered women, troubled adolescents, infants, psychiatric patients, patients recently diagnosed with cancer, or hospice patients with terminal illnesses? Look within yourself and pick a volunteer job that awakes your passions.

Preceptorships

If you want to learn in depth about any primary care or other medical setting, consider finding or setting up a **preceptorship** with a willing physician. In a preceptorship, a sage physician allows a clueless undergrad to tag along quietly each week for an extended period of time, observing the physician's activities, often in a number of different health care environments (office, hospital, community, and occasional field trips to conventions). The best preceptors are doctors with great people skills, patience, and a passion for education. If you are interested in setting up a preceptorship, ask nurses or clinic directors to recommend physicians in your area of interest. Then talk to those physicians who seem agreeable. Offer to do two or more hours a week of clerical or other useful work, in return for the opportunity to shadow the physician a few hours each week in various health care environments. Preceptors who will work with premedical students (as well as medical students) are particularly common at **teaching or university hospitals**, though with diligence, you can find one just about anywhere. Nursing programs also commonly maintain formal preceptorship programs. You may be able to get lists of great teacher-clinicians from your local nursing college, or become involved with the nursing program on an extracurricular level as a premedical student. Doctors of osteopathy (DOs) can also make excellent preceptors, and may write a letter of recommendation for osteopathic medical school later (a letter from a DO is a requirement for admission to osteopathic schools).

Summer Internship Programs

If you are a full-time undergrad, your summer vacation is ideal for building your extracurricular resume. Since you have fewer commitments in summer, you can give medicine some full-time attention. You could also use the season to travel somewhere new in the United States or internationally.

A number of well-known universities, labs, and private companies run summer internship programs for undergraduate students in medically related fields. In addition to internship programs, many students spend their summers doing research in a science lab. If you are interested in basic or clinical medical research, or have little previous experience working in a lab, you might want to consider this option.

In Appendix Three, we list a range of medically related summer internship positions throughout the United States, many of which include a small stipend in exchange for the student's help. In addition, most college and university

A Summer in Spain (or Latin America)

*When looking for a summer program, you may want to consider something in another country where you would have the opportunity to work with underserved communities and become familiar with a foreign language (another potential asset to you as an applicant and as a physician.) An excellent example of this type of summer experience is offered through the **Universidad Autonoma de Guadalajara (UAG)**, in Guadalajara, Mexico. Through the UAG, students may enroll in Intensive Summer Spanish Language and Culture Immersion Programs with an additional Free Clinic option.*

career counseling offices have extensive lists of great local, national, and international summer programs.

When it comes to summer opportunities, **early planning is key!** Don't be like the majority of students, who put off committing their summer to something interesting in medicine, and as a result find little that is available and that interests them when summer finally arrives. Fascinating opportunities for summer work abound, but if you wait until May, all the best choices will be gone. With advance planning and some help from your career counselor, you can find your dream internship, whether it be working at an innovative genetics lab or administering vaccinations to street kids in Mexico City.

Research Experience

If you are planning to pursue an MD/PhD or Medical Scientist Training Program (MSTP) pathway, then getting involved early in medical research is necessary, not optional. If you are an MD-track medical student applying to a top-tier, research-oriented medical school, participating in clinical or basic medical research projects can also clearly enhance your application. In all other cases, research can be interesting and beneficial, but it is not expected. In particular, second- and third-tier medical schools find primary care experience more valuable, on average, than research experience.

To find a good research project, start in your own backyard—your college or university. Every academic department has a free directory or printed booklet, often called the **Faculty Activities Directory (FAD)**, that provides a short summary of all the research being done in every department laboratory. Sometimes these booklets are only printed once every two or three years, but they are still quite helpful for understanding the general research being conducted, as is the departmental website. Some of these projects may look particularly interesting to you, and some of these professors are very interested in having an undergraduate's help.

If you live in a large city and have a very specific set of research interests, don't be afraid to get the FADs, or look at their online versions, from all the major universities and other research centers in your vicinity. Be bold and enthusiastic. Undergraduates can often get positions in amazingly prestigious labs doing cutting-edge medical research. With a little persistence and ingenuity, you could get close to some of the tools and research programs shaping the future of health care.

Working in a lab can be an excellent experience, especially if you are really excited about the topic and can find a great **principal investigator (PI)** to work under. As with any extracurricular activity, however, be selective with lab work. Be careful about *whom* you work for, since your superiors will largely determine what you are allowed to do in the lab. To find an excellent Principal Investigator (PI), see if you can make a lunch appointment with one or more of the graduate students who work in the lab. Do they seem to be happy? Is this PI regularly available to and concerned about his or her students? You should interview your direct supervisors. Also very important: Do you like the graduate student who will be directly overseeing your work? Take all these factors into consideration when you are choosing a lab experience.

Teaching Experience

From your own experience as a patient, you probably know that the best doctors are those who can impart information in a clear and competent manner, and make you feel confident in taking their advice. They can effectively persuade you to follow the recommended treatments, even if you initially don't want to. As a physician, you will be constantly educating your patients, explaining complex and difficult medical information to people who might have no medical background. Therefore, an ability to communicate didactically can be indispensable, especially for doctors who practice in primary care.

Teaching experience is always an asset to a medical school application because it suggests an **ability to communicate with people, confidence and skill when speaking, and experience explaining concepts to others**. If you are also teaching as a volunteer in an underserved community (say, working as a tutor at a Boys & Girls Club), teaching experience can help develop your compassion and humanity.

There are many ways to be a teacher. You can tutor high school students, coach a sports team, teach a musical instrument, volunteer in an after-school program, or work as a teaching assistant in a lower-division undergraduate class in which you excelled. Any of these activities will strengthen your communication skills, increase your confidence level, and teach you to listen to and answer questions.

Premed/Academic Societies

Participating in a premed club or academic society may be useful to you in many ways. Premed clubs often organize study groups, share class notes, or host valuable social events. They also give you the opportunity to **network** with upperclassmen, who can give you advice and provide a group of committed friends who are also applying to medical school. However, unless they engage in unusually active service work, these clubs are of little importance to a medical school admissions committee. Even if you are president of your school's premed group, this position will usually affect your application neither positively nor negatively.

Philanthropic/Socially Aware Experiences

As you know, medical schools are looking for students with a deep dedication to helping others. For example, if you traveled to a foreign country to administer vaccinations, worked on a public health campaign, or joined the Peace Corps after graduation, you may stand out as an applicant because of your exemplary dedication to promoting the well-being of others.

Other Activities and Interests

As we discussed in Chapter Three, medical schools are looking for exceptional, talented, interesting students, who will bring more than just academic competence to the incoming class. Whether you have a refined aesthetic sensibility, extensive travel experience, an interest in public policy and activism, or athletic talent, medical schools will take notice of students who have unique experiences listed on their extracurricular resume. Extracurriculars that give you useful, memorable, real-world experience and maturity, regardless of their pertinence to medicine, will certainly be noted and assessed by the committee.

While primary care and related activities remain the most relevant experiences to present to medical schools, admissions committees are impressed with students who have achieved in non-medically related areas. These types of activities can suggest other desirable qualities in a candidate. For example, participating in a varsity sports team shows that you embody drive, motivation, teamwork, and a sense of fun. If you perform as a concert pianist, the admissions committee is likely to form a picture of dedication, patience, and aesthetic ability, important qualities of a well-rounded, desirable applicant.

Dr. Nelson relates of his experience, "When I applied to medical school, I had a combination of activities. I completed my PhD just prior to medical school and thus was awarded research points at schools that were research-oriented; however, this research background actually hurt me at schools that were very primary care focused, since they assumed I would become a sub-specialist (which in my case is true, since I am pursuing pediatric neurology). But the important thing is this – if doing a certain activity that you enjoy makes a medical school less interested in you, then they are probably not the right school for you; if you love research, then going to a medical school that frowns on research would not only be a poor choice, but could hurt your chances of getting a competitive surgery, dermatology, or emergency medicine residency after medical school (since many of these residencies want research experience in their incoming interns).

Additionally, besides teaching undergraduate and MCAT preparatory classes, I volunteered teaching HIV/AIDS awareness classes at a high school; it was this latter activity that most interested many of the medical schools with which I interviewed. **Be brave**–do something that makes a difference, and don't worry if it is different from what everyone else is doing. **And have fun**– if you enjoy what you are doing, it will show and you will be given more responsibilities, gain more respect, learn more from the experience, and end up with a really excellent letter of reference."

Whatever you choose, we wish you the best in your extracurricular excursions, and we hope that they ultimately lead you further down your path of heart!

Video Assignments for Chapter 5:
The Cider House Rules, Youngblood, and *Slap Shot*

CHAPTER 6
ACING THE MCAT

You're an optimistic, hard-working student with your sights set on medicine. For the past few years you have taken some tough premedical courses and performed quite well in most, receiving a B+ or better, on average. You've participated in meaningful non-medical and medically related extracurricular activities and taken the time to build relationships with key professors and advisors. Now it's time for the MCAT. While its reputation may make you anxious, the good news is that your premedical courses have already taught you most of what you need to know to do well on this test. Your classes have taught you how to memorize large amounts of information, use analytic reasoning skills, perform rapidly under pressure, manage your time, and take challenging tests without panicking. Rest assured that you have already developed the vast majority of skills you will need to ace this test. All you need now is some good advice and a well-crafted plan to focus your talents and bring home the scores you deserve.

THE BASICS

The Medical College Admissions Test (MCAT) is a standardized exam administered by The American Medical College Application Service (AMCAS), designed to test the general critical-thinking abilities and introductory science knowledge of medical school applicants. Since there is a wide range of difficulties in curricula at U.S. colleges, the MCAT helps medical schools to contextualize or "normalize" an applicant's GPA, evaluating his or her basic knowledge and critical-thinking abilities on a standard measure. The MCAT is also designed to be a predictor of performance in medical school, though it serves that function less successfully.

The test attempts to be culturally neutral, indifferent to a student's real-world background, skills, and environmental factors. In that sense, the MCAT has major limits as a tool for evaluating an applicant's unique abilities. Fortunately, most students can do well on it, regardless of background, with a program of advanced preparation. It is far more a test of your preparation technique than it is of your innate learning, verbal, or critical-thinking abilities.

The MCAT tests your ability to **rapidly apply basic sciences and verbal knowledge.** Premedical students acquire most of this knowledge at one point or another in their undergraduate years, but many never learn to retrieve it quickly, some never integrate it, and most importantly, none ever have *all* of this basic knowledge at the forefront of memory at the same time, ready to call upon at a moment's notice. Your preparation pathway, if appropriate, will ensure you get to this special place before you take the test.

The MCAT is a **five-hour and forty-five minute**, multiple-choice, passage-based test, in which students have to quickly read and analyze approximately thirty passages and answer a set of conceptual questions that follow each one. Two-thirds of the passages are on scientific topics (physical and biological sciences sections) and the remaining third are on scientific and nonscientific topics (verbal reasoning section). In addition, there are two thirty-minute essays, which can be difficult for students who have not taken adequate writing-based courses in college.

Since the MCAT centers on science and verbal passages about upperclassman and arcane topics with which you may have little familiarity, it is foremost a test of your verbal interpretive skills. It assesses your general verbal and premedical science knowledge and ability to apply that knowledge in the context of rapidly reading and interpreting text. It is for this reason that humanities majors generally tend to do slightly better than science majors, even though they may not be as well-acquainted with advanced science topics.

What Is On the MCAT?

There are four test sections on the MCAT:

➤ **Physical Sciences**
- 77 multiple-choice questions
- 10 to 11 passages with 4 to 8 questions each; 15 non-passage-based questions
- Tests knowledge of general chemistry, basic physics, and ability to interpret data

➤ **Biological Sciences**
- 77 multiple-choice questions
- 10 to 11 passages with 4 to 8 questions each; 15 non-passage-based questions
- Tests knowledge of freshman biology and simple organic chemistry

➤ **Verbal Reasoning**
- 65 multiple-choice questions
- 9 to 10 passages with 6 to 10 questions each
- Tests reading comprehension and critical-thinking skills

➤ **Writing Sample**
- Two 30-minute essays
- Tests written communication skills

All of the concepts covered on the MCAT are basic, meaning that they are taught in *introductory* science classes at most colleges and universities. Each section of the MCAT (except for the writing sample) contains a series of passages that students must analyze for answers to straightforward multiple-choice questions. Several passages present advanced topics; however, you will not need to be familiar with any advanced-level material for the test. When approaching such

> **What isn't on the MCAT?**
> If you took your standard premed courses, you've got your bases covered. The MCAT has:
> **No** Calculus or Calculus-Based Physics!
> **No** "High-Level" Organic Chemistry!
> **No** Upper Division Biology!

passages, remember that only the basics are necessary to answer the associated questions.

Taking upper division science classes may mean the difference between an 11 and a 15 on the biological and physical sciences sections, approaching perfect scores on the test. Fortunately, medical schools are not expecting their applicants to perform at such an unreasonable level of accuracy. Knowing your basics well is all you need to get a competitive score on the MCAT.

TEST DAY

The MCAT is an ultra marathon, an exhausting, all-day ordeal that requires stamina, confidence, and sustained performance. On test day, you can expect the itinerary to be roughly as follows:

Verbal Reasoning	65 questions	85 minutes	Scoring Range: 1 to 13-15
10-minute break			
Physical Science	77 questions	100 minutes	Scoring Range: 1 to 15
60-minute lunch break			
Writing Sample	2 questions	60 minutes	Scoring Range: J to T
10-minute break			
Biological Sciences	77 questions	100 minutes	Scoring Range: 1 to 15

How Is the MCAT Scored?

MCAT scores are scaled to a curve. Therefore, your score is based on how you performed relative to everyone else who took the test. On more difficult tests, you could miss many answers and still get a very good score. On the majority of tests, you can miss about one out of five questions and still score in the eightieth percentile.

With the exception of the writing sample, the MCAT is scored by machine. Each of the two essays in the writing sample are reviewed and graded by two independent readers. If the readers give scores that deviate by more than one point, a third (master) reader will review and grade the essay. The final score you receive for the writing sample section is the average of the four scores (or master reader re-score) that your essays received.

The Writing Sample
Most medical schools consider the Writing Sample (WS) the least important part of the MCAT, since they have other samples of your written work in your application. Be warned, however, that any school that receives your MCAT scores may request a copy of your writing sample from AMCAS to see how you write under a time deadline. A small number of schools do this, and they primarily look to make sure that certain students (ESL students, technical major students) have reasonable verbal proficiency. Most schools simply use the reported J-T score. A very high WS score can help you, and a very low score can edge you out of an interview, but scores in the middle are not used numerically in the admissions process at any school that we know of. AMCAS itself discourages numerical comparison on this score, which is one reason it is scored as a letter range, not a number range.

The writing sample is graded for its depth, clarity, organization, and comprehensiveness. Effective grammar and syntax are important, though minor grammatical errors will not significantly affect your score.

What Score Do You Need?

Bottom line, you will need a combined score of about **30** on the numerical sections to be admitted to most U.S. medical schools, and ideally around **P** on the writing sample, though this letter score can be more flexible. Medical schools also prefer MCAT scores that are balanced, such as 10, 10, 10, P, as opposed to 8, 13, 9, R. Very few medical schools will accept a score below 7

Learn to Read!
After biological sciences, most medical schools say verbal reasoning is the second most important score on the MCAT. However, because verbal reasoning is the toughest section on the test to ace, a few schools value it as much or even more than the biological sciences section.

on any section. If you want to be admitted to a first-tier medical school, you will need at least two points higher, or an average of roughly 11, 11, 10, P (32P) for top-tier schools.

If you know that you will fall short of the 10/P ideal in one area, don't despair. You will still have a good shot at admission if you can do better than average in the other sections. For example, biological sciences is generally regarded as the most important score on the MCAT. Nonetheless, you can get an 8 in BS, as long as you have other scores in the double digits. In fact, you can also score as low as an 8 in physical sciences or verbal reasoning, as long as other scores, and the rest of your application, compensate. As with all aspects of your medical school application, different schools have different MCAT requirements, some placing higher emphasis on the test, and specific sections of the test than others. Therefore, while poor performance on the MCAT will lower your chance of entrance to some schools, it will be less important at others.

Early bird gets the worm!
Only 40 percent of all medical school applicants take the test in April, but 60 percent of admitted medical school applicants take the test in April. We call this the April Advantage. Try hard to get it for yourself if you can!

When Should You Take the MCAT?

The MCAT is offered only twice a year, once in **April** and again in **August**. In a traditional premed calendar, students should take the MCAT in the spring of their junior year, when they have recently finished the majority of their premed course requirements. In reality, most of students end up taking the test in August when they have the summer to prepare without the pressure of classes.

Generally, taking the test in April will give you a valuable admissions advantage. However, in the real world, there are pros and cons to both test dates. When choosing when to take the test, there are a number of factors you should consider.

April Advantages

- Your admissions file will be complete four months sooner than it will be for August test-takers, giving you first consideration for class spots and an edge over the competition.

- If you choose, you can apply early decision to your first choice school.

- You can retake the test in August if your scores fall below expectations.

- Since you will receive notification of your scores by June, you may better be able to determine which and how many medical schools to apply to.

- If you are satisfied with your scores, you will be able to focus all your energy on completing your applications during the summer, rather than preparing for the MCAT in August.

- The April test is generally a little easier than the August test. Though you will not necessarily get higher test scores (the test is curved so your relative score will likely be the same), you may be less rattled by the questions and have an easier time performing at optimum capacity. Taking the test in April is particularly advantageous for students who get psyched out by taking tough tests.

April Disadvantages

- If you haven't finished all your premed coursework, you may not be ready!

- Unless you prepare the summer before your April test, you have much less time for MCAT preparation while you are still in school.

- Using your time to prepare for the MCAT could adversely affect your grades.

August Advantages

- You will have finished all your prerequisite courses.

- You will have the summer to prepare for the test without having to keep up with your schoolwork.

August Disadvantages

- Your application file will not be complete until later in the application season.

- If you take the test in August *and* are a late applicant, you will have two big strikes against you. In that situation, you may be given several interviews that are only for *alternate* spaces at medical schools.

- You will have to prepare primary applications at the same time that you are preparing for the MCAT.

- You will not have the option of taking the test again in the same application season.

- You will not have the option to apply through an early decision process.

REGISTERING FOR THE MCAT

Once you have decided when to take the MCAT, you will need to register for the test. You must register for the test online at the **AMCAS website** at www.aamc.org/students/mcat. You can register no later than about a week and a half before the test date, though you should know long before that if you plan to take the test. After you have registered, AMCAS will send you an MCAT identification card, which you must bring with you on the test day.

HOW MUCH DOES IT COST?

At the time of publication of this book, MCAT registration costs $190. After paying your fee, AMCAS will distribute, free of charge as part of the application service, your scores from the last three years to all the medical schools to which you apply.

The Association of American Medical Colleges Fee Assistance Program (AAMC FAP) offers a limited amount of financial aid to cover MCAT registration costs and application fees. The FAP is reserved for individuals with extreme financial limitations whose inability to pay the full MCAT registration fee would prevent them from taking the examination in a timely manner.

For more information, contact:

Fee Assistance Program

Association of American Medical Colleges

2450 N Street, NW

Washington DC 20036-1123

202-828-0600

fap@aamc.org

RELEASING MCAT SCORES TO MEDICAL SCHOOLS

When you apply to medical schools using the AMCAS application, your MCAT scores are automatically sent as part of your application materials. For all non-AMCAS schools, AMCAS will forward them a copy of your official test scores for free via the MCAT THX system.

> **Three Swings at Bat**
> Prepare well for the MCAT and be sure you plan to apply for medical school. If you want to take the MCAT more than three times, you will have to apply for special permission from AMCAS after each time. Voided scores also count as one swing at bat.

In previous years, you had the option of releasing MCAT scores only to yourself, before deciding whether to send them on to medical schools or not. Unfortunately, after 2002 this option no longer exists, an example of creeping infringement on the legal rights of test takers. Previously, premedical students could release to medical schools only those tests that they decided were reflective of their true abilities. From now on, if you have the flu, miss-bubble your answer sheet, risk taking the test before you've finished your prerequisites, get test jitters, or do poorly for any other reason, the AAMC and medical schools will know about it unless you void your scores on the day of the test. You may void your MCAT if you feel you have done excessively poorly, up until the time that the biological sciences answer documents are collected. This "last opportunity to void" will be clearly announced by the test proctor. Use this option only under dire circumstances.

HOW LONG ARE MCAT SCORES VALID?

Unfortunately, not very long. Most medical schools will not consider MCAT scores that are more than **two or three years old**. However, this policy varies by institution. In general, it is best to take the MCAT within a year or two of your initial application to medical school.

RETAKING THE MCAT

If you bomb the first time, don't panic. You aren't alone. About 50 percent of test takers retake the MCAT, and all admissions committees will consider more than one MCAT score. Your only option if you are still set on medical school is to retake the test, and to argue in your application that your second is much more reflective of your natural abilities. Fortunately, very few schools will automatically average your MCAT scores. Most will look at trends and take subjective factors into consideration.

That said, it is best to take the MCAT only once. Some schools will consider original low scores to be a negative, regardless of how well you do the second time. For those schools, you will be permanently penalized for your poor performance the first time around. Even at schools that will primarily consider your highest MCAT score in admissions decisions, doing well the first time gives them confidence in your ability to handle pressure and your long-term planning skills. Fortunately, with today's wide availability of timed official practice MCATs, you will know beforehand whether you are ready to sit for the real thing. Don't let yourself fall short simply because you did not adequately prepare for the test the first time around. It's better to let the test date pass than take it if you expect low scores.

Prepping for the MCAT is an extensive process. Depending on your background, we've seen successful students spend anywhere from **10 to 25 hours per week** studying for the test over **one to six months leading up** to it. In the upcoming pages, we will discuss MCAT preparation strategies. If you think you'd benefit from the motivation and expertise of professional coaches and teachers, enroll in a prep course.

PREPARING FOR THE MCAT

The MCAT is a test not only of basic sciences and verbal knowledge, but also of rapid passage reading and critical-thinking ability. Therefore, the best long-term preparation strategy is to study well during college and spend dedicated time improving your conceptual basic science understanding, critical thinking, writing, reading, and communication skills.

As April or August approaches, you will still be wise to spend a few months of dedicated time studying for the test. At some medical schools, MCAT scores are weighed as heavily as your undergraduate GPA. If you lack the discipline to put in many hours studying for the MCAT by yourself, we strongly recommend that you take an intensive MCAT prep course, such as our Hyperlearning MCAT Preparation Course. For over ten years, Hyperlearning has been successfully preparing thousands of students annually for the MCAT. No other national program offers anywhere near as much **in-class basic science review, verbal preparation, sample test work, and supplementary help from a number of specialized, well-trained instructors.** Prep courses like Hyperlearning's help you to organize your approach, pace and formalize your study time, assess your weaknesses early, do many more sample problems, and take more practice tests than you would on your own. Such factors have been long proven to maximize your ability to perform well on the test. Though you may be reluctant to spend significant time and money preparing, the MCAT is very important to your path. Be very aggressive about it; don't let low scores ruin an otherwise excellent chance of admission.

Dr. Nelson further advises, "One important fact to keep in mind about the MCAT is that it is only the first of many tests that you will take on the road to becoming a licensed physician. You will have to take all three steps of the USMLE (United States Medical Licensing Examination), in addition to Board Exams for your specialty/subspecialty. Therefore, an additional contribution that the MCAT makes to the evaluation process is this: medical schools want to graduate students who can become licensed to practice medicine. Since you will have to pass additional standardized exams, it is important that you learn now how to successfully pass these types of exams if you are going to become a doctor. Look at your MCAT preparation not as wasted time but instead as a way of developing **fundamental studying, learning, and testing skills** that you will call on again and again in your future journey."

STELLAR STRATEGIES FOR MCAT PREP

Even with a prep course, you will need to spend a good deal of time studying for the test on your own. Again, do not skimp on this very important commitment to yourself. If you plan to prep on your own or want to get started right away, here are Hyperlearning's eight most important strategies for acing the MCAT.

Create Conceptual Science Outlines

You can fit an entire semester of basic science concepts on ten or twenty pages. Go over your class notes or read a great **MCAT prep syllabus**. Using this information, start creating an **outline** of all the material you need to know for the MCAT. Write these pages in pencil, printing small, but leaving room to erase and add related concepts later. Choose classic, simple examples when needed to make a physics, chemistry, or biology concept clear. The process of **evaluating** information to include and **physically writing it down** will help you commit the formulas and examples to memory.

Do your **physics** outline first, **chemistry** next, and **biology** last, as each will involve progressively more writing than the one before. To make these outlines a reasonable, useful length, you will need to distill complex ideas into simple, short statements. Again, figuring out how to express complex ideas in an efficient way will help you recall it quickly during the test.

Once you have the outline, the fun *really* begins! Review your outlines for a few hours before taking a practice MCAT. When you are done, grade your test and take a good look at every **incorrect** answer. Go back to the outline and find out which concepts you either left out or didn't write clearly enough to quickly recall it. Erase and clean up that section of your outline. As you continue to practice and refine, your outline will quickly become the most powerful tool in your MCAT arsenal.

As you write your outlines, keep in mind that it is better to have a good understanding of important **concepts**, as opposed to building a collection of memorized facts. In particular, familiarize yourself with commonly used concepts and equations from introductory science courses. When referring to class notes, remember that familiar information may take a different format on the MCAT.

Hone Your Critical-Thinking Abilities and Writing Skills

As long as you can keep your GPA up, it is ideal to take one-third to one-fourth of your university courses in any of the following subjects: **philosophy, rhetoric, speech, debate, linguistics, comparative literature, literary theory, political science, anthropology, history, and other humanities and social sciences.** These classes, irritatingly subjective as they seem to many science majors, help build some of the most important general-thinking skills you'll need in the real world, not to mention on the MCAT. Further, many medical schools now require at least a year of English, in addition to other social studies or humanities courses.

STUDY TIP
But I'm not going to law school!
*If you have three months or more to practice improving MCAT verbal reasoning score, look for books that have official released versions of the **LSAT**, **GMAT**, and **GRE** exams. These officially released tests have **excellent verbal reasoning sections,** and the questions are created by conservative committees in a very similar fashion to the way MCAT verbal reasoning tests are constructed. **LSAT reading passages** in particular are tougher than MCAT passages and make great practice.*

At the risk of sounding like a broken record, we repeat: taking at least three years of writing-based humanities courses is the best way to improve communication skills, for the verbal dimension of the MCAT and for your overall admissions candidacy. As we discussed in Chapter Four, if you are worried that humanities courses will negatively affect your GPA, take entry-level courses, take summer courses, or take courses at a local community college.

Practice!

The MCAT is unlike any test you've ever taken and unlike any of the standardized tests administered for other graduate programs. Before you take the MCAT, you must familiarize yourself with the test's format and contents. To achieve the maximum score possible, you will want to do **multiple practice tests** (at least three), spend time scoring them, understanding your score, and ideally, comparing your mistakes to your outline, adding critical concepts as you go.

Test-taking is a learned skill. Sitting through lots of practice tests is the best way to increase your speed, build stamina, discern common errors, and enhance your general intuition about MCAT questions and answers. In the Hyperlearning MCAT Prep Course, students receive the equivalent of thirty MCATs of practice questions and take at least five full-length practice MCATs in real testing conditions during the course of the program. If you are preparing on your own, be sure to have a similar amount of high-quality practice tests and supplementary material available, and be sure to stay motivated to get through all the material.

When it comes to practice tests, be picky about which ones you use. Poor simulations will waste your time, blunt your instincts, and incorrectly channel your energy. Officially released MCATs are always the best. You can find released practice tests on the AMCAS website and on www.PrincetonReview.com. For additional practice, look for high-quality prep books that offer many practice problems with well-worded, detailed solutions to every problem. To practice for verbal reasoning, officially released LSAT, GMAT, and GRE tests are also very good. Avoid non-official tests or tests that have not been developed by a leading test prep company.

How to Use MCAT Practice Tests

The first time you begin **verbal reasoning** practice, don't set your stopwatch for 85 minutes and expect to complete an entire section. Instead, begin with short, concentrated doses, slowly building stamina for longer periods.

After you have completed a passage, grade it, paying close attention to your strengths and weaknesses. Try to understand your mistakes and what the correct answer should have been. In addition to seeing what you did right or wrong, observe how much time you are spending on each type of problem. Which questions are taking up too much time? How could you answer these questions more efficiently? Practice tests are also the best way to develop test-taking intuition. In time, you will **learn to trust your MCAT intuition:** for most people who have obtained some knowledge of a subject, their **first intuition is usually right**. Second-guessing most MCAT answers just wastes valuable time.

As you grade, keep a log of your mistakes. Try to determine the specific passage types on which you need to improve. Don't rush through the grading process. In most cases, it will take longer to grade the test than to take it, if you are really trying to understand your mistakes.

If you are doing **science** passages, each time you take a practice section, return to your outline and revise sections that are giving you trouble. Continue revising your outlines for every test you take. By the time test day arrives, you will have a powerful overview of all the basic information you need.

When you finish taking and grading a practice test, give yourself a little reward! Treat yourself to a healthy dessert, go for a brief walk in the park, have coffee with a friend, make pancakes, get your hair cut, or do anything that makes you feel a bit better and more relaxed. If you didn't perform as well as you would have liked, don't dwell on it. You are one test further down the MCAT prep path than the average premedical student. Just putting in the time and energy every day brings you one step closer to the score you need. Give yourself the positive feedback you need to come back and practice more tomorrow.

Manage Your Time, Energy, and Attitude

Like your premedical journey, MCAT preparation is a marathon, not a series of sprints. Many students have great intentions but procrastinate, reserving all their energy for the last two or three weeks before the test. As a result, they do only as well as their prior undergraduate education allows, which is not MCAT-specific. Doing particularly well on the MCAT requires a **well-balanced and well-planned effort**. Time, energy, and attitude are your three greatest assets. Learn to manage each of these well to obtain the best possible score.

Time

If you want to improve your scores, allow ample **time** for preparation. Take a close look at your schedule. Which commitments can you omit or postpone between now and test day? Don't talk to any but your closest friends. Unplug your TV. Limit yourself to 20 minutes of critical email every day. Use a timer if necessary. If you have to, tune out the outside world for a while. You're going to need some large blocks of MCAT review time.

> **Professional Measures**
> Pull the phone cord out of the jack, or record a new, mechanical sounding greeting: "Message Box is Full."
> Hang "Quarantine by order of CDC" on your front door.
> Darken windows.
> Play trance music on endless repeat.
> Free your pets.
> You get the picture...

Putting in time is the key to successful preparation. **Your first forays into the MCAT are going to be irritatingly, frustratingly unproductive.** Don't become discouraged! Only when you've spent some real time reviewing, outlining, and taking tests will you start to feel like a pro.

First, buy an inexpensive **countdown timer** or stopwatch. Several wrist-watches have this function. You can also purchase a stand-alone countdown timer at stores like Radio Shack. Next, set yourself a weekly time budget. How much time are you going to spend studying for the MCAT this week? 10 hours? 15 hours? 20 hours? Never study more than two hours straight without taking an extended break. A five- or ten-minute break every hour is ideal. At the beginning of each week (or each day, depending on how you like to count), set your countdown timer to the amount of time you have agreed to study. Each time you sit down to study at your MCAT desk, start the timer. When you finish, turn it off. If you need to get up to take a nap, break, eat, stop the countdown. **Restart the timer only when you sit back down in your chair.** By the end of the week, or the end of each day, you should have counted down all the time on your study clock that you agreed to invest. If you haven't, some of your other distractions will have to go. Time management is as simple as this.

If you get bored studying in your apartment, go to cafés, libraries, book-stores, or other venues, where you can reward yourself with some nice study breaks in a new environment. But be sure to bring earplugs for studying and a blanket/pillow for brief naps in the car, so that your **mobile MCAT study environment** has everything important that home does. Whenever you stop the timer, your first priority after a break is to return to your desk/table/nook and finish counting down your time for the day/week. Once you are in a routine, you can stop using the timer, but go back as needed to keep on track.

Energy

Are you at your best in the morning or in the evening? The MCAT deserves your **most productive hours** because it's your highest priority between now and test day. To stay at a sustained peak energy level, you will want to eat well but not too much. Frequent small and healthy meals keep your concentration up. You will want to sleep well but not too much. Several short naps or total relaxation breaks during the day can sustain your mental focus. You will need to exercise regularly but not too much. Several brief (40 minutes or fewer) cardiovascular workouts each week will give you endurance in studying. When you're tired, don't try to push through. Stop the timer and take a nap. Your first priority is always to count down your time, but your second is to be alert, energetic, and ready to learn. Keep tabs on how you feel. Take frequent, brief, and active breaks, like walking in the yard, washing the car, washing the dishes, walking the dog, or folding the laundry.

Attitude

No matter what happens, the one thing you can totally control is your attitude. To make progress on the MCAT, you need to build and keep a **solidly positive, optimistic attitude.** You can fritter away years dwelling on your failures, or you can choose to think about the positive progress you will make towards your goals every day. Review your accomplishments at the end of the day, giving yourself immediate positive feedback for any small gains made. You have control over your reaction to a poor score, procrastination, or a lack of time, energy, or other resources.

Learned Optimism, *by Martin Seligman, is one of several books that cites excellent evidence that your **attitude** can strongly enhance or inhibit your performance. Seligman provides valuable strategies for learning practical optimism in life situations. You can focus and apply such knowledge to your test.*

When things don't go as you had hoped, don't become dejected or berate yourself for days. Make a quick assessment, readjust, and resolve not to lose your pace. You will have some difficult training days, but it is imperative to keep training, keep your head up and eyes on the prize.

Long-Term Prep for Verbal Reasoning and the Writing Sample

For most people, **verbal reasoning** is by far the most difficult MCAT subscore to improve over the 12-week period of an intensive prep course. Your performance on the sciences and the writing sample can be *dramatically* improved in 12 weeks of focused effort. But for most students, verbal reasoning is a tougher beast, rarely ready to let down its guard unless you take extraordinary measures to conquer it. Remember, the *best* way to gain great verbal reasoning scores is to take three full years of writing-based humanities courses throughout college, no matter what your major!

What Scores Do You Need on Verbal Reasoning and the Writing Sample?

The scores you need on the verbal reasoning and writing sample sections depend on your undergraduate GPA. For admission to the top 50 medical schools, the minimum scores you should strive for are:

GPA	Verbal Reasoning Score	Writing Sample
3.6+	10	O
3.3-3.5	11	P
3.0-3.25	12	Q

For admission to the bottom 50 medical schools, your minimum recommended scores are:

GPA	Verbal Reasoning Score	Writing Sample
3.6+	9	N
3.3-3.5	9	O
3.0-3.25	10	P

Generally speaking, medical school matriculants perform better on the sciences section than on verbal reasoning and the writing sample. To determine whether your scores are high enough for a specific school in any particular year, consult the medical school admissions statistics at your campus career center, the MSAR, or The Princeton Review's *The Best Medical Schools*, all of which will help you find average MCAT scores for accepted applicants.

Some schools favor students with an extremely strong liberal arts background and are more likely to admit students with extraordinary writing samples or verbal reasoning scores. The average writing sample score for accepted students at Stanford University School of Medicine, for example, is R. This school clearly seeks students who have above-average writing skills. At New York Medical College, the average admitted student scores below the national average on the writing sample. Nevertheless, a student with a strong writing sample score would still be a unique and desirable applicant to the student body at New York Med.

Three Step Plan for Improving Verbal Reasoning Skills
Step One: Determine Your Skill Level

You can use your SAT verbal score to roughly predict how you will do on the verbal portion of the MCAT if your SAT score is less than five years old and you have continued to take at least two years of writing-based humanities courses in the interim. To roughly predict your MCAT verbal reasoning score in this fashion, **divide your SAT verbal score by 70 and then round it,** up or down to the nearest whole number. Is it already where you'd like to be? If so, congratulations: MCAT verbal preparation will probably not be as challenging for you as for many other premedical students.

If you took the SAT more than five years ago or feel you have made major improvements in your verbal abilities since then, we recommend you take a timed MCAT verbal reasoning section to determine your current baseline skill level. Try to do this in the summer between your sophomore and junior year of college if you are at all concerned about your verbal performance. If your score is low, start preparing for MCAT verbal reasoning over that summer! **You will want to know early if you need to do extra work on verbal reasoning,** as it is the toughest section on the MCAT to dramatically improve.

Step Two: Develop a Study Plan

Based on your GPA and the schools you plan to apply to, determine how well you need to score on verbal reasoning. Remember that verbal reasoning is the only score you can't easily improve in three months. The typical, humanities-starved premed has never carefully read passages in art history, literary criticism, sociology, or anthropology. If you haven't approached this type of subject matter in the past, you will typically have to read **several passages in each subject** before you will begin to feel comfortable. To really improve your reading skills, you will need to carefully read and review several hundred passages. There is no shortcut here, only a long path through the swamplands until you can reach high running ground.

In our experience, a tested rule of thumb is that for every verbal reasoning (VR) point increase you seek, you will need to study roughly **four hours per week for three months** (or two hours per week for six months, or one hour per week for a year). For example, if you want to improve from an 8 to a 10 in VR, you will need to spend eight hours per week practicing with VR passages over a three-month period. If you need to jump from a 6 to a 10, you will need to spend about 16 hours per week on this subject alone. No wonder people usually take longer than three months to really improve their verbal reasoning score! If you have more than three months to prep, you can spread out your prep time accordingly or take advantage of the extra time to really improve your scores.

While you need to put in a lot of time, you should never spend more than three to four hours a day on verbal reasoning preparation. Your efficiency will greatly diminish after that point. If you need to study for 12 hours per week, do so over the course of three or four days. Pick certain days–such as Friday, Saturday, and Sunday–and consecrate them as your hallowed practice time. Once you have picked your days, stick to them. Build a healthy habit of starting at the same time each week so you unconsciously expect it and will perform at your mental peak. As you study, take frequent, brief, active breaks.

Start doing your verbal reasoning passages **untimed**. Read and reread the passages and questions until you are *sure* that you have all the right answers, *then* check to see how you did. If you haven't read a lot of humanities passages before, you will be surprised at how long it takes to understand and use the English language, and how easily you can misinterpret the connotation of a word or the meaning of a phrase. Use a highlighter to mark key words or phrases you would have needed to understand better to correctly answer the questions you missed.

Keep in mind, you need to do new things slowly at first. The first time you rode a skateboard or snowboard, you weren't zooming across the terrain. You stepped on carefully, maintaining your balance, making sure you knew the basic skills before you picked up speed. In the same manner, try to learn to do all the problem types on the MCAT slowly at first, making sure you know the ropes and can prevent needless falls. Only then can you learn to do them faster. With repetition comes agility and speed.

As soon as you are consistently missing **two or fewer questions per passage untimed**, you can begin timing yourself. Until then, you haven't really earned the right to take timed passages. Begin by giving yourself three minutes per question, including reading time. Every time you do several passages and miss only two questions or fewer, you can cut your time down even further. Slowly work up your efficiency and cut down your time until you are flying through the passages at the MCAT standard of 1.25 minutes per question, including reading time.

Step Three: Monitor Your Progress
Take full length, verbal reasoning practice tests every few weeks and grade them to monitor improvement in your scores. Don't expect steady or immediate progress. Just put in the time. If you are not seeing the improvement you want, modify your study plan. Add more hours to your weekly countdown and keep plugging away.

Three Step: Plan for Improving Writing Sample Skills

Step One: Determine Your Skill Level
To determine your current skill level for the writing sample, compose answers to two timed MCAT writing sample questions, called prompts. MCAT writing prompts are always general social, political, economic, technological, environmental, and ethical statements such as: "The object of education should be to teach skills, not values," or "Society is best served by giving people as much freedom as possible," or "The more people rely on computers, the more people become alienated from one another."

Don't give yourself more than the allotted **thirty minutes** to answer each prompt. When you are done, show your work to your premed guidance counselor, an English teacher with MCAT grading experience, or a Hyperlearning MCAT grader to find out your starting skill level. Based on your GPA and school selection, how many points do you need to improve on the writing sample?

Step Two: Develop a Study Plan
Fortunately, even if you don't have a humanities background, you can make great progress on the MCAT writing sample during a twelve-week prep course.

With a strong program of preparation and a reasonable amount of practice time, you will be able to improve your score, on average, by **two to three letters over the course of two or three month**s. If you need to improve your score by more than three letter points, you will want to start earlier, just as with verbal reasoning.

The Hyperlearning MCAT course, which offers twice as much verbal preparation as any other national MCAT prep course, will outline a number of MCAT writing prompts and sample responses and also require you to do many timed writing samples, graded and individually critiqued. A few hundred MCAT prompts are also available in supplementary materials and at the AAMC website.

Your main goal here is to learn how to structure and execute a workable response to a wide range of writing prompts in the thirty minutes available. MCAT essays should generally be written in the classic **Thesis-Antithesis-Synthesis (TAS) format**. In this format, you will begin the essay by showing your understanding of the main point, or thesis statement, of the prompt. In the first paragraph (or section), state all the evidence in support of your point. In the second paragraph/section, offer refuting evidence and opinion. Conclude with a final, synthesis paragraph (or two), which returns to your main points, incorporating the refuting evidence to make your original thesis stronger. With just a little practice, you will become very good at using the TAS format, writing an essay with clear, concise, and interesting examples.

MCAT readers expect you to use good, basic grammar and useful but not-too-fancy vocabulary. If you need a little grammar boost and are preparing on your own, check out Web resources or buy a simple book outlining grammatical concepts. While small mistakes will not affect your score, big grammatical issues will be noted by the MCAT readers, and possibly by your future medical college.

Step Three: Monitor Your Progress

Take timed tests periodically, and have them graded by someone with a composition background who can apply the MCAT Writing Sample grading guidelines (outlined at the AAMC website and in your registration materials).

If you are still two or three letters away from your desired score after a couple of months of practice, you will need to continue to improve your feedback, perhaps taking your essays to a paid tutor-reader who can give careful, line-by-line critique. Again, with only a few months of practice and monitored progress, you will substantially improve your writing sample score, even if you have only a limited humanities background, and English is not your first language.

BRIEF TIPS FOR TEST DAY
(SEE MORE TESTING TIPS IN APPENDIX ONE)

ON THE DAYS LEADING UP TO THE TEST

- At least three days before the test, set your alarm early and accustom yourself to being mentally awake *by test time*, if you aren't already a morning person!

- On the two nights before the MCAT, get good-quality, extra sleep because you will probably be anxious on the eve of the test and may have trouble sleeping.

- On test day, bring a small, healthy lunch for the sixty-minute lunch break, and quality snacks and drinks for your two ten-minute breaks.

- On the night before the test, have a good dinner, hot shower, and go to bed early. If you can't sleep well, just relax and don't worry. You will have had plenty of rest the previous two nights. Many top students end up laying awake much of the night, calmly relaxing as best they can, and then going in and *blowing away the MCAT* on test day. You're in good company!

- On the night before the test, have everything you need ready: your admission ticket, ID, test center map, food, three soft lead pencils, an eraser, two black-ink ball-point pens for the writing sample, and a non-beeping watch.

ON THE BIG DAY

- Get up early and eat a good (but not oversized) breakfast.

- Make sure you know how to get to the test center. Arrive early. There are no late starts on the MCAT!

- Try to use half of your lunchtime, the middle half, to relax, not gab. Ideally, find a place (your car?), to follow up your quick and pre-made lunch with a 20- or 30-minute cat nap or eyes-closed relaxation period, but *only* if you have a reliable timer (perhaps two timers?) or someone available to let you know when time is up. Then drink something with caffeine and/or unrefined sugars and take a brief walk or stretch just before heading back. This lunch-rest-caffeine-walk combination will give you a *lot* of energy for the second half of the test. If you are a muncher, you might also want to pack a paper bag full of high protein (not high refined sugar) snacks, such as protein bars, for your breaks, as well as a thermos of coffee or perhaps a smoothie. Don't drink too much coffee, or you'll lose a lot of time on a bathroom trip.

- Don't talk much about the test on your breaks. Use them to relax, recharge, and focus on the task ahead.

- Think positively. Believe in yourself, and the awesome abilities of your magnificent mind. *You deserve to do well!*

Video Assignments for Chapter 6:

ER, Real Genius, and *Searching for Bobby Fisher*

CHAPTER 7
LYRICAL LETTERS
OF RECOMMENDATION

Letters of recommendation are a golden opportunity to let someone else brag about you in a lyrical way, without the obligatory restraint that you must show when discussing your own achievements. Since medical schools are very interested in your personal qualities, recommendations are a great way to showcase them. Plus, letters offer a third-party confirmation that you are who you say you are in your application.

Recommendation letters summarize notable academic or other achievements and personal qualities of the candidate, and relate how the letter writer came to know the applicant. They may discuss *anything*, even the candidate's MCAT performance, if you have given them that information in advance (for example, their opinion of why your verbal or science scores were so high). Getting great recommendations isn't as hard as you might think. For some people, approaching a professor to ask for a letter can be intimidating. Keep in mind that professors are constantly writing recommendations on behalf of their students. In fact, for some professors writing occasional recommendations is no favor, but part of their job description. Put yourself in their place; professors genuinely want students from their school to succeed and be accepted into medical school—it makes them look good. Even if you don't know certain professors that well, if you approach them with enthusiasm and a positive attitude, they will usually be happy to write you a great recommendation, especially if you follow the suggestions outlined in this chapter.

GETTING RECOMMENDATIONS: THE BASICS

Soliciting and sending letters of recommendation requires a long-term, well-choreographed effort between you, your recommenders, and the premedical office. Unlike all other aspects of your application, you do not have direct control over your recommendations. Since you do not write the letters, you cannot ensure that they will be returned in a timely manner. However, you do have a great deal of influence over them. The key is to start early and be conscientious about following up with your letter writers throughout the process. It may seem hard to believe, but in many professors' minds, the *manner and structure* of your follow-up with them is itself an important indicator of your degree of organization, people-handling skills, and other aspects of your character, which they will comment on in your letter. Were you always courteous and understanding of their frequent delays in writing your letter? Did you follow up and gently remind them again when you said you would? Always keep these communications punctual, brief, and professional.

WHEN DO YOU SEND LETTERS OF RECOMMENDATION?

Letters of recommendation are typically submitted along with secondary applications. Therefore, they do not need to be turned in by June or July, when you will (ideally) submit your primary applications. Instead, recommendations are sent somewhere **between September and January** of your **senior year**, with your secondary applications to various medical schools.

Nonetheless, you will want to ask for letters of recommendation well in advance. Professors are busy and notoriously slow when it comes to writing recommendations. *You should be on the lookout for potential letter writers as soon as you start college.* Start asking for letters in the **winter** or **spring** of your **junior year**. Though it may not be possible in all cases, try to have almost all of your recommendations in your file by the end of the summer after your junior year. There may be one or two letters related to senior fall experiences that you will want to add to your file after this time, as you may be sending out secondary applications as late as January, depending on the school and how early you submitted your primary application.

YOUR FILE AT THE PREMED OFFICE—CONFIDENTIAL OR OPEN?

Before you begin soliciting letters of recommendation, you will need to set up a file at the **Premedical Student Office**. Professors and others will send their letters to the premedical office on your behalf, where they will be kept until it is time to forward them to medical schools.

When you start your file at the premed office, you will have the option of creating a **confidential** or an **open** file. If you choose an open file, you will be able to review the letters of recommendation that are written about you. If you choose a confidential file, you will not be able to see what the file contains.

Unless you have extremely compelling reasons to do otherwise, you should *always* choose a **confidential file**. Medical schools want to feel like the letters of recommendation are unedited, third-party evaluations of your strengths and weaknesses. If you have an open file, this third-party assurance disappears. With an open file, medical schools *know* that you have looked through your recommendations and sent only those that are favorable. No medical school that we know of will consider you a serious candidate if you have read your recommendations before you have sent them.

Even with a closed file, however, you have a tremendous capacity to influence the quality of the recommendations you receive. Taking a friendly, direct approach with your professors and other sources, you can ensure that you will get only strong letters. Later in this chapter, we will discuss techniques for soliciting positive recommendations.

TIP! At some colleges, an advising faculty member who did *not* write a recommendation for you may still review your closed recommendation file. This third-party faculty member can then recommend which letters you send, without revealing their contents to you. Check with your premed advisor to see if this possibility is available to you. Clearly, this is an option that should be made available either to all premedical students or to no students, to level the playing field. Send a letter to AMCAS if you are concerned about the standardization of admissions policy on this issue.

How Many Letters Do You Need?

On their secondary applications, medical schools will indicate how many and what type of recommendation letters you need to submit. You need to show that you can **follow directions** for the primary letters requested, so read their instructions closely. If an admissions committee asks for a recommendation from a premedical sciences professor, sending a recommendation from a psychology or sociology professor instead will count against you, even if you suspect that the recommendation will be stronger. If they ask for a clinical or community letter, sending one from a student organization leader will hurt your admissions chances, unless you call the school and are given specific permission to do so. The admissions committee may even disregard a letter of recommendation if it is not from the specific source they requested.

In most cases, schools request a **minimum of three recommendations,** typically **two from science professors** and a **third from a non-science professor or an extracurricular supervisor**. Each has a slightly different perspective on you as a candidate. Some schools request that you send your recommendations in the form of a **premedical committee letter**, which is either a letter written by the undergraduate premed committee specifically recommending you, or a letter that summarizes comments made by various committee members about you. However, many schools do not have premedical committees. In addition, nontraditional students might not be officially affiliated with an institution that can write a letter on their behalf. In that case, if you are asked for a premedical committee letter, you will typically need to submit a minimum of three letters of recommendation from individual sources instead.

While you need to follow directions for the primary letters requested, unless a school specifically requests that you send *no more than three* letters of recommendation, you should also feel free to send up to **double** the number they request. Thus, unless specifically instructed not to send additional letters, more competitive applicants commonly send **as many as six** recommendations, including those from additional academic sources, clinical mentors, supervisors in extracurricular activities, and research sources.

Consider the following argument for sending up to six, rather than the minimum three letters that are requested in most secondary applications. Since you do not know the strength of each letter beforehand, the chemistry letter you expect to be strong could, in fact, be weak, while the physics letter you think will be lukewarm could actually be great. By sending both, with one going along in a supplementary capacity, you give the medical school a chance to make its *own* decision on which letters count. If the school decides to leave both letters in your file for committee review, the stronger one will stand out, while the weaker one will not necessarily detract.

While it is a good idea to send up to six recommendations, more than six is widely considered overkill, and makes handling your application inconvenient for the committee. Nevertheless, we do know people who have sent even more than this who have been successfully admitted to medical school. So if you think it takes nine letters to show the full spectrum of your scintillating personality, don't let us stop you.

You may want to aim for soliciting seven to eight letters, even though you will typically send no more than three to six to any single school. With this number of letters, you will appreciate having the flexibility to choose specific recommendations for specific schools when completing your secondary applications. You can customize your letter choices based on the type of questions on a school's secondary application, their reputation, or your conversations with admissions officers or students. Furthermore, you can use your letters to draw attention to a certain extracurricular activity in your personal statement, for a particular school. By keeping a decent number of different types of letters on file, you will always have your bases covered. This said, if you can only obtain three or four quality letters for your file, that number is still quite sufficient to gain admittance to a very good school.

WHOM SHOULD YOU ASK TO WRITE YOUR RECOMMENDATIONS?

As a rule of thumb, the minimum application file will contain **two** strong letters from **science faculty**, **one** letter from a **non-science faculty**, and **one** from an **extracurricular supervisor**. We generally recommend that you send one letter from a **biology** professor, one from a **chemistry or physics** professor, and another from a **humanities** professor, thus covering three of the four main subjects tested by the MCAT. When brainstorming for potential letter writers, always check with your premed adviser. They have been reading recommendation letters from faculty for many years, and can sometimes tell you which professors are student friendly, and which might be good matches for your own interests and personality.

Some college career services centers have all U.S. medical school secondary applications on file, which will tell you what type of letters each school requests. Typically, letters of recommendation are requested from three sources: **academic professors, research sources, and other professional sources**, such as your supervisor at work or at a volunteer position.

As with all aspects of your application, your letters should be as well-rounded as possible. If you are going to request a letter of recommendation from more than the minimum three academic sources (and you should), try to get recommendations from several types of references, which point out a variety of your strengths and accomplishments. Don't send letters from six biology professors. Though they may all have very nice things to say about you, each letter is likely to be similar to the next, discussing the same personality traits and accomplishments. Instead, look for additional sources who have seen you in different settings, and who can discuss your non-academic strengths, such as compassion, dedication to service, and professionalism.

Recommendations are also a great way to highlight and balance certain parts of your application. For example, perhaps you worked in a volunteer job of which you are particularly proud. A letter of recommendation from your supervisor at that position would strengthen the comments you make about the job in your personal statement. Or maybe you received a lower-than-expected score on the verbal reasoning section of the MCAT, even though you are an English major. Sending two recommendations from humanities professors who can attest to your written and verbal abilities could help to counter the negative effects of the score.

Building a Balanced Recommendation File: Specific Majors Advice

Whom you ask to write your letters depends also on your major, especially when it comes to academic recommendations. As we discussed earlier, you should submit a minimum of two academic recommendations from science professors and one from a humanities professor. But what if you majored in psychology or computer science? Is there room for a recommendation from a professor in your major field? Below are some common letter suggestions based on your major type. Feel free to check on these with your campus premedical advisor, to see if he or she is in agreement with our advice.

Science Majors in medically related disciplines such as biology, genetics, physics, and chemistry will ideally submit recommendations from the following sources:

- One recommendation from a biology professor

- One recommendation from a chemistry or physics professor

- One recommendation from a humanities professor (can be a professor from an intro-level course)

- Three (ideally) recommendations from other sources, such as supervisors from lab or clinical work, extracurricular activities, and perhaps an additional academic letter

Note that you will be expected to submit at least one science recommendation from a professor in an upper-division course. The other science recommendation can come from a professor in your major or premed prerequisites. For example, if you are a biology major, you should submit a recommendation from a professor of an advanced-level course in biology, and you might also request a letter from the professor for your general chemistry course.

Humanities or social science majors (including English, history, art, philosophy, sociology, psychology, etc) will probably have fewer sources in advanced-level science courses. Therefore, an ideal set of letters from such a student would be from the following sources:

- One recommendation from a biology professor (from prerequisite coursework)

- One recommendation from a chemistry or physics professor (from prerequisite coursework)

- One recommendation from a humanities professor

- One recommendation from a professor of an advanced-level course in major field (humanities majors should send two humanities recommendations, at least one of which is from a professor who instructed him in an advanced-level course)

- Two (ideally) recommendations from other sources, such as supervisors from lab or clinical work, if one did any, or extracurricular activities

Non-medically related science majors (such as computer science, engineering, or math) should submit:

- One recommendation from a professor of a medically related science class, ideally biology

- One recommendation from a professor of an advanced-level class in major area

- One recommendation from a humanities professor (may be an intro-level humanities course)

- Three (ideally) recommendations from other sources, such as supervisors from lab or clinical work, or extracurricular activities

WHO SHOULD NOT WRITE A RECOMMENDATION?

Even though you may be able to talk these people into writing a dazzling recommendation, don't send comments from any of the following sources:

- Family members

- Family friends

- Graduate students (even if they supervised you in a research position or oversaw your work in a class). Postdocs (with PhDs) are acceptable for research letters, but the principle investigator is always the best.

- Bosses or supervisors from jobs that are not related to medicine

- Athletic coaches

MORE ON YOUR PROSPECTIVE LETTER WRITERS

Diverse, well-chosen sources will provide a revealing and balanced assessment of your character. More on each of the three main letter sources follows.

1. Academic Professor Sources

The main purpose of an academic recommendation is to give an assessment of your intelligence, the quality of your class work, and your general approach to learning. When you are deciding whom to ask for a recommendation, think about which professors know you personally and have a good impression of your academic abilities. Keep in mind that letters from academic professors might discuss your:

- Interest/curiosity about the subject they taught

- Academic ability and achievement

- Determination

- Initiative and motivation

- Class participation

> **TIP!** Letters from academic professors should **always** be in courses in which you received an A- or better.

2. Research Sources

The best person to attest to your research skills would generally be the professor who heads the lab at which you have worked, even if you've been working exclusively with post-doctoral PhD students. In such cases, your post-doctoral supervisor may often write the letter that the principal investigator will sign. If the professor has also taught a course that you took, this is an additional bonus. Your research letter might discuss your:

- Lab capabilities

- Accomplishments and results of work

- Work quality

- Reliability

- General knowledge and the practical knowledge gained from lab experience

3. Clinical/Other Professional Sources

The person who served as your supervisor at an extracurricular activity or other relevant position can be an excellent addition to your recommendation file. Letters from these types of sources should, in large part, discuss your personality and character. Therefore, it is particularly important that the writer know you on a personal level. An ideal writer from this category would be able to discuss:

- Personality and character

- Willingness to exceed the basic job requirements

- Professionalism and reliability

- Patient care (if you worked in a primary care position)

- Interpersonal skills

- Enthusiasm

Remember also that if you will be applying to osteopathic medical schools, you will specifically need a letter from a DO in your application. Depending on your state of residence, you may have to get creative to find DOs in your area. Check with the personnel directors at your local medical school, hospital, and the nearest osteopathic medical school for leads.

SOLICITING STELLAR RECOMMENDATIONS

Even though you will not see them yourself, you can sleep soundly knowing that you are submitting a great set of recommendations with your applications. To do so, you will need to start sowing the seeds of goodwill with your recommenders well in advance, **getting to know** key professors and supervisors early. If you have followed the steps of the inward spiral, you have probably begun to form several strong **relationships** with professors, mentors, and extracurricular supervisors by this time. But even if you haven't established enough relationships to fill your recommendation file, you can still obtain plenty of positive recommendations by seeking potential letter writers and taking a direct, friendly approach with them.

SOWING THE SEEDS

The best recommendations come from sources who have known you well for several years and can personally attest to the quality of your work and your good character. The best way to get this kind of recommendation is to start building strong relationships with professors, mentors, and supervisors early in your undergraduate career.

Though it may seem daunting, getting to know your undergraduate professors isn't as hard as you think. It takes very little effort to make the difference between being recognized as an individual or being just another face in the crowd. In classes where the professor might be able to recommend you, stay on top of the material, attend class, and ask questions. It may seem corny, but just sitting in the front half of the class, where you can be seen, and smiling occasionally in an encouraging way when something particularly interesting is said, can do a lot to help the professor understand he is getting through to you. Make time to go to your professor's office hours several times over the semester to chat about the class. Even though office hours are an easy, well-established way to meet instructors, very few undergraduates actually go, preferring to take their questions to less threatening TAs. Professors, however, are usually very happy to spend some time talking with students during their office hours about some particularly interesting question on material related to the course. As an undergraduate, you are often hip to more current events information than the typical professor, so if you discover an article you think she might like, be sure to bring it to her on one of these visits.

If you get along well with a professor in a particular class, consider asking if there are any extra-credit projects available in her course, and ask about research and special project opportunities for undergrads in her lab, if she has one. When the course has ended, visit the professor and ask for feedback or advice, or see if she has a special project you can help with in your extra time. If you did particularly well in the class, you may want to ask if there is an opportunity to teach (TA) for the same class the following year, giving you more time to work directly with that professor. At the very least, you can enroll in another class with the same teacher, giving the relationship continuity.

Beyond recommendations, getting to know professors can be rewarding in and of itself. Professors can make excellent mentors. Many are great conversationalists. Even if you don't end up asking a professor for a recommendation, it is unlikely you will regret the attempt to get to know your instructor. If you do eventually request a recommendation from that person, you will find that a little advanced effort spared you a lot of stress and scrambling in the future.

Choosing Recommenders

Medical schools expect your letters to **positively** recommend you. When they don't, this stands out strongly against you. With the stiff competition to get into medical school, admissions committees are always looking for reasons to *disqualify* particular candidates. You cannot risk sending lukewarm letters, "damning you with faint praise," from someone who does not know you, does not like you very much, does not like students in general, or doesn't like writing letters, period.

Therefore, before you approach a potential letter writer, think about your **relationship** with the person you are considering. Does that person know you? Do they *like* you? Do you feel comfortable talking to him or her, or is it awkward? Do you make jokes or laugh together, or are your conversations so serious and formal that you don't know his or her opinion of you? The best recommendations come from people who **know** and honestly **like** you as a person. People who like you will want to see you succeed and get into medical school, and will be willing to put themselves on the line to recommend you. In addition, think about the potential letter writers who know you best on a personal level. You don't want to send a recommendation that sounds 'canned" ("I recommend candidate X because they did Y...").

Think also about the **personality** of the potential letter writer, to the extent that you know it. Is he a positive person? Has he written positive letters for others in the past? Some instructors' personality types make it very hard for them to write particularly positive letters. Your premedical advisor may be able to give you a hint on that point if you are unsure. Is he often strongly dogmatic about his point of view? Some very opinionated instructors have no problem writing the one scathing letter that will sink a premedical student's admissions chances. Most people, however, would balk at that, and would instead warn their potential letter-requester in advance that they don't feel comfortable writing a good letter. Rather than actively sealing an applicant's doom, most would rather he or she passively fail, simply by not being able to find enough good letters. What kind of personality does your potential source have? Again, your premedical advisor, other professors, and senior students may be able to give a hint in this regard. Certain professors may be too risky to use as recommenders, unless you are 100 percent certain that you are a golden boy or girl in his eyes.

ASKING FOR RECOMMENDATIONS

After you have identified potential letter writers, test the waters. Go to a potential recommender's office hours and remind him or her that you are applying to medical school. Say that you will need academic recommendations for med school by a particular time (say, "within the next three months," or "by June" or "by August"), then ask: **"Do you feel comfortable writing me a strong letter of recommendation?"** Choose a word such as "great" or "strong," then reiterate it several times during the course of your subsequent conversations. Listen carefully to his or her response, or lack of it.

Does the professor seem flattered, happy, and willing, or does he make excuses, claiming that he will be very busy at that time, or that he doesn't have time to write many recommendations for students? If you have any doubt about his feelings, reassure him that you don't want to put him in a position of writing a **strong** letter if he feels otherwise, and you'd prefer he decline if he isn't comfortable, is too busy, or doesn't know you well enough to write a **great** letter. Be direct. If you have any reason to hesitate about a potential writer, you will be better off asking someone else, even someone who doesn't know you as well, to write your recommendation.

HELP THEM HELP YOU

In most cases, your chosen professor will be happy to write you a recommendation, especially if you have already sown the seeds of friendship with this person over the course of a couple of years or several classes. Once your friendly source has agreed to write you a letter, say thank you and inform him or her you will send a package of materials to help write the letter. Shortly thereafter–ideally, no more than a day or two of delay–bring or send a package that contains the following:

1. A concise, friendly, enthusiastic, and well-written letter, which:

   - Thanks your professor for agreeing to write you a recommendation

   - States **in bold** the deadline date for the letter

- Briefly (2–4 paragraphs) summarize your history with this recommender and your account of the experiences you have had working together

Take great care with this! Generally, if you craft a **well-written and informative "first thank you letter,"** the recommendation letter you receive as a result will also be strong. Professors will *refer to this letter* before they begin writing theirs, to give their recommendation a personal touch. Some professors will even borrow phrases from it!

2. A copy of your **AMCAS application**, if available. Some professors will ask for this, since it helps them learn more about you as a candidate. If you have it, provide it automatically, just to be open and candid. In addition, if they can refer to your application while writing your letter, your recommender may draw attention to positive aspects of your application. For example, a professor may mention awards or honors you received in their letter, which will highlight them for the admissions committee.

3. A **stamped-and-addressed envelope** for the premed office. That way, when your source is done writing your recommendation, all they will have to do is print, seal, and send.

"Let Me Help You Help Me"

Before you leave the recommender's office, you may want to ask if there is any way you can assist in the letter-writing process, such as dropping off an old paper or exam for him to remember you by. If he requests any specific material, include it in your first thank you letter/recommendation packet.

Second Thank You Letter

Be sure to send a second briefer thank you card or letter to all your recommenders. They took the time to help you on your way, and you can in turn acknowledge their kindness with heartfelt thanks.

Don't Have Enough Letters?

Maybe you are a nontraditional student who is applying to med school several years after graduation and have lost contact with some of your professors. Or maybe you never saw your chemistry professor outside of lecture and now it's letter time. Don't despair. There is still a way to get additional letters of recommendation if you need them.

Asking for letters of recommendation can be intimidating. Usually, you have developed a relationship with several teachers or supervisors, but to get enough letters, you may have to put yourself out on a limb and ask someone to represent you who you don't know too well. Remember that many of these professors and sources have written recommendations for other students for many years. In most cases, they will be happy to help you.

First, consider what kind of recommendation you need and who is available to help you. Was there a professor whom you don't know well but in whose class you did well? Do any of your former professors seem particularly approachable and personable? If not, think about the professors for the classes in which you have just enrolled. Who seems a likely candidate? If you are a nontraditional applicant and have lost contact with all your old professors, you may want to enroll in a class in a post-baccalaureate program and ask that professor for a recommendation.

Once you have a potential writer in mind, go to his office hours once or twice and get to know him briefly on a personal level. The second or third time you visit, you should feel comfortable telling him you are a premedical student and that you will need letters of recommendation down the road. Tell him you realize he does not know you well, but that you have a solution in mind. Ask him if there is any project you can do in the coming months that will allow you to get to know each other. That way, you can help him, and at the same time he can get to know you on a personal level.

Be sure to **limit the time** of your proposed commitment. Say, "I have Wednesday afternoons free for the next ten weeks. Are there any educational, research, or personal tasks I can help you with?" Stop short of offering to give a back rub, but be sure your offer to help is **sincere**.

Almost always, professors will tell that you don't need to do anything special, just return to office hours to talk. If this is the case, be sure to go back to their office hours the next week. When you go back, **repeat your offer** to work on a project at least one more time. With many professors who are familiar with flaky undergraduate students, this second offer will be the *first* time your offer to help is taken seriously. If there is a big pile of papers in the corner of his office (and with most university professors, there inevitably is), point to it and ask if he is sure there isn't anything you can do to help out. By now, the professor knows that you are sincere. If he has a project for you, enthusiastically involve yourself. If he still says no, you can rest assured that you are even likelier to get a strong letter.

Best of luck with your letters of recommendation, and remember: engage in the one-on-one time you spend with all your letter writers, and be sure to learn personal things about them. They are some pretty amazing people, and it is a gift to have time to get to know them.

Video Assignments for Chapter 7:

And the Band Played On, Gandhi, and *Field of Dreams*

CHAPTER 8
RESEARCHING MEDICAL SCHOOLS, APPLICATIONS, AND FINANCIAL CONSIDERATIONS

You've spent three years taking premedical classes, meeting professors and mentors, engaging in extracurricular activities, and preparing for and taking the MCAT. At last, the big moment has arrived: it's time to apply to medical school.

Submitting your application can seem deceptively simple, but taking an organized approach will greatly increase the positive results you seek. Ideally, you will begin by researching programs you want to apply to. Once you have made **The List** (your list of preferred schools), you will need to send primary applications to those schools, followed by official transcripts, secondary applications, and recommendation letters. You would do well to research different ways to finance your medical school application, as this research will help you decide which schools you can best afford.

RESEARCHING MEDICAL SCHOOL PROGRAMS

Taking the time to research medical programs is a valuable step in the application process. Unfortunately, most students spend little time in this process and end up applying to schools based on school rank or location. While rank and location are important factors, they are just two of the many considerations that should go into the making of The List. A school's rank doesn't say much about its priorities, the character of the students and faculty, or the composition of the student body. It doesn't tell you whether the curriculum is focused on what you most want to learn.

There are real differences between medical school programs, even though they are all standardized enough to give you a good shot at the available U.S. residencies. At the end of your research, at the very least, you will have some specific reasons why you have decided to apply to every school on your list, and a good idea of which things you like and dislike about each program. At best, a small number of highly desirable schools will emerge with factors that speak to your personal passion for medicine.

During secondary applications and interviews, medical schools will put your knowledge of their school to the test. Admissions committees like to hear heartfelt reasons why you applied to their school; some resent interviewing students who know nothing about their institution. On a similar note, you don't need to spend a lot of time and money flying across the country to interview with a school that you discover in the course of your research that you would dislike attending.

As Dr. Nelson advises, if you are a strong applicant with no articulated burning desire to attend a second- or third-tier school at which you are interviewing, you are at a particular disadvantage. Without your expressing a clear reason why you are interested in that school, the admissions committee will simply not offer you a place because it assumes that you are waiting to be accepted at a top-tier school. He states, "You should have a **specific reason for each school** that you choose to apply to. You should know what things you like and dislike about the school before you apply. Why? Because your secondary applications and interviews will put your reasoning and knowledge to the test – just like you do not want to apply to schools that will not accept you, medical schools do not want interview students who are unlikely to attend."

GETTING STARTED

There are 123 allopathic medical schools in the United States, three in Puerto Rico, and sixteen in Canada, all of which are fully accredited and will confer the MD degree on their graduates. In addition, there are nineteen accredited osteopathic medical schools, which confer the DO degree. While you may be aware of one or two medical schools whose reputations appeals to you or that are located near your hometown, there are many more that you know little about.

Due to the fierce competition to get into medical school and the low acceptance rates, most premeds apply to **ten to fifteen programs**. In more competitive states such as New York and California, you will need to apply to even more programs. The average number of applications submitted by California residents, for example, is approximately 25. To find ten to fifteen programs that truly interest you and speak to your passions, you will need to put a few days into dedicated research.

When looking at medical school programs, return again to the inward spiral model. Begin by casting a wide net and surveying as many people and programs as possible. Visit your premed advisor. Acquaint your advisor with your interests and achievements and see if she can recommend some schools for you to consider. You should also talk to your mentor (where did he or she go to school?), to senior premeds (where are they going next year?), and other premeds (where are they going to apply?). You might also look initially into programs based on what you know about a school's rank, reputation, or admissions competitiveness.

KEY RESOURCES FOR RESEARCHING MED PROGRAMS

You can use several methods of researching medical school programs. We've listed the most important here:

- Medical School Admissions Statistics Binders

  The premed advising office of every major college and university receives copies of the **Medical School Admissions Statistics (MSAS)** reports. Reviewing these reports is the most effective way to observe recent medical admissions trends at your school and to evaluate your realistic chances for acceptance into particular programs. MSAS reports contain detailed, but anonymous, information about the previous year's successful and unsuccessful applicants from your university, including breakdowns by major; science, non-science, and total GPA; age; gender; and ethnicity. MSAS binders are by far the best way to find out which schools recently admitted candidates matching your profile.

  Most schools allow students to review MSAS binders at the premed office, sometimes under the supervision of your guidance counselor. A few schools even sell annual copies at the career services center. Unfortunately, some schools do not let students review the MSAS reports at all because they contain sensitive data about minority admission rates. If your school is one of those that has such a restrictive policy, you should talk to high-ranking administrative staff and plead with them to change the policy. Remind them that premeds at your school are at a serious competitive disadvantage if they don't have access to this valuable information. As a last resort, you may still be able to find a university similar to yours nearby that does allow public viewing of their MSAS.

MSAS won't help you find schools that awaken your passion, but they will let you to compile a good list of safety schools, those with the greatest odds of granting you admission. The statistics will help you understand where medical schools on The List stand in terms of their recent admissions difficulty. This can be very helpful for balancing the selection of schools to which you will apply, which is an important admissions strategy for any school.

- Medical School Admission Requirements

Published by the Association of American Medical Colleges, the *Medical School Admission Requirements* (MSAR) contains a data-rich summary of every U.S. medical school, including an outline of the school's curriculum, admission requirements, tuition, application procedures, and acceptance policies. It is helpful, but limited. For example, the MSAR will not help you discover which schools have admissions committees that are biased against certain types of applicant profiles, or faculty with anti-student policies and procedures. The MSAR is, however, a very useful general reference source, and can be particularly revealing in combination with other more subjective information about the school.

Want your own?
You can order the MSAR from the Association of American Medical Colleges for $25, plus shipping and handling.

- Complete Book of Medical Schools

The *Complete Book of Medical Schools* is The Princeton Review's guide to medical schools, which offers a current, unbiased (or rather, multi-biased) description of all U.S. medical programs. The book contains profiles of each medical school in the United States, Canada, and Puerto Rico, including osteopathic medical schools. The profiles, researched and written by The Princeton Review, describe the academic curriculum, student body, and admissions requirements at each medical school. The book also contains vital statistics for each program, such as the average accepted MCAT score and GPA; an outline of tuition and fees; financial aid availability; and the number of applicants, accepted students, and matriculants.

- Premed advisor

Premed advisors have lots of information about medical schools. The older, more experienced advisors can be particularly good at matching a student with an appropriate medical program. If you take time to talk with your premed advisor about your choices, he or she can help match a school to your needs and desires. Advisors can also offer insight as to which schools are most likely to accept you based on your current academic performance, the institution you are attending, etc.

- The Internet

Every U.S. medical school has a website with information for prospective students. Many also list email addresses for admissions officials or current students, who are willing to answer questions and help you learn more about the school.

In addition, you can often learn something about a medical school by looking at the Web pages that are not directly related to admissions. For example, you can see how student-friendly a school is by noting **what kind of Web resources are available to students.** With a bit of innovative surfing, you might even find some student clubs with interests that are similar to yours. If you are feeling drawn to a particular club or activity, you might consider emailing some partici- pants to find out more about that activity at their particular campus.

- School Catalog

It might cost five or ten dollars per school, but no other publication can teach you more about the character of a school than leafing through a school catalog filled with faculty interests, departments, resources, mission statements, and research programs.

- School Brochure

  Medical schools publish their own brochures to attract top students. These are, however, often just marketing materials and therefore should be read with a critical eye. Nonetheless, the free brochure can still provide interesting and important information. You can request brochures from the admissions office, for the price of a phone call or email request.

- Current Medical Students

  If your university has a medical school, talk to current students to hear what they have to say about the program. They may also be able to recommend or evaluate other programs that they had considered. Is your sister's boyfriend's brother in medical school? Give him a call to see what he has to say about the program and the admissions process.

- Campus Visit

  If you can stop by a med school without spending too much time or money, it is always a good idea to visit. You will get a sense of the campus vibe, get to check out the facilities, and have an opportunity to chat with students.

KEY FACTORS IN MEDICAL SCHOOL SELECTION

Once you have an initial list of schools to consider, start evaluating each program in more depth. You may want to consider the following factors, depending on your focus, interests, and goals:

- Requirements for entrance/selection factors

- Curriculum

- Financial considerations

- School rank

- Affiliated hospitals

- Student life

- Any special considerations unique to you

Admissions Requirements/Selection Factors

In choosing to apply to any medical school, one of the most important considerations is whether you will be accepted? As we've mentioned, the best way to evaluate your admission chances is to go to your college's premed office and ask to look at the latest MSAS binders. Your school's MSAS will tell you which med schools recently admitted students from your undergraduate institution, with a background similar to yours. Just as importantly, it will tell you which schools have rarely or never admitted undergraduates from your institution. Sometimes this helps you discover the hidden biases and historical preferences of a medical school's admissions committee. At the very least, it tells you which schools are in your "long-shot" category.

> **Some Historically Research-Oriented Schools**
> The following schools generally prefer students who have engaged in premedical research or scholarly extracurricular activities:
>
> Albert Einstein; Baylor; Case Western Reserve; Columbia; Cornell; Duke; Emory; Harvard; Johns Hopkins; Mayo; NYU; Stanford; University of Alabama, Birmingham; UCLA; UCSD; UCSF; University of Chicago; University of Michigan, Ann Arbor; University of Pennsylvania; University of Pittsburgh; University of Texas, Dallas; University of Washington; Vanderbilt; Washington University; Yale

As the MSAS even contain statistics from unsuccessful applicants, you will get a good idea of what numbers you need to be accepted at the schools in which you are interested. Use this information to help you sort your list of potential applications into three important categories: **long-shots, fifty-fifties** (where you estimate you have a 50% chance of admission)**,** and **likelies/safeties.** There is no harm in sending applications to a few long-shots (perhaps as many as six, if you are applying to twenty-four schools), but smart applicants will concentrate their efforts on applying primarily to schools at which they will be accepted.

> **Rule of Thumb:** We typically advise Hyperlearning premedical students that applications be sent in the following ratio: **one-quarter to long-shots, one-half to fifty-fifty schools , and one-quarter to likely/safety schools.** In easier application years, this ratio might change to one-third long-shot, one-third fifty-fifty, and one-third likely/safety schools. The first ratio is more conservative, but might keep you from being accepted at some top schools. Make your own decision, based on your perceived strength as an applicant, and your risk tolerance.

Admissions requirements and committee preferences vary by institution. In some cases, your experience will not be well suited for a particular school. For example, most medical schools will rely on AMCAS calculations for GPA, considering your performance in all college level coursework in their computation. However, some medical schools will make their own adjustments to these numbers, ignoring or penalizing graduate work and even post-baccalaureate work when calculating a student's application GPA. This means that outstanding performance in a post-baccalaureate or grad program cannot make up for deficiencies in undergraduate performance at those particular schools. Students who have entered master's or post-bacc programs to make themselves a stronger candidate should avoid applying (or at least minimize the number of applications they send) to these schools. Once you have made an initial list of schools, start looking at their admissions criteria in detail, and call or email them if you have any questions. Do you have the right grades, experience, recommendations, and course selection to be accepted to this school?

Curriculum

Medical school lays the foundation for your career as a doctor, and trains you in your initial philosophy of medical care. In that, it is important to seek a curriculum in line with your path of heart. What's more, you are more likely to be accepted at a school whose service mission, goals, and focus are similar to your own.

Some argue that medical schools in the United States are all of such a high caliber that there is no reason to choose one school over another. While it is true that every medical school will give you an adequate medical education, wide variance can be found in medical school pedagogy, elective curricula, philosophy, and resources available to the student. Unfortunately, until you are in the thick of the process, many of these differences are difficult to discern. You may need to do some sleuthing to differentiate among the educational approaches of your top choices.

Some Historically Primary Care-Oriented Schools
These schools tend to recruit students who have participated extensively in community-based, service, or clinically oriented activities:

East Carolina University; Medical College of Wisconsin; Michigan State; Oregon Health Sciences University; Southern Illinois University, Springfield; UCSF; University of Colorado Health Sciences University; University of Iowa, University of Kansas Medical Center; University of Kentucky; University of New Mexico; University of Massachusetts; University of Minnesota, Duluth; University of Missouri, Columbia.

Use the MSAR, our *Complete Book of Medical Schools*, websites, and admissions brochures to initially research the curricula at the schools you want to attend. Once you have narrowed the list to a decent number (say 30 or 40 programs), send away for at least five or six catalogs to obtain more specific information about programs in general. Think about the questions you will want to ask all your programs. If one of the medical schools you are considering is nearby, visit the campus and talk to students, teachers, or admissions officials about academics. If the student affairs office can't help, you can usually find students willing to talk to you in the cafeteria over lunch, at any U.S. medical school. Offer to buy their lunch, as a gesture of your appreciation.

When researching a school's curriculum, you may want to consider the following factors:

THREE RIVERS PUBLIC LIBRARY
MINOOKA BRANCH
109 N. WABENA AVE.
MINOOKA, IL 60447
815-467-1600

- Stated strengths/areas of focus

- Primary care verses research orientation

- Mission and nature of the affiliated teaching hospitals

- Unique programs, learning approaches (e.g., are they mostly case based?), innovative coursework

- Special certificates and degrees

- Grading systems (any Pass/Not Pass?)

- Structure and difficulty of pre-clinical coursework

- Mandate, resources, and quality of the tutorial assistance program

- Approach to clinical coursework

- Service mission

- Types of patient contact

Before you invest the time, money, and effort in a medical education, be sure that you will be attending a school that will support you best on your particular path of heart.

School Rank

A medical school's rank is roughly proportional to its difficulty of admission. Regarding acceptance, the best-reputed schools are generally the most difficult, and the lowest-ranked schools are generally the easiest. The most widely recognized source for school rank is the *U.S. News and World Report's* annual publication, ***America's Best Graduate Schools***. The *U.S. News and World Report* rankings also include useful information about a school's NIH funding, faculty-to-student ratio, and tuition, all of which are important factors in medical school selection.

In some cases, researching how a school's rank has fluctuated over the past several years can lend some insight. For example, if you notice that a school is dropping significantly in rank every year, it could be a signal that that school is in trouble. Many U.S. medical centers have had to continually restructure to accommodate competitive changes in health care financing and delivery, putting some into financial crisis. Though there are obviously some drawbacks to entering a troubled institution, a school in trouble could be a good backup choice as you may have a better chance at acceptance.

Certain factors that go into the ranking, such as rate of alumni giving, can be particularly useful for discovering a school that may not care about its students. Schools that receive little money from their alumni are often caught in a bad cycle, with students who don't particularly care much for the school, and administrators who presently see students more as obligations, or raw material to be molded, rather than as accomplished individuals and future patrons. That would not be a pleasant place to spend four of the most intense years of your life.

While rankings are useful, don't make the mistake of thinking that a higher overall rank necessarily translates to a better education *for you*. The weightings and factors in any ranking system are not only subjective, they also commonly overlook many important factors, such as the character of the student body, the teacher-student relationships, social life, special opportunities, financial aid options, and environment. If you do careful research, you may find a lower-ranked school better suits your own needs than a top-ranked institution.

Affiliated Hospitals

In the third and fourth years of medical school, students do clinical rotations in their institution's **affiliated teaching hospitals**. The hospitals in which you do your first rotations will greatly shape your early clinical experience. The type of experience you will have at a Veterans Hospital, for example, will be very different from that of a city hospital or a swanky suburban clinic.

If you have a particular medical specialty or range of specialties in mind, you should definitely check out *U.S. News and World Report*'s periodic *America's Best Hospitals,* which ranks hospitals by specialty. As a medical student rotating through one of those hospitals, you will have a significantly better chance at getting a residency there after graduation, if you play your cards right. And remember, the medical residency to which you are admitted at the end of your fourth year of medical school will determine your initial practice, lifestyle, and salary options as a physician, much more so than the medical school that you attended. Therefore, be wise and look into the general and residency reputation of the teaching hospitals with which you will be directly affiliated during medical school. No matter where you end up, if you discover a great teaching hospital where you would like to do a residency, you can always apply to rotate through a clerkship at that hospital during your fourth year of medical school. Such rotations are often granted, and can increase your chances of matching with a residency at that teaching hospital.

Financial Considerations

Given the ever-rising price of higher education in general, the **relative cost** of your medical education is an important consideration. If you have a mortgage, children, personal debt, or considerable undergraduate educational loans, the cost of medical school may be among the most important factors in your decision.

Of the 123 medical schools in the United States, 52 are private. The remaining 71 are public. Generally speaking, public schools are much cheaper than private schools for in-state residents. For example, 2003 tuition at the State University of New York (SUNY) Health Science Center at Brooklyn, a public school, cost $10,840 per year for in-state students, whereas tuition at the private New York Medical College (located in Westchester County, New York) was $31,320, or roughly three times the price.

Though state schools provide a cheaper alternative for medical students, the lower tuition cost is usually reserved for state residents, or in some cases, residents of neighboring states. SUNY—Brooklyn, for example, charges double the tuition for out-of-state students.

Great States!
At Ohio State and the University of Colorado, out-of-state residents have to pay the elevated out-of-state tuition rate for **one year**. *For the remaining three, they pay the lower tuition rate for in-state residents.*

To make matters more complicated, many state schools either do not consider out-of-state applicants or subject them to more rigorous admissions standards. Louisiana State University School of Medicine accepts only applicants from Louisiana. Texas Tech University will only consider out-of-state applicants with a GPA over 3.60 and MCAT scores of 29 or higher. Texans, however, can be admitted with lower grades and test scores.

In addition to tuition, you should think about the cost of living in the area you are considering. If you attend Columbia University College of Physicians and Surgeons, you will need to consider the cost of living in New York City, which is a lot higher than the cost of living for students at University of Kansas School of Medicine in Kansas City.

If you are committed to paying less for your education, you will need to spend some time looking into the real cost of programs, including financial aid and scholarship opportunities. Later in this section, we will talk more about options for financing your education.

Student Life and School Character

Where is the school located? Is the environment attractive to you? Is the campus in a suburb or an urban setting? Where do medical students live? Where do they eat, study, and socialize? Is the school affiliated with an undergraduate institution? Is there a campus gym, movie theater, or other recreational facilities that medical students have access to?

Are the people friendly and sociable? Can you imagine yourself fitting in? What is the ratio of minority or female students? Are people politically conservative, liberal, or middle-of-the-road? Are there clubs and students organizations? Are students competitive or collaborative? Are professors approachable? What is the class atmosphere like? Are students heavily penalized, easily put on probation, or expelled for minor academic violations?

All these factors will be important to you as a medical student and should be important to you as an applicant as well. You can read a school's admissions brochure to get a basic idea of the school's character. However, you will get the best information

Minority Medical Education Program (MMEP)
Sponsored by the Robert Wood Johnson Foundation, MMEP offers free, full room-and-board, six-week medical education prep courses during the summer at eleven U.S. universities. These programs give academic and application assistance, as well as a network of committed peers. Graduates of the program presently have a 63 percent acceptance rate to medical school. For contact information for each of the MMEP campuses (as well as other minority oriented summer opportunities), see Appendix Four.

by talking to current students and by visiting the campus. If you can find email addresses for current med students, drop them a line to see what they think. Some career centers also collect feedback questionnaires from alumni who have attended various U.S. medical schools, and these can be very candid and helpful.

If you are applying to faraway schools, you will have to wait until the interview to visit the campus. In most cases, you will get to talk to a student host during lunchtime and may also have the opportunity to spend the night with a current student the night before your interview.

Special Needs/Considerations

For women, minorities, gay and lesbian students, or students with disabilities, other factors may become important in the selection of a medical school program. For example, these groups might be more concerned with the composition of the student body or the campus' general political leanings. They may be interested in supportive student groups, special programs, and the philosophical bend of the faculty. While every candidate has his or her own unique set of needs and desires, there are often some general concerns expressed by students in a nontraditional group.

Underrepresented Minorities

Although minority recruitment programs have tried to attract more qualified minority students to medicine, the number of underrepresented minorities (URMs) entering medical programs remains low, at roughly 12 percent of all enrolled medical students, and has even begun to decrease in the past few years.

AMCAS would like to encourage more minorities to apply to and enter medical school, and some special assistance programs do exist, but admissions to med school is so competitive that underrepresented minorities—like many of their peers in the majority—continue to find it hard to make the cut. That said, medical schools often aim to educate students from a disadvantaged or rural background who profess a desire to return to practice in those areas. Currently, URM students are much more likely to serve in neglected or needy communities after graduation than non-URM students. As there is an increasingly dire need within the medical profession for physicians who will serve in these communities, URMs may receive special consideration if it is their expressed intention to re-enter a disadvantaged community in a primary care position.

Although it varies, URM students often have specific concerns when selecting a medical school program. In particular, many URM students are interested in the following aspects of a medical school program:

- Community-based/primary care opportunities

- Special programs for minority students (such as mentoring programs, academic assistance, summer courses)

- Faculty mentors

- Composition of the student body (% minority)

- Summer assistance programs (helping URMs apply to medical school, and helping them acclimate in the summer before their matriculation)

- Financial aid and scholarship options

The following schools had 30 percent or more URM enrollment in 2002:

Emory University	Texas A&M
Howard University	University of California, Los Angeles
MCP Hahnemann University	University of California, San Francisco
Meharry Medical College	University of Cincinnati
Morehouse College	University of Maryland
Mount Sinai	University of New Mexico
University of Texas Southwestern Medical Center	

Women

Just twenty years ago there was a large gender gap in medicine, with women comprising only 30 percent of entering students. Today, women are entering medicine at virtually the same rate as men. In 2002, 49.1 percent of matriculants nationwide were women. Even so, there may be some special considerations that female medical school applicants will want to consider.

First of all, women may be interested in knowing the gender composition of the entire student body, the medical school administration, and the basic sciences and clinical faculty. Only about 20 percent of practicing physicians are female, and at some U.S. medical schools the female enrollment is a still a mere 35 percent or less.

The following medical schools had 50 percent or greater female enrollment in 2002:

United States

Cornell University	University of Chicago
East Carolina University	University of Connecticut
Mayo Medical School	University of Louisville
Meharry Medical College	University of Maryland
Mercer University School of Medicine	University of Massachusetts
Michigan State University	University of Miami
Morehouse College	University of Missouri, Kansas City
Mount Sinai	University of New Mexico
New York Medical College	University of Rochester
Stanford University	Wright State University
University of California, San Francisco	

Canada

McMaster University, Canada   University of Calgary

Memorial University   University of Saskatchewan
Newfoundland

In addition, female applicants may have other specialized considerations. Some of the factors most commonly considered by female applicants are:

- Campus politics/gender discrimination

- Focus on women's health

- Faculty mentors

- Mentoring programs for women

- "Family friendliness" or childcare options

Students with Disabilities

Due to the growth of assistive medical technology, the increased use of computers in the medical school curriculum, the Americans with Disabilities Act (ADA), and the pathway cleared by disabled physicians in the past, students with various physical disabilities are applying to medical school in increasingly large numbers.

Even so, it can be more difficult for a disabled student to get through a medical curriculum. Though the ADA stipulates that all medical students are to be provided with reasonable accommodation to perform the tasks they need to perform, students with certain disabilities can find it quite difficult to do everything necessary to receive an MD, especially in the physically demanding clinical skills arena. Therefore, students with disabilities would be wise to research medical schools that are particularly welcoming to disabled applicants. In addition, you may want to consider:

- School location, including proximity to home, mass transit, and other urban resources

- Curriculum, including clinical requirements

- School facilities, including the physical access to classrooms, dorms, and lab facilities for students with mobility-related disabilities

- Political climate and general attitude toward disabled students

- Programs/facilities to assist disabled students (such as sign language interpreters, readers, and testing accommodations)

Gay and Lesbian Students

A large number of **openly** gay and lesbian students are studying and practicing medicine throughout the United States. When choosing a program, gay and lesbian students may consider the following:

- Location (schools located in a traditionally gay-friendly city or urban environment usually offer more resources and support networks)

- General campus political climate

- Clubs/student support services

Nontraditional Applicants

The special needs of older, nontraditional students will be discussed in detail in Chapter Ten.

MORE OPTIONS
Osteopathic Medicine

There are nineteen medical schools in the United States that confer the **Doctor of Osteopathy (DO)** degree. DOs are general medical practitioners who are licensed in all U.S. states and who work alongside MDs in hospitals, usually taking on the role of primary care physician. Although most DOs engage in primary care, there are some present in all medical specialties. They participate in the same National Residency Matching Program (NRMP) that MDs do, and have the option of entering osteopathic or allopathic residencies. That said, it is usually more difficult for a DO to obtain a position in a competitive allopathic residency program, particularly in **specialty** residency programs.

The difference between osteopathic medical programs and allopathic programs is that osteopathic schools usually have a greater focus on preventive medicine, holistic healing, and patient care skills. They also incorporate training in "manipulation," a traditional form of healing that is intended to promote musculoskeletal health.

An advantage to osteopathic schools is that admissions standards are generally less stringent than for allopathic schools. Matriculants generally have MCAT scores of 25 and a GPA around 3.4. For older applicants or students who lack a perfect academic record, but have a strong desire to be a doctor, osteopathic schools can be an excellent fit and a smart entry to primary care. For students who are interested in entering specialized allopathic medical fields or engaging in basic and specialized clinical medical research, the DO may be a poor choice. Osteopathic schools will significantly limit certain choices, so do your homework first.

Foreign Medical Programs

If you want to broaden your options or would like the experience of living in another country, you may want to consider applying to a foreign medical program. At McGill University in Canada, for example, U.S. citizens not intending to practice in Canada comprise about 15 percent of every medical school class. In addition, students there have the opportunity to experience Quebec-French culture.

If you do choose to study at a foreign school but intend to practice in the United States, you will need to do careful research as to that school's U.S. Boards passing rates and residency matching. (Many Israeli schools have an excellent U.S. Boards Passing Rates and generally good U.S. residency matching.) Every year, there are more available residency spaces than there are U.S. medical graduates, particularly for non-specialist positions. To fill these matching positions, hospitals perennially admit foreign-trained medical students into U.S. residency programs. If you choose correctly, you should be able to practice in the United States immediately after foreign training.

Even so, you will be less likely to get top residency spots if you go to a foreign medical school, with the exception of a few particularly reputable foreign schools such as those we've listed on this page. If you are interested in a specialty position that is not too competitive, you may need to do an additional year or two of internship in a U.S. hospital before landing a U.S. residency in that position. Some competitive specialties, such as cardiology or dermatology, would be **extremely** difficult to enter after attending a low-ranked foreign medical school. The post-graduate training necessary to have a reasonable chance of admission, after your return to the U.S. might simply be prohibitive in terms of time.

In addition, you'll be paying 20 percent to 50 percent more per year for your education in a foreign country, and you may not be eligible to receive as much financial aid. On the other hand, if you will be practicing in a noncompetitive field, such as general practice, internal medicine, or gerontology, and don't mind doing an internship in a less desirable inner city hospital, you may find the slower, and for some, more humane pace at a foreign school to be a very acceptable path of heart.

PRIMARY APPLICATIONS

The majority of medical schools admit students on a **rolling** basis, which means that spaces in the program are offered to qualified students until all the spots are filled. Once all the places have been allocated, additional qualified candidates are placed on the **alternate list** and are granted a space only as accepted students decline their acceptance or, rarely, drop out of the program in the initial days.

The way rolling admissions operates varies by institution. At some medical schools, the entering class fills up within a month. At most schools, only a certain percentage of the class is admitted in each cycle. Many of these schools periodically re-rank candidates, inviting the top percentage to interview with every cycle. The standard U.S. interview season is between **September and February** (occasionally March). Foreign schools (like Technion, in Haifa, Israel) interview later (April, June). Mid-May is the end of the standard admissions cycle. By **May 15**, the AAMC asks all students who have been admitted to more than one medical school to **choose one** to attend. Many acceptances off the alternate lists will occur in the next few weeks, and rapidly diminish after that.

Needless to say, the most qualified applicants always have the best chance of acceptance to medical school. However, applications that are submitted early are reviewed first and therefore have a better chance of acceptance at almost all schools. Even a very strong candidate may be denied a space if they apply too late in the admissions cycle. Therefore, you must submit your primary application early in the cycle.

AMCAS v. Non-AMCAS

Most medical schools participate in the **American Medical College Application tion Service (AMCAS),** a centralized, third-party organization that administers and processes medical school applications. Since 2002, the AMCAS application can only be submitted via the AMCAS website at http://www.aamc.org/students/amcas.

AMCAS primary applications annually follow the same rough timeline:

Transcripts Accepted Beginning:	March 15
Applications Available Beginning:	April 1
Applications Accepted Beginning:	**June 1**
Early Decision Application Deadline:	August 1

Again, plan to submit your applications as early as possible —ideally, in **June or July.** Even if you are not taking the MCAT until August, you should strive to send out your applications "in the Js," so that medical schools can open a date-stamped file on you. August applicants are usually processed in the order their applications are received. If you send your application early, you can be sure that there will still be ample places available in the program when the admissions committee gets around to reviewing your application.

If you want to be considered for anything other than alternate spaces, you must submit your applications **no later than September!** Applicants who wait until October or later often spend a lot of time and money flying to interviews when there are *only* alternate spaces left (many don't know this). These students will only get a space if someone else declines an offer of admission.

NON-AMCAS SCHOOLS

The following schools do not participate in AMCAS and must be contacted individually for an application:

1. Brown University School of Medicine (Providence, RI)
2. Columbia University College of Physicians and Surgeons (New York, NY)
3. New York University School of Medicine (New York, NY)
4. State University of New York, Rochester (Rochester, NY)
5. Texas A&M University School of Medicine (College Station, TX)
6. Texas Tech University Health Sciences Center School of Medicine (Lubbock, TX)

7. University of North Dakota School of Medicine (Grand Forks, ND)
8. University of Missouri, Kansas City School of Medicine (Kansas City, MO)
9. University of Texas (Southwestern Medical, Galveston, Houston, San Antonio)

In addition, none of the sixteen Canadian Schools of Medicine participate in AMCAS.

Though you cannot apply to non-AMCAS schools using the AMCAS application, most of their individual applications have only a few questions that you won't see on the AMCAS version.

> University of Texas Medical and Dental schools operate their own central application service, similar to AMCAS. For details, go to their website: http://www.utsystem.edu/tmdsas/

APPLYING TO OSTEOPATHIC MEDICAL SCHOOLS

The nineteen accredited U.S. osteopathic medical schools operate a centralized application service similar to AMCAS. It is administered by the **American Association of Colleges of Osteopathic Medicine (AACOM).** You can submit a paper or Web application through AACOM to any or all of these schools. Like allopathic applications, it is best to apply early.

The AACOM application for osteopathic medical schools is similar to the AMCAS application (described below); however the personal statement is even shorter (just half a page), and it has one additional requirement: all osteopathic candidates must submit a **letter of recommendation from a DO.**

EARLY DECISION PROGRAMS

Currently, more than ninety allopathic medical schools operate **Early Decision Programs (EDPs).** Students who apply for early decision take the April MCAT (or in the year prior to applying) and typically submit all their application materials between June 1 (some schools) and August 1 (for AMCAS schools). Early decision applicants are prohibited from applying to any other school until a decision on their application has been rendered, by October 1 or earlier. If they are accepted, they are obligated to accept the offer.

One benefit of an EDP is that you will only have to apply to one school, thus reducing the cost and hassle of the admissions process. You will have your answer early in your senior year and if it is positive, will be able to enjoy your last year of college with less stress and worry.

An additional advantage to EDPs is that you are clearly stating your first choice of school, which can be advantageous to your application. As we mentioned before, medical schools prefer to admit students who have a strong interest in their particular program.

Generally speaking, however, schools do not admit students via early decision who would not be admitted during the regular admissions cycle. If you are a marginal applicant, you will not improve your chances of admission, except slightly to third-tier (bottom 50) medical schools, by applying early decision.

If you are considering applying to a program early decision, be aware they have some drawbacks. First, you must be absolutely certain that you want to attend the medical school you apply to. If you are accepted, you have to attend, even if you later discover something that makes you less inclined to go to that school. Second, if you are not accepted early decision, you will enter the regular admissions cycle late, some time between September 1 and October 1. AMCAS says this still provides sufficient time to apply nationally, meeting all final deadlines (which occur between November 1 and December 15). But the reality is that you will be at the tail end of the admissions cycle, at a measurable disadvantage, unless you are a particularly strong applicant.

If your admissions profile is **above average** in GPA, MCAT scores, and otherwise, the advantage of applying early generally outweighs the risks. Doing so may also be a smart move for marginal candidates applying to third-tier medical schools, though this approach is controversial. For average candidates, the decision is more difficult to assess.

Some universities, such as Tufts, also have **Early Notification Programs (ENPs)** for their undergraduates, allowing them to apply to their associated medical school at the end of sophomore year. These programs occur early enough that they have none of the timing or commitment drawbacks of typical EDPs.

How Many Schools Should You Apply To?

The typical premed applies to **ten to twelve** medical schools. However, this number is an average, and varies greatly by student, undergraduate institution, and geographic location. In California or New York, which are more competitive states in terms of medical school applications, most students apply to more than twenty medical schools. (Twenty-four is a recent UCLA average).

If you think your chances of acceptance are lower than average, you may want to apply to many institutions. Students with a higher chance of acceptance may choose to apply to fewer schools, or just one school via an EDP. No matter how many schools you apply to or how strong you are as an applicant, if you are not applying via EDP you should make sure that about one-third to one-half of your applications go to safety schools—schools at which your chances of acceptance are high.

SUBMITTING YOUR APPLICATION

If you are applying to any non-AMCAS schools, you will need to send away for their applications individually. Again, the AMCAS application is only available via the Web. To access the online application, you will need to register with AMCAS, which requires a valid social security number and email address.

Once you have registered, you will be prompted to fill out the application, screen by screen. You are not allowed to advance through the application without putting something (anything) in each field. You are allowed to save your work and return later, to change and edit answers.

The AMCAS application consists of the following ten sections:

Biographical Information
> General biographical information, such as name and address, gender, birth date, etc.

Post-secondary Experiences

  Extracurricular resume

  Awards and honors

  Distinguished publications

  Research experience

Essays

  There are two essay portions of the AMCAS application, the Vision
  Essay and the Personal Statement. The Vision Essay is a half-page
  statement that discusses your vision for your future and your career
  as a physician. The Personal Statement is a one-page essay that
  gives the admissions committee the opportunity to better understand you as a candidate.

Schools Attended

  Basic information about all previous education (even incomplete),
  schools attended, and degrees received

Transcript Request

  An application is not complete without an official transcript from all
  college- or university-level coursework. AMCAS provides a transcript
  request form, which you can forward to your college's registrar.

GPA

  Grades from all college level coursework

Coursework

  Details of any college- or graduate-level coursework, including
  courses for which you did not receive credit. Information you will
  need includes dates of attendance, credit received, and all degrees
  completed.

  Many advisors suggest listing your high school AP classes in
  freshman year and marking the intro-level college classes you were
  exempted from with "EX."

  Tip: Order a copy of your transcript early so you can have it with you
  when you are filling out your application. Write down course names

exactly as they appear on your transcript. AMCAS will check your application against your transcript.

Designate Medical Schools
Place where you select the medical schools you are applying to.

Application Audit
Before you can submit your application, the website does an audit of your entries to make sure that you have filled in all required fields.

Certification and Transmission
Final authorization of your application. Once you certify and transmit your application, it is sent off to the medical schools you designated. You cannot return to the application to modify the information further.

APPLICATION CHECKLIST

As you fill out your primary applications, keep these pointers in mind:

Be Honest

In no case should you fabricate, alter, or omit information that is requested on your application. Honesty is revered in the medical field, and the physician who lies will be a liability to himself, his patients, and his colleagues. If you are caught lying on any part of your application, even after being accepted or starting at a medical school program, you will be barred from entrance, put on probation, or expelled. Medical schools occasionally receive **anonymous calls or e-mails** (from jealous competitors?) alleging that various students have fabricated on their application, and they will often follow up on these tips. If you are worried that you will be judged poorly or discriminated against due to some aspect of background or experience, you can try to counteract negative conclusions by directly addressing deficiencies on your application. Beyond that, keep in mind that those schools, institutions, and friends that don't want to accept the real you are not associations that you want to have anyway.

Prioritize

Resist the urge to put every little thing you've ever done on your list of post-secondary experiences. While you should not hesitate to record anything pertinent—even if your list is very long—don't undermine the strength of your extracurricular activities by listing unrelated, substandard, or short-lived experiences. For example, don't list any activities or honors from high school, unless they continued in college in the same subject. In addition, prioritize the list itself, putting the most impressive extracurriculars first and the least impressive last.

Be Clear

Be sure that all your time is clearly accounted for. If there are gaps or ambiguities in the chronology of your education or career, it will send a red flag to the admissions committee. Even if you innocently forget to account for six months during your junior year, admissions committees may suspect that you are trying to hide something.

Note Inconsistencies

Don't let grades and test scores speak for themselves—especially if they are saying bad things about you! Be sure to explain poor performance on your application, in a manner such as "Please consider period A to period B most representative of my capabilities," or "Please note that period C to period D, when my grades took a noticeable dip, was the time of my hospitalization."

Proofread

Don't get caught making simple mistakes and spelling errors. Careless errors demonstrate inattention and a general lack of regard for the application process.

THE VISION STATEMENT

A half-page essay on the AMCAS application, the vision statement is an opportunity to demonstrate that:

1. You understand the field of medicine well enough to have a grounded, realistic, and positive view of your role in the profession over the long term.

2. You are goal-oriented and have identified at least one or two places in medicine that you know would fit with your strengths and sensibilities.

3. You identify with medical professionals who are older than you and consider at least one of them a mentor.

4. You know that the future is uncertain and that, in medicine, the journey is as important as the destination.

If you took the time to reflect on your goals and explore medicine through the inward spiral, the vision statement is a chance for you to shine. Take the opportunity to illustrate the commitment you have made, and seek to make, to the medical field. If you have gained some specialized exposure to or experience in any medical field, refer to that experience.

THE PERSONAL STATEMENT

The personal statement is the best opportunity to give a human face to your medical school application. Don't underestimate the power of this statement to make a strong, positive impression on an admissions committee. Your written words will give shape and life to your application.

Choosing a Topic for the Personal Statement

The best personal statements focus on a single theme supported by a few well-chosen, illustrative examples. Most personal statements address one of the following general themes:

- The decision to pursue a medically related career

- A life-changing personal experience with medicine, as a patient or as a person close to a patient, which led to an interest in a career as a doctor

- An experience that challenged or changed your perspective about medicine

- A relationship with a mentor, or other inspiring individual

- A challenging personal experience and its effects on your life

- An insight into the nature of medical practice or the future of medical technology, and your perceived relation to this insight.

Shelve it
- *Don't write about something that is not at least partially related to medicine.*
- *Don't tell an overly self-aggrandizing story.*
- *Don't go on a **long philosophical rant** that isn't linked to your personal experience or medicine.*
- *Don't criticize other people or be overly negative about situations or experiences.*

When brainstorming ideas for your personal statement, dig deep. Consider first those experiences that have most strongly influenced or changed you. If you have been following your path of heart, you have probably had a number of experiences that have affirmed or challenged your sense of purpose. Write them down and begin to look for a connection between them. What have you learned in the past few years? How have you and your perspectives changed? What part of medicine was not like you expected it to be? What has been most difficult or enlightening for you to accept or learn?

Whatever topic you choose will require thorough care and consideration. For example, you may decide to write about a complex, tragic experience that challenged your faith in medicine, such as the death of a loved one. You could simply retell the story, explaining what happened, how you felt about medicine before the event, and how you felt after. A better approach, however, would be to consider the deeper issues related to this experience. It might explore how the health care system functions on the individual level, what preventive care was missing from your loved one's experience, or it might define the lack of technology or science that could provide a solution to your loved one's problem. It might discuss the physical aspects of the health care setting, describing the hospital room, the ambulances, or other environments. The essay might also discuss the positive aspects of the experience, such as the influence of a trusted doctor or nurse. In addition, the essay could explain how this experience affected other parts of your life, what you did and didn't do as a result of it, and how it might impact you as a medical student or a doctor.

The point is: whatever you say, it shouldn't be simple. Medicine is a complex, interdisciplinary, and ultimately human profession. When discussing your feelings and experience in the personal statement, take the time to write something truly heartfelt and original.

At a Loss?

Writing a personal statement is a unique experience. In fact, it is something of a genre of its own. Even if you are an English major and have written 101 papers on the writings of famous authors, you might find yourself tongue-tied when drawing over-arching conclusions about your own life experiences. A good way to get an idea of the personal statement genre is to read other students' attempts. Several books and websites contain **sample personal statements** for medical school applications. Your premed advisor also may have some examples of exemplary personal statements on file. For an even wider perspective on the experience, you might consider reading law or business school applications, to see what students in other professions have written about themselves; our own *Law School Essays That Made a Difference* and *Business School Essays That Made a Difference* are good resources for this task.

You can find strong sample statements in any of the following publications (listed here in order of authors' preference):

> *How to Write a Winning Personal Statement for Graduate or Professional School*, Richard Stelzer, 1997.
>
> *Resumes and Personal Statements for Health Professionals,* James Tysinger, 1999.
>
> *Essays That Will Get You Into Medical School*, Daniel Kauffman, 1998.

Qualities of a Great Personal Statement

Great personal statements are **personal, medically oriented, well organized, thoughtful, clear, honest, and unique.** It's a tall order, but an essay that contains all of these qualities can make an application truly memorable. As you write your essay, keep all of the following points in mind. Where does your essay shine and where can it be improved?

Personal

The best personal statements are those that tell a real story from your real life. Adding an original, intimate component will make your statement stand out among the thousands seen by admissions officials every year. Though you may feel like you have the same standard experiences as every other premed, that is never the case. We all take unique paths. If you take the time to think back on your life and review your experiences, you will come up with many small (or large) ways that you are an original person.

Medically Oriented

A good personal statement clearly explains why the applicant is interested in a medical career. In fact, the central theme of the essay should illustrate the applicant's interest in or commitment to medicine. If you choose to write about an experience that was not directly related to health care, you need to immediately explain how that experience contributed to your desire to go to medical school or how it will specifically inform your experience as a medical student.

Well Organized

Choose one central theme and make sure your essay has a thesis statement or overriding purpose. Before you begin writing, organize your essay into clear paragraphs, with a beginning, middle, and end. Organization is key to a great personal statement. It demonstrates your mastery of the English language, and it makes your points understandable.

Thoughtful

Writing your personal statement will take some time and effort. Take the time to develop a theme for your essay and pick out some memorable experiences that related to the theme. Before you begin writing, explore each idea or experience more deeply. Why did that experience affect you? How does it pertain to medicine and the type of physician you want to become?

Clear

Don't try to outshine other essays by using fancy words and terminology, and do not underestimate the power of a short declarative statement. If you use a flowery or overwrought writing style, you may muddle your main point. Though you should certainly try to vary your sentence structure and word choice throughout the essay, resist the temptation to pull out your thesaurus and replace adjectives with bigger, more impressive variations. Simpler and shorter sentences are often the clearest way to convey your message.

Honest

Admissions committees are generally able to distinguish between an essay that describes a real personal experience and those that describe an exaggerated or contrived event. In addition, your interviewers will occasionally follow up on the things you said in your personal statement, asking you further questions about the experiences you describe. It does not pay to be dishonest. What's more, there is no reason to be. If you feel like something you have to say is inadequate or uninteresting, consider why, rather than trying to mask it with synthetic emotion. For example, if you worked in the oncology ward of a hospital for two years but found yourself generally uninspired by the job, don't pretend that the experience was life changing or moving, just because you think that is what an admissions committee wants to hear. Instead, consider what your reaction to the situation says about you or about medicine. What could have been improved? Why weren't you able to make an emotional connection with the patients? How did the shortcomings of that experience inform your view of medicine? The answers to your questions will not always be the "right" ones; however, if you take the time to carefully reflect and consider your experience, you will ultimately find a satisfying, original, and thoughtful response.

Unique

Admissions essays have a tendency to sound the same. Knowing this, some applicants try to make their essay stand out by telling jokes, saying somewhat extreme or controversial things, writing in the third person, inserting heady intellectual quotations or commentary, or telling a story from a very unusual perspective (e.g., a patient or a child). While you do want your statement to be unique, you do not need to resort to such gimmicks. Instead, make it special by telling a personal story in a personal way. Why is your essay about *you* and not about any other medical school applicant? What qualities are special about you or the circumstances you are describing? Bring your own voice, perspective, and experiences to the story to give it a truly unique and memorable flavor. Finally, you can make your essay unique by occasionally using strong, original language, as long as it is not overdone. You might start with a great opening line that catches the reader's attention, expressing an original sentiment or thought.

Personal Statement Dos and Don'ts

DOs

Do focus on a single theme or thesis. Elaborate on your theme through details, opinions, and experience.

Do outline your theme and main points before you start writing. Aim for an organized, direct statement.

Do tell a personal story, rather than making generalizations.

Do write about something medically oriented.

Do start your essay with a solid, attention-grabbing sentence.

Do end your essay with a strong conclusion.

Do spend time on your personal statement – this isn't a "throw away" part of the application.

Do proofread carefully.

Do spell check and spell check again.

Do have three different reviewers, but not many more than this.

DON'Ts

Don't write an autobiography, list all your awards and achievements, or try to include everything you have ever done on a single page.

Don't be overly philosophical and abstract (a common mistake).

Don't be self-aggrandizing or try too hard to impress the admissions committee; tell a real story and let the details speak for themselves.

Don't use clichés or resort to attention-getting gimmicks to stand out. Use real, honest detail to make your personal statement unique.

Don't lie or exaggerate.

Don't use too much detail. Aim to be succinct and direct.

Don't be too controversial. Avoid topics that may raise eyebrows.

Don't make negative statements unless you can show how they lead to a positive counter-argument.

Don't use the word "I" too often. Instead, tell a story and let the details speak for themselves.

Getting Help with Your Essay

Writing is an ongoing process of drafts and revisions. If you have been taking mandatory writing-based humanities courses, you know how long it can take to perfect a paper. (And to be brutally frank, it never will be perfect. It's a subjective evaluation about and by you. How could something like that ever be perfect?) To improve your essay's quality, seek out a small circle of reviewers to help in this process.

Recruiting Your Reading Circle

To maximize the chance that your personal statement has broad appeal, you will want to recruit at least **three types of readers** to look at it in draft form. The first person will be someone with an **admissions background**, such as your premed advisor, who can tell you whether the essay is addressed appropriately to your medical school audience. The second reader will be someone who **knows you very well** and who can analyze the content of the essay based on what they know about you and your passions. The third reader should be someone with a **composition or English background** who can address whether your statement is appropriately organized, tells a compelling story, and is interesting and grammatically correct. If you think you are particularly weak in your insights about medicine, in your composition abilities, or in your personal introspection abilities, you might recruit more than one of those three reader types.

As a rule of thumb, your essay will benefit from as many qualified readers as you can convince to read it. But at the same time, after three or four readers you will discover that most of the additional comments touch on areas that you've already thought through sufficiently. There will come a time when you will know your personal statement has been well crafted, a time when further modification would only reduce its impact and originality.

Questions for Your Admissions Reader:

- Does my personal statement compliment my application?

- Is my interest in medicine and medical school evident?

- Are there any other aspects of my premedical experience that I should address?

- Have I forgotten to include any important aspects of my background or personality?

- Does this essay reflect me as a person?

- Do I represent myself well?

Questions for Your Composition Reader:

- Is my essay well structured?

- Is there a central theme?

- Are my ideas expressed well?

- Do I use proper vocabulary?

When looking for readers, start by asking people who are in your immediate circle. In particular, you may have trouble recruiting your composition reader. If no one of your acquaintance is a great writer and willing to spend an hour carefully critiquing your essay, you

will need to specifically recruit someone for the job. Your best bet is to find a trained writer, such as a humanities TA or a paid writing tutor, who will review your essay for grammar, syntax, organization, and content.

SECONDARY APPLICATIONS

If you've taken the MCAT in April, then you will get a short breather after submitting your primary applications. Traditionally, premeds take advantage of this time with a well-deserved **vacation**. But keep the phone handy, because only a few weeks after you submit your application to AMCAS, medical schools will start mailing secondary applications.

WHAT TO EXPECT

Unlike primary applications, secondary applications can vary substantially from school to school. However, most consist of:

- A set of short essay questions

- Instructions for sending your recommendation letters

- A photo request

- An additional fee (ranging from $35 to $120 per school)

WHO GETS SECONDARIES?

Most schools indiscriminately send secondary applications, meaning that every living, breathing candidate who submitted a primary application will likely get a secondary, regardless of their chances for admission. There are, however, a few student-friendly schools that will review GPA and MCAT scores to be sure you meet their minimum admissions standards before they send a secondary application. In many cases, however, you will receive a secondary application even if you have no chance of acceptance. In fact, some admissions committees will simply wait to review a student's file until after they have submitted their secondary applications, even when an early review would have saved the candidate hundreds of dollars, and saved U.S. medical school applicants several *million* dollars annually. Needless to say, this is a source of irritation for many premeds, who spend countless hours filling out secondaries for schools that would not interview them based on their primary applications. Keep this in mind, and don't have false hopes that a secondary application means more than it does.

I want to attend University X because...
Secondary applications often ask why you want to attend their specific school. Take this opportunity to show that you have researched the school and why you are specifically interested in it. Don't simply parrot back a phrase or two from their marketing brochure. If you want to earn the maximum points you can, take the time to answer this type of question well. If you have learned that the school has particular strengths, describe what you like about their medical program. Use specifics. You may even want to quote the name of a particular physician that you would like to learn from during your medical undergraduate or graduate training. It would be particularly impressive to say (truthfully) that you've talked to that physician, demonstrating initiative that few students have.

HOW TO APPROACH SECONDARY APPLICATIONS

Unlike primary applications, secondary applications ask specific questions about your goals, experiences, and your personal views on a range of topics, including your decision to go to medical school. Copying and pasting boilerplate responses from a previous draft of your personal statement is not acceptable. Your secondaries will be read to see how they complement what you have said in your primary application. At the most basic level, your secondary is another test to see whether you can adequately understand directions (this time, the school's specific directions), and focus yourself to answer the question that was asked.

If you are willing to put in a little effort, secondaries are a great time to elaborate on elements that received less attention in your primary application. As you answer secondary questions, refer briefly to the themes in your personal statement but focus more on **new material**. For example, if you write in your personal statement about a primary care experience, you may want to point out some research experience in your secondary applications, showing that you are an even broader applicant than your initial application suggested. Yet do not bring in new material in a way that casts doubt on your original statements. In this case, a discussion of how research broadened or deepened your interest in primary care might be appropriate.

If you are given enough room on certain questions, you may want to follow the thesis, body, and conclusion structure that you would use for a longer essay. Don't, however, try to squeeze in extra words by using a font more than a point smaller than your AMCAS application. That approach always appears forced, and you come across as a rule bender—not an ideal image to portray.

SAMPLE SECONDARY APPLICATION QUESTIONS

Secondary questions run the gamut from personal to political to pointless. If you want to see what a school's secondary application entails ahead of time, many premed advisors keep a file with the previous year's secondary applications. To give you an idea of what to expect, here are a few questions from recent applications:

- "Write a short autobiography of your life. You should include childhood and elementary school experiences, all the way to college." (University of California, San Diego)

- "Compare and contrast managed care and traditional fee-for-service medical care." (University of California, Irvine)

- "Describe a challenge or obstacle you have overcome, and what you learned from the experience." (Duke University)

- "Describe an instance where you helped someone in need." (University of Chicago)

- "Describe your greatest accomplishment." (University of California, Los Angeles)

PRIORITIZING SECONDARY APPLICATIONS

As you begin to receive secondary applications, you will have a few potential approaches. Some students focus their energy first on the schools that they would most like to attend. Other students realize that their last secondaries will be better written than their first. Thus they hold off sending secondaries to the more competitive schools until they've sent out a few to the less competitive ones. Still other students reply first to schools whose secondaries ask questions to which they can easily give solid answers. This allows them to work their way up to the more difficult applications. Finally, a few students practice writing secondary statements even before they get their first ones, so that they can send out well-written, personalized responses to their top choices first.

In many cases, schools betray what type of student they are looking for in the type of secondary question they ask. If you have strong answers for their questions, it is possible you have the characteristics they are most looking for in an applicant.

Only you can know which approach will work best for you, but keep these factors in mind when you make your decision. Also keep in mind that if you want to make sure that you are not wasting your time and money filling out secondary applications for particular schools, you should be sure you've done some research with the MSAS and MSAR *before* writing those big checks.

TIP FOR STRONGER CANDIDATES (SECONDARY TIERING)

If you are a particularly strong candidate, you may want to save yourself the expense and stress of an interview request from a less desirable school. You can do this by staggering your secondary application responses in time, so that you may actually receive an acceptance from one of your first choice schools before you hear back from your second- or third-tier choices. Tiering involves waiting just a few weeks (typically, two to three) before sending your second and third batches of completed secondary applications. The stronger an applicant you are, the longer you can wait between sending each batch.

	School	Send
Tier One	First choice schools plus two or three safeties	Immediately
Tier Two	Second most desirable schools plus two or three safeties	Two to three weeks after first tier
Tier Three	Least desirable schools	Four to six weeks after first tier

Many admissions committees will tier their interview candidates as well, so don't feel guilty about using this strategy. Just as you ideally don't want to buy a plane ticket or take days off work to interview at all your safety schools, medical schools don't want to waste their interview resources on a candidate they think is unlikely to come to their school. Of course, if you are a well-qualified applicant applying to a third-tier school, you can probably convince them to interview you with a well-written secondary that indicates your deep personal interest in their particular program. Nevertheless, many third-tier medical schools decline to interview particularly strong candidates because they know they are very unlikely to entice them to come to their school.

FINANCIAL CONSIDERATIONS

Deciding how you will **finance** your degree is an integral part of selecting a medical program that is appropriate to your needs. As you research medical school choices, you can also begin exploring your financial aid options. Few people *enjoy* the process of thinking about and researching financial aid. What's more, no one will require them to do so. As a result, most students manage their medical school finances poorly. With a little effort, you can avoid that mistake.

Most students put this issue off until the last minute and end up taking out big loans to pay for school. Though you may not want to put in any time on financial issues, think about it this way: if someone were willing to **pay you $10,000 for a week or two of your time**, you probably wouldn't hesitate to take the job. But with financial aid planning, you could save far more than $10,000 if you take just a few days to research and consider your options.

For specialized tasks that you don't enjoy, get help. Ask a parent who is good at managing the family funds or see a financial planner. Every medical school also has a **financial aid officer** who is usually happy to give advice over the phone, even to prospective students. Most current medical students don't talk to financial aid officers nearly as much as they should, perhaps because they are afraid of dealing with money issues or thinking about displeasing topics like debt. You will quickly overcome your fears simply by taking proactive steps, talking to the helpful experts at your medical college (or prospective medical college), and making a plan.

What is Financial Aid?

Financial aid is money given or loaned to students to help cover the gap between their and their families' resources and the amount needed to pay for a medical school education. Some schools and independent foundations offer scholarships, grants, and fellowships to students based on their academic performance or other factors. In most cases, however, medical students receive financial aid awards based on their demonstrated financial need.

Applying for Financial Aid

Given the high costs of medical education, almost everyone is eligible for at least some financial assistance. To apply for financial aid, you will need to file an application and a standardized need analysis form. Generally, medical schools require you to submit the **Free Application for Federal Student Assistance (FAFSA)** as well as their own financial aid forms. The FAFSA is available via the Web at http://www.fafsa.ed.gov

FINANCIAL ASSISTANCE: YOUR BASIC OPTIONS

The majority of medical students need some form of financial assistance to help cover the costs of medical school. Students usually fund their education through one or a combination of the following:

Loans

Taking out student loans is the most common form of covering medical educational expenses. Medical students may participate in subsidized federal loan programs (e.g., Stafford Loans), as well as proprietary loan programs through private schools, associations, and financial institutions (e.g., Bank of America's Student Maximizer program, Key Bank's MedAchiever program). As we will discuss shortly, each has different terms and conditions, and you will **save thousands** over the life of the loan by finding one that is best suited to your needs.

Scholarships and Grants

Qualified students can receive "free money" (scholarships or grants) through the school they are attending. The amount of this money can vary significantly from school to school. In addition, some private sources of scholarship money are available for medical students, though these resources are limited and harder to locate. If you are looking at these types of awards, check to make sure that any third-party grants and scholarships will offset your loans and not your school-based grants. If they offset your school-based grants, third-party awards will not lower your overall costs; they will just save your school some money. Generally, scholarships and grants are awarded to students who display both financial need and academic prowess.

Savings

Though it is unlikely that you will have extra money after your undergraduate years, those lucky few who were thinking ahead may have some savings to help cover the cost of med school. If you are an undergrad, ask your financial advisor if there are any savings programs they would recommend. We have some great articles on this subject on our website at: http://www.princetonreview.com/medical/finance/finSaveFor.asp

Check out our handy tuition cost and aid comparison calculators, and sign up for the free financial newsletter.

Military/Service Programs

Federal service programs, like the **National Health Service Corps,** can cover the entire costs of a medical education in exchange for several years of service in the military or underserved communities. These programs can be particularly excellent choices for students with primary care practice interests. Be sure to investigate them thoroughly to understand the options they provide.

Teaching Assistant/Research Assistant Fellowships

Some institutions will cover a significant portion of a student's tuition in exchange for their services as a TA to undergraduate classes or as a graduate research assistant. Availability of this type of opportunity varies by institution and is usually limited to a small subset of students.

KEY RESOURCES: GETTING HELP WITH FINANCIAL AID

To get more information about the variety of available loans, scholarships, and grants, you will need to dedicate some time and resources to researching these topics. Here are some of the best places to start looking:

Financial Aid Brochures

To get started, call the financial aid offices of at least three prestigious, private medical schools and request their **financial aid brochure**. Most will send this to you at little or no cost. Expensive colleges typically do the best job finding and explaining financial aid options, to help struggling students and parents to offset their high annual tuition cost. Review these brochures to acquaint yourself with the wide range of possible financing tools available to you.

The Internet

The Internet is one of the cheapest and most efficient ways to get information about scholarships and loan programs. In fact, it is usually more effective than private aid search services, which differ greatly in quality. A number of independent websites can help you locate free money and financing options (some of which are listed in Appendix Four). Also be sure to check official financial aid sites for information, eligibility requirements, and forms.

Books and Publications

There are several good books published on the topic of financial aid and scholarships. The Princeton Review's *Paying for College Without Going Broke* and *Paying for Graduate School Without Going Broke* are among the best and most comprehensive.

Private Consultants

Financial aid options are so vast and confusing that it can be difficult to navigate the terrain alone. Consider seeking the help of a professional, such as a **certified financial planner (CFP) or certified public accountant (CPA),** whose independent perspective will help you create a viable, long-term financial strategy. Many CFPs, as well as the more expensive CPAs, can also handle your annual tax returns for a low fee.

DETERMINING FINANCIAL NEED

The basic formula for determining financial need is:

Financial Need = Costs of Education – Expected Family Contribution

However, this formula can become more complicated in reality.

COSTS OF YOUR EDUCATION

By any standard, medical school is extremely pricey. Tuition and fees are the most sizable factor, especially for students attending private institutions. Even students at public schools may discover that the cost of their education is far from reasonable, given living expenses, equipment, transportation, and incidental costs. How much can you expect financial aid to cover?

When determining your eligibility for financial aid, schools factor in the following:

- Tuition and fees

- Room and board

- Supplies, including lab equipment

- Medical and licensing exams

- Transportation to and from school or hospital

They do NOT generally include:

- Family expenses for married students or student-parents

- Relocation expenses

- Debt or other financial obligations

When you consider these factors, you can actually begin to determine what you will have to pay to attend medical school.

DETERMINING EXPECTED FAMILY CONTRIBUTION

In most cases, your expected family contribution (EFC) is calculated based on the "federal methodology." The contribution consists of the student's share and parents' share. The formula takes into consideration income and assets of both the student and parents, then subtracts taxes, standard living expenses, and asset protection allowances (in the case of the parents, this depends on the age of the oldest parent). If more than one family member is attending college, the parent contribution is divided into equal portions for each student.

*Can you **live less expensively during medical school**, so that you can avoid taking an additional loan or two? Talk with your financial planner. The money you save now will never have to be paid back with compound interest later.*

Many students are surprised to hear that their parents' income is factored into their financial aid package, especially if they have already graduated from college and have been living independently for several years. Nonetheless, all U.S. Department of Health and Human Services programs, as well as most institutional loans, grants, and scholarships, consider students dependent by default, regardless of their age or whether they actually receive financial support from their family. For U.S. Department of Education programs, however, all students are considered independent, meaning that their family is not expected to make any contribution to their education.

Your financial aid package will change every year, based on the changing factors in your and your family's life and finances. For example, if one of your siblings graduates from college, you may be eligible for less financial aid the following year.

Basic Aid Options
Loans

Most students take out loans to pay for medical school. Since doctors are, on average, the highest paid professionals in the United States, most schools assume that you can deal with the consequences of a significant amount of debt. You need to be aware, however, that student loans vary widely in terms of interest rates, terms, repayment plans, and deferment options.

The average debt among 2002 medical school graduates was $91,389 at public schools, and $123,780 at private medical schools. These are very substantial amounts, associated with long-term payment plans that are quite sensitive to interest rates and loan terms and conditions.

Federal Loans

Loans offered through the federal government are generally attractive to students because they offer lower interest rates than commercial student loans. Medical students who demonstrate financial need are eligible for the following loans from the federal government: **Stafford (Subsidized and Unsubsidized) Student Loans, and Federal Perkins Student Loans**. These programs differ in their borrowing limits, interest rate, repayment method, deferment options, fees, application procedures, and eligibility requirements.

State Loans

If you are planning to attend medical school in the state in which you are a resident, you may be eligible for need-based state loans. State loans have lower interest rates than commercial loans and are generally available to minority or disadvantaged students. Some states also have service programs that grant full tuition in exchange for service in disadvantaged communities after graduation.

Institutional

Many schools offer their own loan programs for medical students. However, the amount of money available, interest rates, and repayment methods vary greatly by institution. While some schools have a great deal of money to offer students, others have none. If you are offered a loan through your medical school, you will need to carefully evaluate whether that loan is better than something you could find through a federal, state, or private source.

Private Loans

Students can also get loans from banks or private lending institutions. The federal government does not subsidize these loans. Many private loans are not very good options, as they have high interest rates and strict repayment plans. But terms and conditions vary, and a private loan may be very helpful in a pinch.

In addition to loans from traditional lending institutions, some private foundations, corporations, charities, and associations make *charitable loans* to medical students. These loans have lower interest rates or other benefits over traditional private loans. Charitable loans are usually designed to assist a certain segment of the population, such as minorities or students with disabilities. To find the best option or to locate a good private source for which you qualify may take some research.

Scholarships

Though they are considerably harder to come by, some students are eligible to receive scholarships, which are awarded to cover tuition costs. Scholarships are administered, like loans, through federal funds, state funds, private institutions, and associations. Usually, scholarships are aimed at helping students of a particular demographic. They are either merit based or awarded based on a combination of need and merit.

Loan Programs

The Access Group (www.accessgroup.org) offers the Medical Access Loan, Residency Loan Program and Dental Access Loan programs

Bank of America (http://www.bankofamerica.com/studentbanking/) Maximizer loans for medical students and residents

Citibank (www.citibank.com) Citibank CitiAssist® Loans

Key Education Resources (www.key.com/education) offers the MedAchiever loan for full-time students in allopathic or osteopathic school and the Alternative DEAL, for students pursuing dental or post-doctoral dental degrees

Student Loan Marketing Association (www.salliemae.com) offers the MEDLOANS program, funds for federally guaranteed student loans

TERI (www.teri.org) offers the Health Professions Loan (HPL) for medicine, osteopathic medicine, and dentistry

Federal Scholarships
The U.S. Department of Education and Department of Health and Human Services have some limited funds available for medical students. Usually the awards are need based, but they also consider other factors. **Scholarships for Disadvantaged Students (SDS)** are awarded through the U.S. Department of Health and Human Services. These scholarships are reserved for students from disadvantaged backgrounds, who are extremely financially needy. You can obtain more information about these from your school's financial aid office.

Institutional Scholarships
Most medical schools have some proprietary funds, which they award to qualified students based on merit or a combination of merit and need. Through these scholarships, students receive what amounts to a discount on their tuition. These funds often come from an endowment and involve specific criteria, such as a student's ethnic background or research interests.

Service Options/Obligatory Scholarships

> *Native Americans and Native Alaskans who are the children or grandchildren of tribal members are eligible for special **Scholarships for Native Americans**. In return, they contribute a minimum of two years service to the community.*

A number of federal scholarships are available to students who are willing to serve in the **Army, Navy, or National Health Service Corps** immediately upon graduation. The service "repayment" process usually begins as soon as you finish residency and is usually directly proportional to the number of years you received support.

Most programs cover up to $25,000 of tuition cost annually, as well as a monthly stipend for living expenses. On top of that, the subsequent service experience can often be in a very desirable training environment. However, students should be prepared to fulfill their obligation for seven to ten years after leaving the classroom. For those who require more independence, these programs may not be ideal, but for those with an interest in community service, they are an option to carefully consider.

Some examples of obligatory scholarship/service programs are described below:

- **National Health Service Corps**

  If you are interested in primary care medicine, you have the option of participating in the National Health Service Corps (NHSC), a scholarship program that covers a medical student's tuition and expenses and offers a monthly stipend. In return, students are obligated to work in Health Manpower Shortage Areas, assigned by the NHSC. Again, the number of years a recipient is required to serve is directly proportional to the number of years he or she received support, usually about 4 to 7. These scholarships are very competitive. For more information, check out their website: http://nhsc.bhpr.hrsa.gov/.

- **Armed Forces Health Professions Scholarships**

    The Army, Navy, and Air Force operate scholarship programs for students training in professional health fields. Students who participate in these programs spend forty-five days on active military duty each academic year, usually during summer, or when the school's schedule permits. Upon completion of residency, scholarship recipients must serve a year as a medical officer for every year of support they receive. The minimum number of years you must serve is three. In exchange for their service, students receive full coverage of their tuition and fees, reimbursement for books and supplies and a monthly stipend. These scholarships are very competitive.

    Consider Dr. Nelson's experience: "I funded my medical school through the Health Professions Scholarship Program. I am now completing my pediatric residency while on active duty in the Air Force, will be spending next year as a Flight Surgeon (deploying with a fighter wing, doing operational medicine, flying in the jets), and then will start my pediatric neurology fellowship. I owe the Air Force four years of service after residency for my medical school training, and will incur an additional three years of commitment for my fellowship (since my fellowship is three years). Do not think that military scholarships will prevent you from doing the residency that you want, because the military trains physicians in all specialties. Furthermore, because you do your residency on active duty, you make about $15,000 per year more than your civilian colleagues. As a fellow, you may receive about $45,000 per year more than your civilian counterparts. Also, you gain many unique experiences that they will never have, such as going on medical missions to other countries, military transports of patients to other hospitals/states/countries, medical care in field environments, and many other unique benefits. During medical school you hold the rank of Second Lieutenant (Ensign in the Navy), and after graduation are commissioned to the rank of Captain (Lieutenant in the Navy). I highly encourage anyone who has an interest in serving his or her country to explore this option."

- **Army National Guard**

    Medical students can be commissioned as Second Lieutenants through the Medical Student Commissioning Program. While in medical school, these students train sixteen hours per month and two weeks annually. Upon graduation, the student is transferred to the post of Captain in the medical corps. In exchange, the Army National Guard covers roughly $6,000 to $28,000 of annual fees. For many medical students, Guard duty could make the difference between significant or insignificant debt by the end of medical school. In addition, the Guard is a great service option and one that is less time intensive than the others listed above.

EVALUATING YOUR FINANCIAL AID PACKAGE

After you have been accepted to med school, you will be offered a financial aid package to help cover your estimated need (as determined by the FAFSA) through a combination of loans, scholarships, grants, or employment. If you have other options, don't automatically accept everything in the aid package (or any of it, for that matter). Don't automatically accept the school, either, even if it is your first choice. Before you start packing, you need to think about how you will pay for your education. Is the offer sufficient to accept? How will you cover the difference? When you are finished with medical school, what will your debt be? What is the interest rate and repayment schedule?

If you have more than one offer, you should compare the two options carefully. If one school makes you a great offer but you have your heart set on another, use the difference between the two packages as bargaining leverage. Students in the enviable position of having multiple acceptances can save thousands to tens of thousands of dollars by negotiating better financial aid packages.

COMMON PITFALLS IN FINANCIAL AID

While today's financial aid programs make it possible for almost everyone to pay for higher education, there are some common pitfalls in the financial aid process, which can inhibit your ability to participate in loan programs, especially low interest and subsidized loans. Watch out for the following problems:

Missing Deadlines

Like all aspects of your application, the earlier you submit your financial aid materials, the better. Financial aid deadlines are strongly enforced. Keep careful records and be sure to send everything *on time.*

Poor Credit History

As long as you have good credit, you can borrow money to pay for your education. If your credit is bad when you start medical school, however, you may be ineligible for loans, even high-interest loans. If you have a bad credit rating, get started on credit repair now. In this case, you may need to seek professional assistance. There are a number of credit-rating repair services, but beware: some are merely scams. Get a referral to a reputable agency from a certified financial planner. Even if you don't have bad credit, you should check your credit rating before applying for financial aid. Sometimes, even a few late payments on your car or credit card will show up in your credit history.

Defaulting on Undergraduate Loans

If you have not met your undergraduate loan payments, you will have a hard time qualifying for medical school loans, especially federal loans. Before you apply for aid, try to clear up any problems with your undergraduate student loans. Again, you may want to seek professional assistance from a financial planner. If you have undergraduate loans and are still in school, talk to financial aid officers about deferment options.

Congratulations on taking your finances seriously. Cultivating good financial habits now will help you to quickly get to a place where family, home, vacations, emergencies, caring for your aging parents, and eventually, your own retirement, can all be taken in stride.

Video Assignments for Chapter 8:

City of Joy, Endurance, and *Running Brave*

CHAPTER 9
ROCK THE INTERVIEW

You have arrived at the **final stage** of the admissions process: the interview. You've done so much to get here that you may just want to coast through this last little section of rapids without putting in much effort. You won't get such half-hearted advice from your coaches, however. The interview, like every other peak you've scaled, is a crucial test that deserves its own careful preparation.

Think about it: no other profession except the clergy invests the time, money, and resources it takes too personally interview every potential admit. Medical schools know that **emotional and interpersonal intelligence** are the cornerstones of a great doctor's character. These fundamental skills can't be formally taught in academic programs; they are a product of your life experience, insight, and self-mastery.

Medical schools also know that the full cost of a medical education is much greater than the tuition you pay, so they want to make sure that they are making a worthwhile investment of their resources; they want to be sure each space goes to a deserving student. **Are you someone they could easily see becoming a likeable, trustable physician?** That question will be in the back of the mind of your evaluators on interview day.

After the MCAT, the interview causes the most anxiety for typical medical students. Fortunately, if you are lucky enough to get more than one interview (John and Steve both had over ten each) you'll discover that your fears rapidly subside with experience. The first one or two will be the most challenging. Fortunately, you can also dramatically decrease pre-interview jitters by doing some high-yield advance preparation. This chapter is an edited version of a preparation program that we have recommended and refined for Hyperlearning premedical students since 1991. If you give it serious attention, you'll be ready for anything.

HOW IMPORTANT IS THE INTERVIEW?

To many admissions committees, the interviewer's opinions matter even more than recommendations, partly because recommendations often come from unknown sources. Again, if you consider the expense and hassle involved in setting up a personal interview for every possible admit, you have an idea of how much medical schools value the process. The interview is a chance to get a real sense of the candidate as a person, and the school's opportunity to hear a medical professional's first-hand evaluation of an applicant.

For highly desirable applicants, the interview will not be a deal-breaker unless something dramatically bad happens. For top-tier candidates, the interview is primarily an opportunity for the medical school to confirm credentials and verify that the actual person roughly matches the impressive application. Even if they don't dazzle their interviewers, top applicants are still very likely to be accepted.

For students who have high potential but are not at the top of the stack, in other words, for the average applicant, the interview is an important opportunity to make a positive, distinctive impression on the admissions committee.

WHAT ARE MY CHANCES OF ACCEPTANCE GOING INTO THE INTERVIEW?

If you have been invited for an interview, you have officially joined the ranks of "desirable" applicants. It would be too costly and time-consuming for the medical schools to interview all possible candidates; therefore, it is only the most promising who are invited. That said, about 50 percent of interviewed candidates are not offered admission.

SCHEDULING THE INTERVIEW AND TRAVEL ARRANGEMENTS

The earlier you interview, the sooner the admissions committee can begin evaluating you for a position. Whenever possible, you should take the earliest interview date you are offered. As a rule, don't put off or delay interviews unnecessarily.

Nonetheless, you will probably want to control travel costs by scheduling interviews for schools that are in similar geographic regions within the timeframe of a single trip. Schools understand students' desire to minimize costs and will often accommodate changes. If you receive an interview request from one school and have applied to another school in the same area, you may consider calling the second school and asking politely if they are planning to interview you. Explain that you have **another interview at a school in the same area** and were wondering if you should also be planning to visit their campus. In that case, schools are often happy to let you know whether they would be able to interview you in the same timeframe.

Interviewees often have the option of **staying with a current medical student** the night before the interview. If you are comfortable with new people and short on cash, this option is always a good way to save some money and get to know more about the school. Be sure to ask them for their honest opinion of the **strengths and weaknesses** of the school. A friendly host may be able to offer a couple last-minute interview tips. If, however, you would feel stressed or unwilling to sleep on someone else's sofa, look for accommodations on or near campus.

INTERVIEW DAY

There are two main reasons you have been invited to campus. The primary reason is **positive**: they want to give you, a clearly desirable and impressive applicant, a good impression of the school, while assessing your unique personality and the kind of contribution you will make to the entering class. Secondarily, as critics, they have a **negative** reason: they will look for any obvious interpersonal drawbacks that were not evident on in the application.

Individuals who are particularly **arrogant, aloof, negative, emotionally fragile, politically incorrect, and otherwise less desirable applicants** are occasionally weeded out in this process. If you've ever been accused of having these or other less desirable traits, you will want to start working on minimizing them now, conducting mock interviews until you've improved the image you present to the world.

When you arrive at the admissions office, you will probably find a number of other applicants who are being interviewed that day. Here's what to expect:

ORIENTATION

Once everybody has arrived, an admissions officer will give a short introduction to the school. This may include a slide show or Q&A.

TOUR

After the orientation, applicants usually take a tour of the campus and facilities. If you have never visited that campus before, the tour is a great time to get a feeling for the school environment. You may also want to ask some questions of your tour guide, who will most likely be a student volunteer, eager to sell you on the school.

LUNCH

There is always a lunch break, during which time you may be assigned a student host, who can answer more questions about the school and give you a general idea of what to expect in your first years at the school.

INTERVIEWS

Each applicant has from one to three interview sessions, beginning either before or after lunch. Interviews can run anywhere from 15 minutes to an hour.

A word to the wise: you are actually "interviewing" the whole time you are on campus, so act accordingly. Even when you are bunking in a student's apartment, going on the tour, or having lunch, all those around you are evaluating you. Admissions committees often select students whom they like and respect to lead tours or host interviewees for the night. Though these students might not be directly involved in admissions decisions, the administration is always interested in their feedback about a candidate, especially if it is strongly positive or strongly negative. **Be polite and friendly to everyone you meet, and try to stay relaxed.** Tense people make other feel people uneasy. It helps to remember that **your relaxed and positive attitude makes their life easier, and takes the focus off you.** This is ideal as a default situation.

WHO CONDUCTS INTERVIEWS?

In most cases, one, two, or occasionally three people will interview you over the length of your time at the school. You will usually be interviewed one-on-one. Very few schools will conduct group interviews, in which a panel of med school faculty members interviews a group of students. Interviewers will be one or a combination of the following: a faculty member from the clinical sciences, a faculty member from the basic sciences, a current medical student, or an admissions staff professional.

OPEN- VERSUS CLOSED-FILE INTERVIEWS

The most influential factor on the content of your interview is whether it is an **open-file** or **closed-file** format.

OPEN-FILE INTERVIEW

In an open-file interview, the interviewer has access to your **entire admissions file**, including grades, coursework, recommendations, and the personal statement. In an open interview, the interviewer will probably ask you questions about your application, encouraging you to elaborate on an experience you've had or a research project in which you were involved.

You may also encounter a semi-open interview, in which your interviewer has read your personal statement but has not seen your grades, MCAT scores, or coursework. Schools often choose the semi-open format to give the interviewer an idea of the candidate but to prohibit them from judging the student based on his or her GPA and test scores.

Open or semi-open interviews generate the most personal questions. For some students, such questions are the most challenging.

CLOSED-FILE INTERVIEW

In a closed-file interview, your interviewer has **not seen your application folder**. Therefore, the interviewer does not know anything about your undergraduate studies, what grades or MCAT scores you received, or your personal experiences. For better or for worse, the interviewer cannot have any preconceived notions about you, and you will have the full responsibility for making a good impression.

A closed-file interview is likely to begin with general, open-ended questions about you and your background, such as "So, why do you want to be a doctor?" or "Tell me a little about yourself." Interviewers ask these questions to get a general sense of who you are and how you relate to others verbally.

For students who have difficulty talking generally, these open-ended questions can be more challenging than penetrating personal ones for which you may have more specific answers. You will need to prepare in advance so that you can explain yourself succinctly without rambling, or sounding like you are reciting a speech. Richard Nelson Bolles, in his award-winning job hunting book, *What Color is Your Parachute?* states that studies show employers like interviewees who 1) don't talk more than **50 percent** of the time, and 2) don't talk more than **two minutes** at a time. These are ideal guidelines for any interviewee. If you can keep your responses short, yet full of information, you give your interviewer a lot of space, both to ask additional questions and to make points as well.

GROUP INTERVIEWS

Although it is unlikely that you will have a group interview, if you do, remember to be polite and to acknowledge all the other applicants. Unlike individual interviews, where the objective is to express your unique personality in a positive way, in panel interviews, it is important not to stand out in a negative way. In a group interview, there may be time for no more than one question per interviewer per student. Don't hog the attention. Keep your answers succinct enough that you aren't taking time away from others. If you can, in your own answer refer to something others students said, and show courtesy by using their names when referring to them.

AREAS OF ASSESSMENT

The point of the interview is to gather reliable information about your personality, temperament, and fitness for the profession, as well as your interpersonal skills. Generally, interviewers will be evaluating you in the following ten most common categories:
1. Communication and interpersonal skills
2. Maturity
3. Strengths and weaknesses
4. Analytical skills
5. Open-mindedness
6. Ethics, compassion, and sensitivity
7. Motivation, commitment, and goals
8. Knowledge of the issues and of the field
9. Extracurricular activities
10. Leadership and cooperative activities

Of course, the majority of these qualities are rather subjective. But subjective or not, interviewers will seek to form an opinion about you on any or all of these areas. If you know that you are weak in any now, start discussing them with trusted friends and come up with strategies to improve them before your interview date. Do not be afraid to be open with those who care about you.

Simply acknowledging and talking about your possible weaknesses will do wonders toward making you a more balanced applicant.

HOW ARE THESE QUALITIES ASSESSED?

How does one judge abstract qualities like compassion, ethics, or open-mindedness? The following chart provides a few **sample questions** to give you an idea of how interviewer opinions are formed, and some tips for answering in a powerful fashion. You can think briefly about these in preparation for a more comprehensive list of **fifty** valuable questions we'll introduce a bit later in the chapter.

Quality	Sample Questions	Interview's Objective	Tips
Communication and Interpersonal Skills	Tell me about yourself.	To learn what vocabulary and sentence structure you use. To find out if you are easily understandable. To find out whether you answer the question.	Prepare for these types of questions ahead of time. Outline brief answers in your journal. Reveal some favorite bits about yourself. You don't want to sound rehearsed, but a little preparation will greatly help your presentation with open-ended questions.

Quality	Sample Questions	Interview's Objective	Tips
Maturity	What sacrifices have you made in getting to where you are today? How have you handled big disappointments in your life?	To see if you have a sense of the constraints, costs, and challenges of a medical career. To discover how you handle adversity.	This is one of your best chances to be authentic and honest. Showing a combination of vulnerability and strength, capability and humility, will go a long way toward demonstrating your maturity.

Quality	Sample Questions	Interview s Objective	Tips
Strengths and Weaknesses	Probing questions about your application (GPA and MCAT scores, extracurriculars). What would you say are your strong and weak points? What would your friends and family say? Any difference?	To find our what you will bring to the program. To find out whether you recognize your own shortcomings and how you can improve them.	Brainstorm areas in which you most need improvement. Whenever you discuss your weaknesses or shortcomings, follow up this admission with positive supercedents—factors that lessen them, actions and plans for overcoming them.

Quality	Sample Questions	Interview's Objective	Tips
Analytical Skills	You may be presented with a hypothetical problem, either specific (e.g., How might you deal with a patient who did not want to take your medical advice?) or general (e.g., How might we develop more effective prevention of disease in our society?).	To see if you can organize a problem and support your conclusions when challenged.	If your interviewer asks you to discuss a hypothetical situation, don't try to find the "right" answer. The interviewer is less interested in your opinion than in how you think through a problem. Don't be a know-it-all or say things you aren't sure about.

Quality	Sample Questions	Interview's Objective	Tips
Open-Mindedness	Can you name a medical controversy where you can see more than one possible solution? Why do different groups take the positions they take?	To see whether you can see both sides of an issue. To see how comfortable you are with ambiguities or moral dilemmas.	If your interviewer contradicts your position, don't get defensive. Instead, try to understand and carefully articulate your interviewer's point. Only then should you mildly take the counter-position, if you choose. Interviewers often contradict interviewees to gauge their reaction.

Quality	Sample Questions	Interview's Objective	Tips
Ethics Compassion Sensitivity	What do you think might be more important for a physician: "doing no harm" or "being of benefit?" Why? Where do you think our nation's health care system may be currently falling short in serving society?	To discover your major ethical precepts. To see whether you are sensitive to the feelings and positions of other people.	Don't sugar coat! It's easy to come across as false when delineating your concern for others. Speak honestly and be modest. As above, don't become defensive if your interviewer contradicts or presses you on an issue.

Quality	Sample Questions	Interview's Objective	Tips
Motivation, Commitment, and Goals	Why do you want to become a doctor? What will you do if you are not accepted to medical school? To which other schools did you apply?	To find out whether you have the drive and desire to make it through medical school and residency, even in the face of adversity. To find out whether your commitment to medicine is long term.	Be honest about the schools to which you have applied. Don't say you have only applied to top schools unless you are a top-tier applicant. If asked about your back-up plans, be sure to have one. How will you improve your overall admissions candidacy? Don't just say that you will reapply without presenting a strategy.

Quality	Sample Questions	Interview's Objective	Tips
Knowledge of Issues in the Field	What topics in medicine interest you? What is one of the issues or controversies you have heard about in that area?	To get a sense of how deep your medical knowledge base and interest is.	Try to stay away from relaying opinions (after all, you are only starting out in this profession) and relate carefully what you do know. Ignorance is always forgivable; prevarication is not.

Quality	Sample Questions	Interview's Objective	Tips
Extracurricular Activities	What have you done outside of your studies? What are your personal interests and talents?	To get a sense of why you are attracted to these activities. The way you spend your free time says something about you.	If you are asked about your extracurricular activities, try to discuss those in which you have had a long-term, in-depth involvement. Explain why you enjoyed them and have followed through with the activity, rather than just recounting what you've done.

Quality	Sample Questions	Interview's Objective	Tips
Leadership and Cooperation	What kind of positive experiences have you had working as part of a team? Have you played in any team sports?	If you seem standoffish or a bit of a loner, the interviewer may be particularly interested in assessing your cooperation and teamwork abilities.	Speak positively of your experience working as a part of a team with shared responsibility. Mention sports teams, volunteer activities, organizations, and study groups. Be honest, yet positive, about learning experiences you built in this area.

FIELDING TOUGH QUESTIONS

Most interviewers have no intention of demoralizing or intimidating hopeful interview candidates with unnecessarily tricky questions. Usually, an interviewer's objective is simply to learn more about the candidate's background and critical-thinking and communication skills. If you happen upon one of those rare interviewers who seems to be particularly needling, don't panic. First, realize that you are simply being tested

General Interviewing Tips
- *Think before you speak.*
- *Don't talk too quickly.*
- *Don't talk more than two minutes at a time.*
- *Make and maintain eye contact.*
- *Make human contact. Enjoy something about your interviewer's background, interest, personality, or perspective.*
- *Don't try to talk about something you don't know anything about.*
- *You are always better off being honest about your limitations.*
- *SMILE!*

to see if you'll fall for the bait. If you have figured out their game, you can use that knowledge to become **even calmer and more collected.** Don't rush. Take a deep breath and think for a moment longer, if you need to, before answering their questions. Don't beat yourself up if you can't easily think of the perfect, spot-on answer. If stumped, share some of your thinking out loud, and let the interviewer know the kind of research you'd want to do to find the answer.

When you are being challenged, ask yourself if you are communicating well. Looking for mistakes in your own communication first can often defuse a tense situation. Stephen Covey, in *The Seven Habits of Highly Effective People*, sums up this attitude in his fifth habit: **"seek first to understand, then to be understood."** See if you can **restate** what the interviewer has said, even if you disagree with his or her viewpoint. Let him know that you hear what was said and are trying to understand the problem, even if you don't yet see the solution. Covey sums up this habit as, **"diagnose before you prescribe."** Good communication advice for all would-be physicians!

Some interview questions are technically "illegal," meaning they have been deemed inappropriate either by medical schools or by law and so should not be asked by an interviewer. Illegal questions include those that delve into a candidate's personal life in a way that is irrelevant to overall candidacy. For example, an interviewer should not ask a female candidate whether she plans to have children and how she thinks that will affect her success as a doctor.

If you are asked a rare "none-of-your-business" type of question, don't become upset. It's **their** *faux pas*, not yours. In most cases, your interviewer just wants to know if you have considered difficult life issues. Ideally, you should try to answer any question you get in a polite, tactful way; but don't let the power dynamic scare you into sacrificing your rights as a candidate. Tell the interviewer if a question makes you uncomfortable. Give him the benefit of the doubt as to his intentions. If you feel that your interviewer was inappropriate and did not treat you decently, you may want to make a note of it on your evaluation form after the interview.

BACK 'ATCHA

As the end of the interview nears, the distinguished medical school faculty member often peers over her spectacles and asks, *so now that I have heard about you, do you have any questions for me?* Relieved and ready for the interview to be over, the stressed premed shakes his head "no" and makes a fast break for the parking lot. The smart premed, however, nods his head yes and asks a few **interesting questions**.

Asking a thoughtful, insightful question will differentiate you from other candidates. Often a good question can spark a short **conversation** between you and your interviewer, which can be the most natural and memorable part of the entire interview for both parties.

What Questions Should I Ask?

The best questions are those that can be answered with expertise by your interviewer. If you are perceptive, you will be able to come up with a personalized question or two during the interview. In most cases, you'll find out who your interviewers are by name at least several hours in advance (typically, in the packet you pick up on the morning of your interview). You can begin thinking then about questions appropriate to their backgrounds. There are also a number of classic questions related to:

The Interviewer's Experience

- What do you like most and least about your work?

- Where did you go to medical school? How is med school different today?

- Where did you do your residency? How do residencies here compare?

- What do you think are the most important aspects of a medical education?

- What did medical school and residency best and least prepare you for with regard to your practice?

- Who are the clinical mentors and medical role models in your background? At this university?

The Medical School Program

- How would you rate the strengths and weaknesses of the faculty here?

- Do students here receive any formal training with medical expert systems, such as diagnostic systems, Medline, or any other computer training or educational software?

- What do you think will be the future role of computers in medicine?

- How many students get their first-choice residency matches?

- If you were dean, what single thing would you most want to improve in the medical school?

Research or Clinical Opportunities

- What kind of special research or clinical opportunities exist here in your discipline?

- Have you had medical students do independent study or research projects with you?

- Does the residency in your specialty accept many students from this medical school?

- Do you have exchange or off-site programs with other teaching hospitals? What are your favorite hospitals and why?

PREPARING FOR THE INTERVIEW

Even if you are naturally charming and charismatic, resist the temptation to wing it in the interview. Though you want to be candid and extemporaneous while answering questions, you can benefit greatly by preparing ahead for all the types of questions that an interviewer might pose.

FIFTY SAMPLE QUESTIONS

Though each interviewer will word his questions differently, here are fifty classic questions, arranged in nine categories. We compiled them from several years of post-interview reports by premedical candidates, made available publicly within the University of California system.

Skim the questions, **highlighting the ones that scare or challenge you most**. Be sure to **outline brief responses** to those in the margins in coming weeks. Put together a very short, one- or two-sentence outline at first. Later, if you can make the time, consider writing a one- or two-paragraph longhand response in your trusty journal for the most challenging ones. Do this as late as a night or two before your interview, if you have no earlier time available. Keep your responses short enough to deliver quickly, never more than a **minute or two**. Practice delivering them to a friend a few days or even longer before the interview, or out loud to yourself, at least. But remember: *don't* stay up late doing this the night before your interview. Relax instead!

The key is to *think through* your answers to the more difficult questions here before you walk in the door. You will be miles ahead if you have already given any serious thought to them beforehand.

Group One: *Education-Related Questions*
1. Why did you choose your undergraduate major?
2. How have you tried to achieve breadth in your undergraduate curriculum?
3. How has your undergraduate research experience, if any, better prepared you for a medical career?
4. How have the jobs, volunteer opportunities, or extracurricular experiences that you have had better prepared you for the responsibilities of being a physician?
5. How do you envision using your medical education?

Group Two: *Candidate-Related Questions*
6. What are your greatest strengths and weaknesses?
7. What travels have you taken and what exposure to other cultures have you had?

8. Thinking of examples from your recent past, how would you assess your empathy and compassion?

9. As a premed, what skills have you learned to help manage your time and relieve stress?

10. If you could be granted three wishes for making the world/society/your community a better place, what would they be and why (or, If you were given a million dollars to achieve three goals, what would you work on and why)?

11. What do you do for fun?

Group Three: *Medicine-Related Questions*

12. What excites you about medicine in general?

13. What do you know about the current trends in our nation's health care system?

14. What do you believe to be some of the most pressing health issues today? Why?

15. What do you feel are the negative or restrictive aspects of medicine from a professional standpoint?

16. If you had to choose between clinical and academic medicine as a profession, which would you pick? What do you feel you might lose by being forced to choose?

Group Four: *Society-Related Questions*

17. What do you feel are the social responsibilities of a physician?

18. What do you consider an important/the most important social problem facing the United States today and why?

19. How do you think national health insurance might affect physicians, patients, and society?

20. In what manner and to what degree do you stay in touch with current events?

21. What books, films, or other media come to mind as having been particularly important to your sciences/non-sciences education?
22. Can you think of any examples in our society when health care is a right? When is it a privilege? When is it not clear?

Group Five: *Ethics-Related Questions*

23. Are you aware of any current controversies in the area of medical ethics? List and discuss some of these.
24. Have you personally encountered any moral dilemmas to date? Of what nature?
25. How do you feel about euthanasia or medically assisted suicide?
26. What different feelings and issues might you experience with a terminally ill patient, as opposed to other patients?
27. How would you feel about treating a patient who has tested positive for HIV?
28. What are some of the ethical issues that our society considers in regard to teenage pregnancy?
29. Assume there are limited resources available and you must make decisions in a major emergency with a wide assortment of patients from all ages, backgrounds, and degree of injury. Assume also that there is no "right answer" to this question, only considered and unconsidered responses. Who would you direct to receive the treatment first and why?

Group Six: *More Candidate-Related Questions*

30. What is "success" in your opinion? After twenty years as a physician, what kind of "success" would you hope to have achieved? Please explain.
31. What qualities do you look for in a physician? Can you provide an example of a physician who embodies any of these ideals? How do they do this?

32. What kind of experiences have you had working with sick people? Have these experiences taught you anything that you didn't know beforehand?

33. Do you have any family members or role models who are physicians?

34. What family members, friends, or other individuals have been influential in your decision to pursue a medical career?

35. If you could invite four people from the past to dinner, who would they be, and why would you invite them? What would you talk about?

36. Do you have any "blemishes" in your academic record? If so, what are they and why did they occur?

Group Seven: *Underrepresented Group-Related Questions*

37. If you are a minority candidate, how do you feel your background uniquely prepares you to be, and will influence your role as, a physician?

38. If you are a woman, how has your gender impacted your decision to pursue a medical career?

39. If you are not a minority, how might you best meet the needs of a multiethnic, multicultural patient population?

40. If you are economically disadvantaged or have limited financial means, how has this adversity shaped you?

41. To what extent do you feel that you owe a debt to your fellow man? To what extent do you owe a debt to those less fortunate than yourself? Please explain.

Group Eight: *Medical School-Related Questions*

42. What special qualities do you feel you possess that set you apart from other medical school candidates? What makes you unique or different as a medical school candidate?

43. What kind of medical schools are you applying to, and why?
44. Pick any specific medical school to which you are applying, and tell the interviewer about it. What makes this school particularly desirable to you?
45. What general and specific skills would you hope an ideal medical school experience would give you? How might your ideal school achieve that result?

Group Nine: *Motivation-Related Questions*

46. Discuss your decision to pursue medicine. When did you decide to become an MD, and why?
47. Why did you decide to choose medicine and not some other field where you can help others, such as nursing, physical therapy, pharmacology, psychology, education, or social work?
48. How have you tested your motivation to become an MD? Please explain.
49. What will you do if you are not accepted to medical school this year? Have you an alternative career plan?
50. Is there anything else we have not covered that you feel the interviewer should know about you or your interest in becoming a physician?

MAKING A PERSONAL OUTLINE

"Tell me your life story in a hundred words or fewer." (That's roughly 30 seconds of talking time, the length of this paragraph). It seems like an unrealistic request, doesn't it? However, an interviewer—especially one who hasn't seen your admissions file—is likely to want just that: a **concise, efficient summary of who you are**. It can be hard to hit on all the best points of your personality in an honest and humble way. Many candidates walk away from their interviews saying, *I wish I'd mentioned....* The best way to avoid that feeling is to write a short personal outline.

Your personal outline should include all the important elements of your background, including your **influences, mentors, personality traits, strengths, weaknesses, goals, and education.** You don't need to make the outline long or self-aggrandizing. In fact, you should keep it short enough that you can show it to a parent or loved one to see if you have forgotten something. List your weaknesses near the end of the outline. Follow them up with **positive progress you've made in improving on them**, including your ongoing plans to ameliorate those weaknesses. The interview is not a time to hide weaknesses, but rather to acknowledge them honestly and explain your path of personal and educational development. You are a work in progress!

> **TIP!** When doing formal mock interviews, wear your interview outfit so that you feel comfortable in it. If you find that you just can't get comfortable, you will have a chance to make changes if you are unhappy with it.

Right before you go to the interview, look over your personal outline in a relaxed and unhurried manner. Try to remember which points you want to bring out about yourself. When you are asked a tough question, take a deep breath and run through the outline in your mind. What is the *most* important thing you want to say? Don't wander into it. Lead with that statement.

PRACTICE

You will get a great idea of your interviewing strengths and weaknesses by running through sample questions with another person. If you have a few weeks to prepare in advance, recruit a friend or family member who likes to play devil's advocate to gleefully act as your scrutinizing interviewer. This is the time for criticism. You have nothing to lose and everything to gain from constructive, even negative feedback, so ask for it. Ask your mock interviewer for critiques of your enunciation, vocabulary, body language, and anything else that comes to mind.

> **TIP!** Borrow a **video camera** and have a friend tape you doing a mock interview. If you have never seen yourself on tape before, this is an excellent way to evaluate yourself. Do you smile appropriately? Make good eye contact, but not stare, blink madly, or wink? Do you fidget too much or sit stone-faced and immobile? Do you have any nervous tics? Anxious posture or laugh? Play the video on fast-forward to notice any repeated gestures. Are you happy with those? Do you want to lose some and add others? Repeat the exercise until you are more conscious of your body language and can express **confidence, warmth**, and **poise**. As professional actors know, **enhanced interpersonal awareness** will help in all your interactions on your future path.

DRESS

Just as a picture says a thousand words, how you choose to dress for the interview says a lot about who you are, whether you like it or not. Your posture, poise, and yes, your clothes will be the first thing to make an impression on your interviewer.

> **TIP!** Guys, if you aren't used to wearing a suit, buy a shirt with a **slightly oversized collar** (one or even two inches more around the neck than the typical salesperson recommends) so your tie won't feel like it's choking you while you talk. Generally speaking, you should choose clothes you feel as comfortable in as possible.

Nonetheless, you don't really want your clothes to be make a statement. As a rule of thumb, dress professionally, erring on the conservative side. You can choose something fashionable, but don't be too trendy or flashy.

You may wish to *slightly* tailor your outfit to complement your personality. For instance, if you are generally shy or conservative, you may want to counterbalance that by choosing a suit that is slightly more modern and fashionable.

Men should generally choose tasteful blue, black, or gray suits and an attractive tie. Don't wear sneakers or baseball caps. Avoid flashy ties and generally minimize jewelry, if you wear any.

Women should choose a formal outfit, like a pantsuit, dress, or matching coordinates. Avoid short hem lengths and lots of makeup.

Think of this as a first date with your medical school. Be clean, well groomed, and free of bad breath and body odor. If you take away the potential negatives, your most positive attributes will leave a lasting impression.

TIPS FOR LATE-SEASON INTERVIEWS

If you are interviewing late in the season, during the last month of a school's interview cycle, which ends as early as January and as late as April, depending on the school and the number of applicants they have received that year, most of the spots for the incoming class will have already been filled. Admissions officials are reluctant to admit that late interviewees have lowered chances of acceptance, but at many schools, the fact remains that most interviewees are only vying for the alternate list at that time.

If you are a late interviewer, don't despair—take the earliest interview time that is offered to you, even if it inconveniences your schedule. In fact, if you are late in the interview cycle and you think the admissions committee may be flexible, you might want to ask if you can schedule the interview a week or two earlier than the earliest date offered to you, particularly if you have some reason to be out in that area of the country at that time. A friendly admissions official may be able to slip you in to an earlier appointment.

Whatever date they give you, go do your best, and wait patiently for May, when a last burst of acceptance letters might find a way to your door. **When you've done your best, with balance, you can feel content with yourself, no matter what happens.** It doesn't matter which gates open or close in any particular year, for reasons that are beyond your control. What *matters* is that you have found, and are walking, your path of heart.

SUCCESSFULLY ADMITTED? PREPARING AHEAD AND THE DEFERMENT OPTION

Congratulations! Let's assume you have made the cut, that you recently received a thrilling acceptance letter in the mail, which you've taped to your wall, and will soon be off to medical school. (Those who haven't might skip ahead to Chapter Ten). Welcome to the ranks of Hippocrates and Vesalius, of

Schweitzer and Salk! The most exciting and demanding phase of your educational journey still lies ahead of you.

You're about to enter a new phase of your life, so the first priority, again, is to know your options. You are beginning at the outermost loop of another inward spiral. Start acquiring catalogs, maps, and directories, and reading up on the people and programs at your new educational institution. Try to get an idea of the curriculum ahead so you can study during your senior summer for those first-year medical school subjects where you will be at a disadvantage. If possible, get course syllabi and actual handouts for the most difficult courses, in advance, from a second-year medical student, and start looking at them now.

Once you are there, everything about your medical school study will be prioritized around *one* theme: what is the highest-yield use of my time? See if you can start chanting that mantra *now*, as it will be your friend for many years to come. Study ahead now if you like, but don't get bogged down in details. Get the **big picture overview;** learn first the critical concepts. The details will come later, if you can afford the time, when you are learning to sip water from the medical fire hose. Keep your highest-yield priorities in order and enjoy the process.

More specific preparation suggestions are beyond the scope of this book, but a general guide to medical school, such as our *Medical School Companion* (Princeton Review/Random House), might be a good place to start.

One final bit of advice: medical schools typically give all their admitted students the **option to defer matriculation** for one year. If this request is made early enough after your acceptance (often prior to June 1st), it is automatic, meaning no petition is needed and no reason is required. After the automatic date, typically a simple form is required, and deferment is often granted for any good reason, such as the ability to spend time caring for a family member.

Some students see deferment as a last chance to take an extended break before starting into the long-term, high-pressure environment of medical training. But perhaps its greatest advantage is as a backup strategy if you are accepted to a medical school that you think is particularly difficult, and you have no other "easier" schools you can attend. Some top-tier medical schools can be very grueling environments, places where less-strong students will have to seriously struggle to survive. Choosing a less-demanding medical school can make it much easier to be near the top of your class, which maximizes your chances at a top residency. But if you are set on attending a medical school with the most prestige, or if you think you may have trouble adjusting to any medical school given your academic background, consider this option carefully during your transition.

Taking a year off to prepare ahead, audit classes, and work on your weakest areas, if you can afford it, can be of great benefit if you are a slow learner or are simply looking for some balance before the storm. Some students who have done this have followed a program of working on their basic science skills in the morning, ideally through the medical school's tutorial center, and learning some basic clinical skills in the afternoon, ideally with a preceptor affiliated with the medical school. Don't be pressured to automatically follow the standard route, however, if it seems less effective for your particular path of heart.

We wish you the best as you live the life of a passionate future physician!

Video Assignments for Chapter 9:

Cancer Warrior, *Dead Poet's Society*, and *Chariots of Fire*

CHAPTER 10
LONG-TERM AND NONTRADITIONAL PATHS

REAPPLICATION STRATEGIES

If you are reading this chapter, the following scenario could very well apply to you. You did your best, but you didn't get into medical school the first time around. So what's next? Actually, anything you want. Students who apply to medical school are a very talented social subgroup with reasonably strong verbal skills, analytical minds, drive and dedication, and an ability to master complex science concepts. **You're one of the most talented young (or reasonably young) persons in the country at the present time.** The question to ask yourself now is: What do you want to do next?

Search your mind again and ask yourself if medicine is what you really want to do. Go back to your journals and see what it was that most excited you about the prospect. Are you sure that medicine remains your dream? What else might you do if you don't become a doctor? If the practice of medicine remains your goal, ask yourself what you can do now, during a reapplication cycle, to get closer to what excites you most about medicine. How can you gain experience now? How can you keep walking your path, taking small but satisfying steps each day?

Let's assume you're going to reapply. Repeat applicants are accepted at roughly the same rate as first time-applicants. So you have a great shot at getting in with the next application, if you **do anything to improve your profile**. In fact, the re-applicant pool is always smaller than the first-year applicant pool, and you have an additional year (or more) to travel further down your path of heart before you make another attempt at gaining admission.

You may think you can't afford to lose the time, but for 99 percent of applicants the reality is that the majority of one's life is still ahead. Taking another year to discover if medicine is your calling is time well spent. Even if you ultimately don't go to medical school after reapplication, by then you'll have a better understanding of the nature and profession of healing than the vast majority of people, and you will have that understanding for the rest of your life. That is valuable in itself.

It is natural to feel defeated, angry, or humiliated if you weren't accepted to medical school on your first try. You put a lot of work into your preparation and the news of rejection can be a big downer. But try to put the whole experience into perspective. Every year, about 35,000 highly accomplished, intelligent, talented students apply to medical school, and roughly half to one-third of these applicants do not gain entry, simply due to space limitations. Those who don't make it in on the first try still have a wide range of options for acquiring further academic or medical experience and improving their chances of ultimately becoming a physician.

Consider, for example, what a unique and desirable applicant you would be if prior to your first, second, or even third application, you were to become a nurse, physical therapist, medical technician, or other allied health professional. If you like biomedical research, or public health policy and administration, perhaps you should consider pursuing an advanced degree, like a master's of public health, and in the process writing a thesis valuable to medicine. Or what about serving for two years in a free clinic, perhaps learning a second language in the process, or managing a patient education or support program? The point is that there are many paths to physician-hood. If you have an inkling of what kind of physician you want to be, that makes your choices now even easier. Don't let early rejection steer you away from your path of heart.

Dr. Nelson advises, "I think the most important thought to keep in mind after a first application is this: **Why** do you want to be a doctor? Whatever your reason, you can usefully pursue these same goals while reapplying to medical school, and even if you never get into medical school. Focus on your **life goals** (such as to help others), not just the short term issues (to get into medical school) to maintain your sense of perspective, balance, and tranquility."

STEP ONE: ASSESS YOURSELF

The key to success the second time around is to **improve yourself as a candidate** during your reapplication year. If you can identify and improve upon your weaknesses, your chances of acceptance will go up significantly. Another thing is also certain: if you don't improve upon anything (including realistic school selection), then you will not improve your chances by simply reapplying.

The first thing you need to do is take a good look at yourself and your application. You will need to try to improve on any deficiencies in your first application. Review your strategy, tools, map, and your climb. Which mountains did you scale easily, and on which did you never quite reach the summit? How could you make yourself unique or more well rounded? Most commonly, students need to improve their application most in one of the following four areas:

- GPA

- MCAT scores

- Communication/interpersonal skills

- Medical school selection

Where can you get trustworthy third-party feedback?

Obviously, *you* think you are a qualified applicant. Though you may be reluctant to spend time discussing your rejected application, don't let pride get in the way of your dreams. For a while, you might steer clear of the well-meaning but often misguided advice you will receive from friends or family members who are probably a bit biased when it comes to your worthiness for medical school. Fortunately, many qualified individuals and groups can give you solid advice about your reapplication.

Premed Advisor

Your premedical advisor can review your application and evaluate your strengths and weaknesses, making recommendations for areas of improvement. Since advisors have access to statistics on each premedical class, they may have particularly good insight into where you were deficient. If you haven't bonded with the premed advisors at your school, consider going to drop-in hours for those advisors at one of the other good universities in your area. Bring your application, of course.

Schools that Rejected You

Many schools are willing to give you some feedback as to why your application was ultimately rejected, especially those at which you interviewed but were not accepted. Call the admissions office and politely ask if you can speak to an official who reviewed your application "to get advice on reapplication." Be friendly and appreciative. No matter what they say about your application, do not be defensive. If you feel confused on a point or think that something that they are saying is untrue, you won't be able to change anything for this admissions cycle. Clarify uncertainties by asking polite questions. This *may* be an opportunity to learn, and to impress on someone that you will be back, knocking on the door in a year or two (or three); it is not an opportunity for you to talk your way into the program.

Medical School Admissions Statistics Binders

Return to the **MSAS binders**. Did you pick the right schools after all? What was the median GPA at the schools to which you applied? MCAT scores? Did you apply to enough schools? Did you apply early enough? Did you pick only the most popular likely/safety schools? In some years, there are certain popular schools that are not "safe" at all, but actually way over-applied to.

Other Premeds

Which seniors from your university were accepted into medical school? Where are they going? Did you apply to the same medical schools? What were the qualifications of accepted applicants? Compare your credentials to the successful applicants and try to evaluate where your application was deficient.

Independent Consultants

If you feel you need more structured advice, you may want to look for an independent admissions consultant in your area. Consultants often are people who have worked in admissions in the past and can give you an insider's view of the selection process. These services can be pricey, and the people providing them aren't necessarily qualified. Ask for references before you make an appointment.

Step Two: Commit to a Plan for Self Improvement

After you have evaluated your application and have some idea of its deficiencies, you will need to devise a plan of action. Following are some of the many ways you could improve your profile for the following year:

GPA Boost: Take More Courses

If your undergraduate GPA needs improvement, you may want to enroll in some additional college coursework. The options include **formal post-baccalaureate programs**, **graduate schools**, and **informal courses** at a local college. (For more information on academic study after your undergraduate degree, see **Post-Baccalaureate Programs**, below).

It is worth noting that while AMCAS and most medical schools will factor all college-level coursework in with your original undergraduate GPA to create a new GPA, some top-tier schools will not accept superior post-baccalaureate coursework as compensation for weak undergraduate grades. If you need your reapplication post-grad GPA to be calculated along with your original application GPA to get yourself up to acceptable numbers (3.45 or so), then you should inquire at individual schools to be sure that doing more coursework won't be a waste of time (at least in terms of GPA). You might just skip the top-tier schools when you reapply. Fortunately, most second- and third-tier medical schools will treat all undergraduate GPA equally.

If English is your second language, perhaps your oral and written verbal skills are significantly weaker than the average applicant's. If so, this weakness was probably an important factor acting against your admission. If you did not prioritize humanities coursework during your undergraduate education, it is not too late to do so. A year or two of *intensive* work in such courses now, in combination with medical extracurriculars, could significantly improve your non-science GPA, application, interview, and your overall profile. Enroll in some writing-based courses at a local state or community college.

If you want to apecialize in . . .	Consider pursuing a graduate degree in . . .
Othopedics	Anatomy Biomechanics
Pathology	Histology
General Practice Gerontology	Pahrmacology Physiology Immunology Pathophysiology
Oncology	Histology Immunology
Infectious Disease	Microbiology Genetics
Pediatrics	Child Psychology
Psychiatry	Abnormal Psychology Clinical Psychology
All Specialties	Nutrition Pharmacology Immunology Public Health Medical Informatics

Graduate degrees can add real depth and strength to an application. At most medical schools, excellent performance in medically related graduate work can counterbalance a lower-than-average undergraduate GPA. (Again, many of the first-tier schools will not allow graduate work to replace or make up for poor undergraduate performance, while second- and third-tier schools will be much more forgiving. Do your homework first before sending in reapplications.) In many cases, a future in general or specialty practice can be *greatly* enhanced by an advanced degree. These degrees could certainly improve your chances of being admitted to medical school; however, they also may be an **end in themselves** for students who are interested in research or administration in a particular field, or those who have a special interest in a topic that is not well-covered in traditional medical school. Few courses in nutrition, alternative medicine and preventive medicine are offered at most U.S. medical schools. These are just three examples of "areas of opportunity" to improve the allopathic tradition of medicine.

Apply Earlier

If you didn't get in this time, perhaps you did not submit all your materials early enough in the application process. The sweet spot, as premeds call it, is being "in the Js." If your primary application doesn't get out the door in **June or July**, statistics start working against you. The farther you are away from the Js, the lower your chances of acceptance.

Since you have already been through the application process once, you should have no problem completing all the steps in a timely manner on your next application, right? If you are a terrible procrastinator, **tell family and friends about your goal** to apply in the Js. If you are one who is habitually late to events (and medical school is the event of your life), it may take superhuman effort to get your application in early, but don't sell yourself short!

Pursue Further Clinical Experience

If your extracurricular or volunteer activities did not include any **primary care work**, your re-application year (or years) is a great time to add some of this highly beneficial experience to your resume. Maybe you were so busy with varsity soccer and an after-school tutoring program in college that you didn't have time to do work in a hospital or clinic. Though other types of extracurricular activities will also impress medical schools, they are always interested in students who have real-world experience in health care and an informed view of the field.

Doing more primary care work will almost always improve your chances for admission, and will also give you more opportunity to find the type of medical practice that fits your path of heart. If you have graduated from school and are looking for a job, you may want to consider looking for a primary care related position, as opposed to working in a bio lab. If you take a lab job, be sure to spend at least a few hours a week working in a primary care extracurricular activity, especially if your resume lacks primary care experience.

Reconsider School Choice

This isn't so much a self-improvement process as it is a remaking of your application strategy. With at least some experience in the entire medical school application process (provided you interviewed with at least one school), you can look at your plan for your first cycle and see where it was too optimistic, or worse, totally unrealistic. With the data in front of you, ask yourself some questions. Do you meet the average GPA and MCAT requirements at the majority of schools to which you applied? Did you include enough lesser-known safety schools in your application? Did you apply to schools whose mission or educational focus was similar to your background? Did you make the mistake of applying to those out-of-state schools that rarely accept candidates from your state? Did you get any interviews? Were there some schools whose secondary applications seemed particularly ill-suited to your experience?

Now that you have completed the application process once, you have a better understanding of what qualifications and achievements medical schools are looking for. Visit your premed advisor and look again at the MSAS binders at your school. Look at the MSAS binders at nearby colleges also, if you need more data.

Improve Your MCAT Scores

Many schools will not even consider students who did not get a certain score on the MCAT. Weigh yourself against the standards laid out in Chapter Six. Did you measure up? Review the preparation strategies we suggest. Did you put enough time into your MCAT prep, or did you try to wing it? Were you getting consistently high scores on your practice tests and then simply choked when you took the exam? With rededicated effort, you will be able to raise your scores to where they belong. Eat, sleep, and breathe the MCAT—until the next test date, if necessary. Buy prep books. Practice stress management and test-taking techniques. Read our attached study "bible," the **Basic Study System**, included in Appendix One. If you have extra time and money, enroll in the best MCAT prep course in this corner of the universe (that would be the Hyperlearning/ Princeton Review MCAT prep course, of course.)

Improve Your Interpersonal Skills

Human interaction is part of a physician's daily job description. Even stellar MCAT scores and an above-average GPA will not compensate for a lack of **communication skills** or the ability to be **warm and authentic** in an interpersonal setting. If you interviewed at some schools but were not accepted, the most likely reason that you were eliminated is substandard communication skills.

Some people are naturally shy. Shy people can still be good doctors. However, they still need to have strong communication and conversational skills so that they can effectively provide information to educate and advise their patients. If you need to improve your speaking ability, conversational skills, or overall emotional intelligence, the best way to do so is to get a job, paid or volunteer, in which you will be required to interact with strangers. There are also conversational classes and a number of books about improving your emotional or interpersonal intelligence. The very best way to learn is to engage in natural, candid conversation with people who are not close friends or members of your immediate family.

At a Loss?

Every year, so many qualified students apply to medical school that some significant fraction is bound not to be accepted initially, even if they did everything "right." If you can't find any deficiencies on your application and your premed advisor agrees that it was just a case of bad luck, take that as great news. You have another opportunity to become an **even stronger candidate** in the interim, and if you apply again in the next year or two, you'll look even more dedicated and experienced.

If your GPA and MCAT scores are below the national average, you might want to consider a formal or informal post-baccalaureate program of study, as discussed in the next section. But if both your scores and grades were already above the national average, it would likely be a waste of your time to either take more undergraduate classes, or to take the MCAT again. Work instead on one of the other premedical peaks. Devote time to a new volunteer job, an advanced degree in a medically related field, full-time work at hospital, teaching, a service or creative project, building verbal skills, or to any other thing that will both enhance your overall admissions candidacy and passion for your chosen profession.

POST-BACCALAUREATE PROGRAMS

Post-baccalaureate programs are pathways designed for **career-changer students** who have completed their undergraduate degree, either recently or a few years back, but have not yet taken all the prerequisites necessary to apply to medical school or other graduate programs. There are also programs intended to improve students' **undergraduate science GPA**. Many post-baccalaureate programs have been designed specifically to improve the **acceptance rate of minority and disadvantaged students** into medical school. Any of the above may accept students who have previously applied to medical school but not been accepted. The AAMC maintains one the best of several online searches for these programs at http://services.aamc.org/postbac/. They list programs serving four different student types: career-changers, academic record-enhancers, underrepresented minority students, and economically or educationally disadvantaged students. Be sure to ask admissions officers the program's **success rate** in gaining medical school admittance for the students who successfully complete it each year. This percentage is the best indication of the effectiveness of the program.

Formal Post-Baccalaureate Programs

Formal post-baccalaureate programs are ideal for those students who can quit working and prepare for medical school **full time**. One advantage of this type of program is that you will apply, or reapply, with the reputation of your post-baccalaureate institution. As a student, you will have access to the same resources and advantages that you would have had as a traditional college premed at that school. Perhaps the most important advantage is motivation. You will be in classes filled with other focused students like yourself, preparing for a medical education. For students who did not perform up to general admissions standards during their undergraduate career, obtaining excellent grades in a high-ranked post-baccalaureate program is the single best way to get accepted to medical school.

The major downside of formal post-baccalaureate programs is their **cost**—most are significantly more expensive than simply taking similar coursework at a local junior college or extension program. If you have just spent a lot of money on four years of undergraduate tuition, you may be hesitant to take on even more debt. In addition, many programs require that you stop working almost entirely and devote full time effort to the premedical curriculum. Thus, for slower or more financially strapped students, a disadvantage of these programs is their intensity.

Informal Options for Prerequisite/Additional Post-Baccalaureate Coursework

After graduating from college, you may need to work full time to make ends meet. That makes it almost impossible to enroll in a full-time post-baccalaureate program. But if you are self-motivated and don't mind taking a little extra time to finish your premedical prerequisites or to take additional undergraduate work to improve your GPA, there are other options available. You can save a lot of money by taking courses through a university extension program or a local community college.

School status is an important factor in this situation, so take your science and non-science coursework at the best local college you can find. Even the most selective colleges (Harvard, University of California, Berkeley, etc.) usually allow easy access to their science courses through their extension programs, on a course-by-course basis, subject to enrollment availability. Premedical advising offices and career services centers are often available to extension students for an additional fee. With a little planning, you can gain access to most of the same services and create a program of study that is well balanced with your other responsibilities. One to two years of such coursework, combined with a good set of extracurricular activities, can greatly improve your chances during a reapplication cycle.

Again, if you want to safely create your own **"Personal Post-Baccalaureate Program,"** we suggest you take your courses at a school that has *at least* *as good a reputation* as the school you attended for your undergraduate work. We know one reapplicant who took three years of community college biology courses *after* graduating from a nationally competitive university. This effort successfully brought his GPA back to where it belonged: a 3.6-plus GPA after a much worse one in his BS program. Yet admissions committees look at trends carefully. What motivated this applicant to return to the "easy" community college environment? If he needed to work on his sciences background, couldn't he have continued working at the university level? This may have hurt the success of his second application.

Nursing Programs

Medical schools are very interested in students who are serious about medicine. Perhaps nothing demonstrates that seriousness more than a student working in the field, as a **licensed nurse, paramedic, or allied health professional, for example**. Surveys have shown that nurses (BSN or MSN) with competitive college backgrounds, GPAs and MCAT scores, have a very high acceptance rate to medical school (more than **85 percent** in one study). Nurses have already learned much of the clinical foundations of the field and are clearly committed to the practice of patient care.

You can take one of two accelerated pathways to become a nurse as a medically oriented student who has finished the BS degree. The first is a **second bachelor's degree (BSN)**. These programs take two (occasionally three) years to complete, allowing you to sit for licensure as a registered nurse (RN). The second is a **direct-entry master's degree**. These are three- or four-year programs that start BS students off with RN coursework and licensure, give them some clinical experience, and graduate them with an MSN.

These programs can also train you for advancement to additional nursing credentials, such as clinical nurse specialist, certified midwife, or nurse practitioner (the last has many similarities to an MD). Programs vary widely by type and reputation, so do your homework first, and apply to a program that is at least as well-regarded as your undergraduate institution so that it is clear you are continuing to challenge yourself. A list of direct-entry programs used by U.C. Berkeley BS students can be found at: http://career.berkeley.edu/Health/NursApp.stm#direct. All of these programs prefer that you will have spent time in primary care settings beforehand so that you know what to expect when you choose a nursing credential.

Nursing is perhaps the most powerful reapplication strategy, and we know several students who have taken this pathway, usually applying to medical school during their first or second year of nursing practice. Nevertheless, we wouldn't recommend that you pursue a nursing, physician's assistant, or medical technologist degree simply to get into medical school. You should also be willing and able to pursue a career as a nurse regardless of its benefits to a medical school reapplication, and be satisfied with all the traditional nursing growth options if you do choose to go to nursing school.

RADICAL STRATEGIES

Sometimes, being a little more creative than the norm can help your candidacy. Here are admission strategies that we don't automatically recommend. We do, however, know students who have used each of them successfully.

Changing Residency to a Less Competitive State

Medical school admission difficulty varies from state to state. In some states, like **California** and **New York**, the competition for state schools is so fierce that only the top graduates will be considered at these schools. Other states, like **Texas** or **Ohio**, have a substantial number of state school choices, some of which have traditionally less competitive admissions standards. Since all public and some private state schools strongly favor in-state residents, changing your legal residency to a less competitive state, if you are willing to take that step, can give you more options and advantages in the admissions process.

To get an idea of how this strategy might help, consider a few statistics. In both Texas and California, roughly 50 percent of recent applicants matriculated (got accepted and went to medical school). But in Texas, **88 percent** of these successful applicants got into in-state schools, while only **41 percent** of California's successful applicant's got into in-state schools. Yet in both states, students overwhelmingly apply and desire entry to in-state schools.

To qualify for legal residency in a state other than the one where you currently live, you would need to **move** to that state and **work full-time for at least a year or two**, depending on residency qualification requirements (different for each state, so investigate carefully), ideally in a **medically related field**. If you have relatives, or know particular institutions that you'd love to work at in one of these other states, this could be a particularly effective strategy during your reapplication cycle.

Foreign Medical School Option

If you have already applied to U.S. medical schools for two application cycles without any luck, this might be the time to consider foreign medical programs. We generally advise our students still intent on getting into medical school to apply to some well-chosen foreign schools concurrent with their *third* application to U.S. schools. This option is best for students who are:

- Academically strong and disciplined, but perhaps a bit slow or shy

- Primary care oriented (intending to practice in a primary care field)

- Willing to initially practice in less desirable areas during residency (e.g., inner city New Jersey)

- More concerned with practicing medicine than with having status

- Willing to pay more for their medical education (depending on the foreign program), to put up with more qualifying tests and bureaucracy, and to get by with less financial aid (again, available aid depends upon the program).

Foreign schools train some very fine U.S. physicians every year. Many have become leaders in their communities and occasionally academic medicine. So-called **International Medical Gradates (IMGs)** pursue clinical and occasionally research paths, and generalist and occasionally specialist residencies. But taking the foreign school pathway will definitely limit and delay some of your choices, so be sure to research this choice carefully.

There are introductory books on this topic, but you can learn much more valuable specific information on each school, including the initial options you will have for residency practice in the United States, by simply sending away directly for the information packet for all of your schools of interest, comparing them, and then talking with U.S.-based graduates of each of these schools (ask each school for such **references**).

OLDER AND NONTRADITIONAL APPLICANTS

Although most students apply to medical school during college and start their program within the first year or two after graduation, a small percentage of students apply to medical school several years after they finish their undergraduate education. Typically these individuals go back to college to finish premed coursework or to refresh their skills before applying to medical school programs.

Unfortunately, AMCAS and application services tend to assume that most students are of traditional age, making the older student feel somewhat isolated during the process. The acceptance rate to most U.S. medical schools decreases gently at first, then faster each year after your late twenties. Only about 20 to 30 percent of applicants between the ages of 24 and 37 are admitted to medical school, much lower than the 47 percent admission rate for traditional applicants.

Some American schools welcome older applicants, and some do not. Bias against the older applicant strikes widely and randomly across the three medical tiers we have discussed, is not easily generalized, and is not something about which most U.S. medical schools will readily talk. Fortunately, many foreign medical schools do not exhibit an age bias with late-20-somethings and 30-somethings. By carefully checking the MSAS, possibly at several university career centers to get more data, you can find those U.S. schools that have accepted older applicants with your profile in recent years. You will want to look for those medical schools that will welcome the maturity, experience, and diversity that the rare older applicant can bring to an incoming class.

Older applicants will take the same steps to prepare and apply to medical school as the traditional applicant. However, you may need more time to prepare than your younger counterparts. It may take a bit longer to review your subjects before you get a top MCAT score, so allow extra time in your preparation plans. You may need to put more effort into tracking down sources for letters of recommendation. When you start planning for medical school, be realistic. Depending on your age, if the international medical graduate option is something that would work, you might consider applying concurrently to a few foreign medical schools, either on your first or second application to U.S. schools. Many foreign schools have biannual application dates as well.

SPECIAL CONSIDERATIONS FOR OLDER APPLICANTS

Why Medicine?

Older applicants come to medicine in many different ways. Some come as a result of a recent, **life-changing experience** with illness and recovery. Others discover a **latent desire** to be a doctor that wasn't obvious in earlier years, or a **new self-confidence** and ability to handle premedical coursework. Still others are looking to make a **career change** to a more prestigious, meaningful, and interesting job.

Like traditional applicants, older applicants should take time to deeply investigate medicine and examine the reasons why they want to be a physician. If you are thinking of becoming a doctor just because you feel unsatisfied with your current career or you simply want a more prestigious and lucrative job, there are many such pathways available. You should carefully consider whether the tremendous investment of time and money in the medical pathway will be worth the outcome.

If you are attracted to primary care but are not in need of the top status job in medicine, you might think about the physician's assistant, nursing, or nurse practitioner options. Each requires less training and has many benefits, such as opportunities for professional advancement, the ability to help people, and a health care focus. If you are interested in prestige or influence, there are a number of other fields, both in and out of health care, where you can make a positive difference in the world and be financially comfortable.

Lifestyle and Long-Term Goals

If you have not yet taken any of your medical school prerequisite coursework, then you are looking at a minimum of **two additional years** of academic preparation to apply to medical school, **four years** of medical school, and **three to seven years** of internship and residency training. If you want to do a fellowship at that point, that will require an additional **one to three years**. Add to that another **five to ten years** of paying off your loans and you can expect **15 to 20 years** to get to where you want to be. This can be quite daunting if you are looking at medicine for the benefits in growing and maintaining a mature practice more than for the benefits of the educational pathway itself.

Are you willing to wait that long? What else could you do with yourself in one-and-a-half to two decades of time? If you'll be able to apply by your **mid-thirties** (or even a bit later), and are willing to take the foreign school route if necessary, your age at entry is not really a factor that will prevent your ultimate success, and don't listen to anyone who tells you it is. Instead, consider carefully the true **time and cost** of medical school, including the somewhat **longer time** (with more repetitions!) it will take you to learn fundamental medical concepts and skills as an older applicant, unless you've already had a background in the profession. Also consider the somewhat higher **social costs** of taking the medical path at an older age. For students who have been out of college and working full time, it can be a big sacrifice to lose control of their life for so many years. The amount of time can be straining on relationships, especially if you are already married, or make it difficult to begin one if you are still looking for love.

An issue commonly discussed by medical students and young doctors is that they did not sufficiently consider the effects of medical school on their **personal life**. Bottom line, you are going to medical school to improve your life in the long term. How much can you cut back on your personal life without feeling isolated or miserable during the education process? Will your social and family network support the focus you need?

Academics

Older students can bring unique academic backgrounds to the class. But if you are an older applicant who did not achieve up to general admissions standards as an undergraduate, or if you have a non-science background, doing well in a formal post-baccalaureate program can be even more important. Remember also that medical schools vary in the way in which they consider post baccalaureate and graduate coursework.

Extracurricular Activities

Medical schools expect that the older applicant in particular has explored and is committed to medicine. If you have had a brief career after college that is in some way related to health care, like working in a lab doing biomedical research, or if you have been managing youth education for the American Red

Cross, you may not need to have as many extracurricular activities as the average premed. If you have not done this, again, entering a formal post-baccalaureate program and doing two years of medical extracurriculars may be your wisest choice for a reapplication strategy.

Selecting Medical School Programs

Given the varying opinions of medical schools on the age issue, you should steer your applications toward schools that have already demonstrated a tendency to accept older students. It will not only help your chances of acceptance, but you will be more likely to feel comfortable in a school that has other nontraditional students. If you are enrolled in a post-baccalaureate or extension program, check the MSAS binder at your school's pre-health office. Try to find schools that accepted older students from your school in past years.

Primary Applications and the Personal Statement

Your status as an older applicant is an important part of what you bring to the table. When you are writing your personal statement, you may wish to focus on the course of events that lead you to medicine. Explain who you are. Explain why you came to medicine later in the game and **how your unique experience will make you a better physician.**

For example, if you spent two years working as an insurance adjuster before coming back to the medical path, how can this experience help you as a physician? Do you have a passion for improving relations between physicians and insurance/oversight bodies? Have you considered volunteering for any physician advocacy groups working to reduce the insurance busywork faced by today's doctors? Each of us, depending on our background and interests, can bring unique and compelling contributions to the profession of medicine. Even if insurance (or whatever) is no longer your central passion, you may be in a unique position to use your experience to complete an important "final project" in your field of experience that has recognized value to the medical community.

CONSIDERING OTHER LIFE PATHS

Many people who are interested in health care are drawn to doctoring because it is the most publicized and venerated position in the industry. But if you are truly committed to helping others through medicine, many career paths will take you there. If you are not sure that you want to apply or reapply to medical school, take another trip through the inward spiral. Ask yourself again why you were attracted to physician training in the first place. If you are committed to **helping people through primary care work,** then a career as a nurse, a physician's assistant, a nurse practitioner, or as an allied health professional may be a great alternative path. If you see the **creative and intellectual challenge** of being a physician as a major attractor, then perhaps an advanced degree in a medically related field will be an excellent alternative path. Each of these could also be used as reapplication strategies, but you should feel comfortable and satisfied pursuing them for their own sakes.

Do you like the **business** side of things? Working in biotechnology, health administration, or in pharmaceutical sales might be perfect for you. Do you love **science and learning?** Perhaps a career in pharmaceutical research would suit you. Do you have a passion for **teaching?** Maybe you would enjoy pursuing an advanced degree and a career in primary or secondary or even college education.

If you simply want to help people, you can do so through many other career fields in education, government, law, or nonprofit careers, to name just a few. If you were attracted to the power and responsibility aspect of being a physician, you might look into jobs in management or administration. In most small and mid-sized organizations you can rise to a level with managerial responsibility similar to that of the typical physician, if that is an interest and a goal.

In short, people choose to become doctors for many reasons, not all of which are directly related to health care. If you learn in this process that you **don't really want to be a physician after all,** remember that knowing that is in and of itself a very helpful discovery. Some people don't make this discovery until well into their medical careers. Return to the inward spiral and ask yourself what you really want to do. What path will give you the greatest satisfaction on the journey?

Related Advanced Degrees

Being a physician is not the only way to have a powerful, important role in the health care industry. There are a large number of professional credentials, advanced degrees, and career fields that would be well suited to someone who is interested in health care administration, legal affairs, or other influential roles in the industry.

Students interested in health care might also consider pursuing advanced degrees in the following:

- MPH/MPP (Master's of Public Health and Public Policy)

- MBA (Also consider Tufts MBA/MD Program).

- JD (Also consider MBA/JD Programs)

- Clinical Social Worker

- Clinical Psychologist

Physician's Assistant

If you are interested in primary care medicine, you may want to consider an alternative path as a physician's assistant (PA). Developed in the 1960s as a response to the shortage of primary care physicians, PAs fill the role of primary care provider in many hospitals and clinics, doing anything from preventive medicine, patient education and physical exams, to bridging the gap between physicians and nurses in a hospital setting.

Physician's assistant programs are generally **three to four years long** and include extensive clinical rotations. They take the accreditation exam administered by the National Commission on Certification of Physician Assistants (NCCPA). After passing the exam, physician assistants receive the PA-C license and may practice medicine under the supervision of a doctor.

What a PA does depends on their training, experience, and the laws of the state in which they practice. Physician's assistants conduct physicals, diagnose and treat illnesses, order tests, counsel patients, and even assist in surgery. In 47 U.S. states, PAs are licensed to write prescriptions. About 50 percent of PAs practice in primary care medicine, meaning family and community medicine, pediatrics, internal medicine, or obstetrics and gynecology. About 20 percent work in surgery. Unlike the supply of physicians, which has stayed constant for decades, this category of health professionals has grown steadily in numbers, reputation, and prestige in recent decades.

Nurse Practitioner

Nurse practitioners and other **advanced practice nurses** (e.g., clinical nurse specialist, nurse administrator) work in a variety of primary care settings, and have a wide range of practice options. Advanced practice nurses usually hold an MSN [Master's of Science in Nursing] degree. Master's programs are open to the BSN or to an RN with an extensive amount of prerequisite coursework. There are also a number of **Master's Entry Programs in Nursing** for students who hold an undergraduate degree in an unrelated field.

After completing the MSN degree, the nurse practitioner has an increased scope of practice in the primary care setting. A variety of specialties are available, the most common being gynecology, midwifery, and family medicine. There are also many interesting specialties available, such as intensive care, oncology, infectious disease, psychiatry, pediatrics, geriatrics, and school nursing.

Nurse practitioners increasingly work on the front lines in primary care, serving as the doctor that many patients will see in lieu of a physician. Fairly or not, their job has sometimes been described as "two-thirds the responsibility, status, work hours, and salary of a physician." If that sounds more in line with your path, take a closer look at the various direct-entry nursing programs.

Allied Health

If you are interested in a **specific medical specialty**, pursuing an allied health credential is an excellent way to learn more about the field as a path towards becoming a physician, or as an end in itself. Allied health professionals can also pursue credentials in a wide range of specialties, including anesthesiologist assistant, athletic trainer, audiologist, cardiology technologist, clinical lab technician, dietician/nutritionist, diagnostic medical sonographer, dental hygienist, and many others not named here.

Pursuing an allied health or other specialized credential on a path toward becoming a physician can be a valid strategy, but it is risky, as these credentials have not been designed for that purpose. Be sure you value the credential and experience in and of itself and aren't obtaining it simply as a means to get somewhere else. Be wary also of being perceived as doing a year or two of "drifting," rather than improving your medical experience and candidacy. You don't want to wake up twelve- to twenty-four months later and realize you are farther from your goal rather than closer to it. If using the credential helps pay for school, gives you unique specialty experience, a great letter of recommendation, contacts, or other specific advantages, that is fine. But be sure to keep working toward your larger, longer-term goals, whatever they may be.

Make specific dates, put them on your calendar, write weekly in your journal about them, and tell your family and friends. Keep your momentum on your path of heart, and envision the inspiring mountains ahead, whatever they may be.

Video Assignments for Chapter 10:

Survivor M.D., Stand and Deliver, and *Days of Thunder.*

Appendix 1
Hyperlearning's *Basic Study System* for Pre-medical Students

Doctors are lifelong learners. To become a doctor, you will need to develop **superior study skills** to help you through tough premedical courses, then medical school, residency, continuing education, and recertification courses for the rest of your career.

This *Basic Study System*, used by Hyperlearning premedical students who have asked for study tips for over a decade, outlines the keys to the mindset of a lifelong learner. If you read and consider this advice, you will greatly strengthen your personal study techniques.

There are nine components to the *Basic Study System*. They are:

1. **Commitments:** Recognizing your long-term and deep motivations to learn
2. **Time Management:** Creating a regular time structure for studying
3. **Compartmentalization:** Achieving simplicity and specialization of learning through structured planning and execution of goals
4. **Rewards and Reflections:** Evaluation and positive reinforcement of learning behavior
5. **Concentration:** Improving awareness, understanding, and intake of new information
6. **Emotion:** Remaining emotionally receptive and maintaining a balanced perspective on the studying process
7. **Repetition and Cognitive Maps:** Improving retention and recall of new information
8. **Testing:** Efficiently integrating and demonstrating knowledge of learned information
9. **Mantras:** Brief instructive sayings that remind you of your commitments and attitudes, and the strategies you use to keep them

We will review each of these nine in turn. No matter how accomplished a studier you already are, our experience has shown that you will learn some new information in at least one of the areas discussed in coming pages. So consider them carefully, and ask yourself whether your premedical study engine is **firing on all nine cylinders**. If not, we hope you will be motivated to test for yourself what we advise here, adapting and adopting what works.

1. COMMITMENTS

While it may seem all too obvious, reflect for a moment on the fact that the **first key** to truly effective studying seems to be the ability to make and keep commitments, both to yourself and to others. Read biographies of your own role models. Successful people always experience "lucky breaks" to get to their place in life, but as many famous achievers have said (Vince Lombardi, Ben Hogan), "Luck is the residue of hard work." Or as Louis Pasteur put it, "Chance favors the prepared mind." Those who know what they are committed to, know which lucky breaks are worth pursuing, and which are diversions of their precious time, energy, and resources. Winners commit themselves to excellence in a specific area, honing the skills and acquiring the knowledge relevant to their specialization. Future doctors must also maintain a strong and at times single-minded commitment to their long-term goals. To be a truly good studier, whether prepping for the MCAT, writing a paper, or studying for a bio test, try to always keep your ultimate goals in mind. A good study system recognizes the value of commitments, both small and large. You must respect yourself enough to make the commitment to studying because it is primarily through effective studying that you will become a physician.

Before you can take the first step, you need to define your goals and decide how you plan to achieve them. Get out a sheet of paper and begin to write down everything that you expect from yourself. After each goal, write a sentence or two about why it is important to you and what steps it will take to reach that goal. Use your experience with the inward spiral and return to questions like these: Why do you want to be a doctor? How much time are you willing to devote to the process? What results are you working toward? What past priorities are you now giving up? Start with your commitments to your education and your future profession, then add others, such as family, relationships, and finances.

After you have defined your goals and made a commitment to pursue them, strive to **keep your commitments in mind**. What does "in mind" mean? Many cognitive scientists believe that most of our waking life is spent operating in less-than-conscious states of mind, carrying out lots of mostly unconscious behavior patterns and rituals, punctuated by only **a few minutes each day of truly conscious reflection and action**. It is in these moments that we evaluate and choose to begin or stop any path of behavior. The rest of the time we may spend mechanically "going through the motions" until a chosen process is complete. The more regularly you can draw your consciousness back to the greater picture, to **watch yourself** as you execute even your habits, the greater your resolve and the more intentional and effective your life's thoughts and actions will be.

2. TIME MANAGEMENT

How many times have you thought that there just aren't enough hours in the day? While that may be true for busy premeds, you need to learn to make the most of the time you do have. If you don't procrastinate, if you manage your schedule well, if you make the most of your studying hours, and if you are careful to keep up with your major commitments, you will have the time you need to get through each day. Though you may have to force yourself to adopt a few new habits, good time management will allow you to **spend a little to save a lot of time each day**, once you get the hang of it.

Many products and strategies are available to help you manage your time, from scheduling programs like Microsoft Outlook to wall calendars. Make use of anything you find that is fast, simple, and effective so that you will regularly consult it.

We recommend a couple of tools that are especially effective for today's student. First, we suggest a digital watch with a timer. Look for a watch that has all of the following: a countdown timer, unlimited alarms with simple message input ability, and a stopwatch. Casio's inexpensive "Data Bank" models work well in this regard. If you have an **important appointment** that you are afraid you might forget, put a reminder in your scheduling watch. As we will discuss in the next section, you can also use your watch to count down the time commitment that you make to yourself, on a daily or weekly basis.

Second, you will need a daily diary/appointment book or handheld organizer. If you choose a paper organizer, pick out one with any design that appeals to you. Just be sure that it is large enough to include a full day's activity on a page, but small enough to take with you everywhere: in your backpack, back pocket, or purse. Use your planner to keep track of every appointment you must schedule. **Don't try to schedule everything each day, but always try to schedule *something* every day** to keep your scheduling habit strong. Use the planner to block off *special* study time, as well as *special* time for relaxation and exercise. As we will discuss in the following section, study time is an important commitment that you make to yourself. You should treat it as an obligation and dutifully schedule some of it into every day.

When you get up every morning, spend a minute to consult your planner to see what you plan to accomplish that day. Before bed, spend a minute writing some **reflections** on how the day went, and another minute to plan the next day, and to check for **early appointments** in the morning. Those are **two very important minutes**, and doing them near bedtime will allow your dreaming brain to come up with creative solutions you never anticipated. Make them a daily habit.

3. COMPARTMENTALIZATION

Compartmentalization is a conceptual approach to scheduling and executing activities that will greatly improve your productivity over time. Using a compartmentalized system, you will divide your time into discrete blocks, during which you devote all your thought and energy to a specific activity. **When you are in a certain "compartment," you can and must leave behind all your thoughts or worries about the others.**

The concept is not new. In fact, you probably already have several compartments built into your life. For example, you may have a part-time job. When you are at your job, a very well-defined compartment, you do not study for biology, talk on the phone with your friends, sleep, eat, exercise, or watch

TV. (At least we hope you don't.) While you are at your job, you work until your shift is over, and you generally get a lot done. Unfortunately, most students do not give the same respect and priority to their study time. Just as you set aside all other commitments when you go to your job, so you should **compartmentalize your study time**.

How do you set up a compartmentalized study system? The following are a few simple ground rules for organizing your study time into compartments:

COUNTDOWN YOUR TIME COMMITMENT

As part of your commitment to studying, you need to determine roughly how many hours you are going to devote entirely to each activity. At the beginning of each week, set your **countdown timer** to the amount of time you have agreed to study. Each time you sit down to study, start the timer. When you finish, turn it off. If you need to get up to take a nap, break, or eat, stop the countdown. You can restart the timer when you sit back down in your chair. By the end of the week, you should have counted down all the time on the clock that you agreed to put in. You can stop using the timer as a reward for a few weeks of good performance, but go right back to it if your weekly time commitments to studying start to suffer.

When it comes to studying, you will need to make an exact hour commitment to yourself. If you are preparing for the MCAT, use the guidelines we recommend in Chapter Six to estimate the average number of hours you need to study.

KEEP YOUR SCHEDULE CONSISTENT

Pick a **regular time each week** when you will sit down and work through your study commitment. If you are preparing for the MCAT four hours per week, you may choose to work for one hour at 5:00 PM every Monday, Tuesday, Wednesday, and Thursday. Two hours every Tuesday and Thursday will be practically easier to schedule, but mentally harder to start. Either way you're going to face obstacles, so expect them. Keeping your schedule consistent will make it easier to concentrate when you sit down and easier to plan your schedule around. Remember, studying is a commitment you need to plan your life around, just like a job. Don't worry about how much you are getting done at first, **just putting in the time is an important accomplishment in itself.**

CREATE PHYSICAL COMPARTMENTS

You must, whenever feasible, have some **preferred physical spaces** where you consistently return to study. Eventually, your brain will associate learning with these places and will make you more receptive to new knowledge. Don't bring your biology textbook to bed with you; doing so will interrupt your sleep compartment. Don't do chemistry homework in the student lounge if you usually socialize there. Don't study for the MCAT at the kitchen table if others use it to eat and talk. You will not be able to concentrate, or effectively compartmentalize.

If you are studying for two major but different subjects simultaneously, see if you can create two physically distinct spaces for them. For example, if you are preparing for the MCAT while still in school, you might have two separate physical compartments for both MCAT prep and schoolwork. Ideally, you would set up two desks, preferably in different rooms. Even if your MCAT prep desk is just a little folding table in a corner somewhere, try to find a place to set it up, and respect the space by using it regularly.

Keep only materials for school or MCAT on your respective study desks, and keep them free of the clutter of other materials. If you cannot find space in your apartment, find a comfortable, unpopulated space in the **library** or a **quiet coffee shop** (bring earplugs) where you can always sit. Return to the same desk or area regularly, and bring the same type of materials.

SHUT OUT THE OUTSIDE WORLD

The time you spend at your desk is a job. Respect yourself enough to do it. Never take distractions like newspapers or other work to your study desk. Read such things in other locations, or on your breaks. Don't turn on the TV or radio, or any kind of music that distracts you. Unplug the phone.

MANAGE DISTRACTIONS

If you find your **attention drifting** away from studying while you're counting down time, relax and do your best to draw your attention back to the subject. If something is persistently bothering you, you may want to **jot it down in your diary**, let it go for now, and then try to focus again. If you cannot focus, don't beat yourself up. It is natural to daydream, plan, or worry when you feel bored. The creative, imaginative parts of your mind, your arguing, diverging mindsets don't want to all focus on the same thing, so you will need to gently train them all to do so for short, uninterrupted compartments of time. You may need to reward your wandering mind with a **very short break every hour**, or even to **meditate briefly** in order to draw your consciousness back to the task at hand.

A regular schedule will help combat a wandering mind. Eventually, when your brain realizes it *must* spend that special time each day engaged in the same activity, it will start to become interested in studying.

You may also find that as soon as you start working, you feel **sleepy or hungry**. You can bring some healthy food to your desk if you want to, but not junk food that you have to reach into the bag 100 times for, costing you 100 interruptions to your train of thought. It's much better to take occasional **food breaks** (countdown timer goes off when you stop studying). If you are sleepy, **take a nap**! Don't waste your important study time when you cannot focus. Remember that there's nothing wrong with taking one or two naps while working through a study compartment, especially if you've had a long day or are doing a lot of difficult learning. Psychology studies have even shown that **retention of information** *increases* **if it is learned just before and after sleeping.**

Four Tips for Power Naps
1) Sleep for only a **half an hour or so** (20–40 minutes).
2) Set the **alarm across the room** from where you are napping to force yourself to get up when the nap is over.
3) Loosen your clothes, kick off your shoes for circulation, and sleep with minimal covers (extra clothes are better than heavy blankets), so that you will **carry most of your heat with you** when you get up.
4) Take a **brief stroll** to wash your face and jumpstart your circulation when you wake up. You'll be refreshed and ready for at least one or two more good hours of studying.

CREATE BALANCED COMPARTMENTS

Try to imagine a schedule in which you **eat, sleep, study, work, and relax** every day. When you plan your week, don't over-schedule each day, but do try to create a few compartments for both studying and non-studying activities. For example, you should plan for eight hours of sleep per night. If you follow a standard time for it, your body will respond by dropping right to sleep and waking up a minute or two before the alarm rings in the morning. That's a natural, powerful **compartmentalized rhythm** that you can use to great effect. You may also want to make a compartment for exercise and for at least one well-balanced meal each day.

Very important advice: When you are not studying, don't dwell on your schoolwork or MCAT prep. You have already allocated plenty of time to worry about those things. When you aren't doing them, take care of yourself and have fun.

4. REWARDS AND REFLECTIONS

If you took intro psychology, you may have heard that **positive reinforcement** is usually much more effective in stimulating long-term behavior change than punishment or negative reinforcement. Giving yourself **rewards** for the work you do is essential to any successful study system.

When you have completed a study compartment, you should always do something fun right afterward, even if you still have more work that you "should be doing." (Remember, you are committed *first* to putting in the time, not reaching a certain goal amount of memorized information.) Call a friend, take a jog, bake cookies, garden, play a game, or do whatever will lift your spirits. If you have more work, only return to study *after* you have taken a good break. You should also reward yourself every time you reach smaller goals, like successfully raising your Verbal Reasoning score one point on your practice MCAT. The bigger the goal completed, the bigger the reward should be.

Everyone has his or her own sense of fun and relaxation. Think about what you like to do and allow yourself time to do it as a reward for the time you put in studying. Go out for an all-you-can-eat meal at a salad bar, take a trip to the healthy section of the grocery store, workout at the gym, nap in the sun, swim in the ocean, soak in a Jacuzzi, do a short weight-lifting session, or get a haircut. Some of the best rewards are often related to a good diet and exercise program, so they are both fun and good for you at the same time. But there are many others that are just plain fun. You may also want to reward yourself with some regular activity that's a little more daring or unusual than you would ordinarily do after your study time. How about learning a new sport with a friend?

Just as rewards are important to your studying habits, so is **reflection**. As you make your way through your premed curriculum, you should continue to set aside time to think about past mistakes and future challenges and how you want to approach them. Reconsidering how things are going every so often should be natural and enjoyable, but it is surprising how few people do it regularly.

When people fall short of their commitments, they often start beating themselves up, but don't generally take time to actually examine **why** they did not meet their commitment. When reflecting, especially on shortcomings or failures, it's easy to start rationalizing, giving yourself reasons why something happened. Don't write off you rationalizations as excuses. Instead, examine them. Are they valid? Why did you *really* blow off your biology midterm when you had all that time to study for it? What are the easy and obvious answers? What might be the hidden ones? How can you stop a repeat of this script next week?

If you notice that you are routinely falling short in a certain commitment to yourself, reflection is particularly important. Let's say you counted down one hour on your MCAT study compartment, took a break, went out to a long dinner with a friend, and never went back to finish your studying. By the time you arrive home, its bedtime and you don't have the energy to complete the 1.5 hours you still owe yourself. What should you do? Don't beat yourself up. Instead, **sit down at your desk for a few minutes, look at your books, and think seriously about why you broke your commitment.** It will only take a few minutes to consider your subconscious choices and get a **better understanding** of the weaknesses in your current approach or thinking patterns. Over time, you will create a slow, steady buildup of resolve that eventually demands control of your study behaviors. Reflection will allow you to turn yourself in to the amazing studier you know you can be.

5. CONCENTRATION

This *Basic Study System* emphasizes making and keeping time commitments to yourself, rather than reaching certain goals. If you follow the advice here, you will find that it will become easier and easier to concentrate during your study compartments. However, it is **always hard to maintain focus on a single topic**, especially when you are busy, worried, have a number of other commitments on your mind, or are feeling stressed or tired.

Generally, when people have trouble concentrating, it is for one of the following reasons. Consider each of them carefully, and ask how they play a role in your own daily study experience.

YOUR CONSCIOUSNESS IS ON A CONTINUUM

Becoming conscious was a **gradual process** that happened over the course of many months of development during your infancy. Even as a grownup, there are many, many moments in a typical day when you aren't fully conscious. During waking hours we have the *potential* for consciousness, but even then, many researchers believe we have **full, *self-reflective* consciousness for just a few minutes each day**. Sigmund Freud, for example, told subjects under hypnosis that they would feel the need to open a window in the room if he wiggled his tie. Then he would bring them out of hypnosis, instructing them to forget the hypnotic session. In later conversation, whenever he wiggled his tie they would very frequently get up to open a window. When he asked them *why* they did this, almost everyone, after a brief pause, quickly came up with a conscious rationalization for their action, such as, "I had to stretch my legs" or "I wanted some fresh air." Subsequent experiments by more modern psychologists, such as Roger Sperry's work with "split-brain" patients, have led to a model of brain function that includes a structure called the **interpreter**. It is the interpreter's function to make sense of everything that happens to the organism, and it is the interpreter in all of us that **deludes us into thinking we are acting consciously when we actually go through much of our day unconsciously reacting** to external stimuli. Ask this question: How much of your daily thought and action is based simply on **reacting** to who you meet, or what you see and hear that day, versus what you **choose** to do, both before and while events are happening all around you? Cultivate the habit of regularly noticing your state of consciousness during the day, and marking those all-too-long periods where you dropped out, went automatic, and therefore did *not* seem to be self-aware. This is an important first step toward better concentration.

ALL STATES OF CONSCIOUSNESS REQUIRE COORDINATION

How do you give your undivided attention to something you wish to learn? Psychologists tell us that the human mind has an attention span of about **90 seconds**, after which it moves on to something else. As you read this, your brain is probably occupied with about **three or four different threads of activity**, all babbling away with varying degrees of clarity.

Many scientists have suggested that our brains contain multiple, semi-independent neural networks, each operating more than one thinking sub-system or mindset in your head at any given time. Have you ever had this experience? You are watching TV. **Part** of you wants to study, **part** of you wants to eat, **part** of you wants to go outside, **part** of you wants to see what's on the next channel. You have a lot of willpower here, but no coordination of will. You are a veggie, a sessile organism.

Our minds need to veg out like this a little every day, thinking/dreaming at random and doing very little coordinated action, but when you are rested, they don't need very much of it. That's what sleeping is for, and you've already given a third of your life to that task. But the worst thing to do is to try to mix two compartments, and get rest while watching TV, in which case you will do neither well or quickly. The thing to remember is that our minds get pushed out of consciousness and into daydreaming whenever they are tired and don't want to do the difficult work of choosing a particular **direction** for our thought and behavior. The key is to stay **aware** of your conscious self throughout the day, and make frequent **decisions** according to what is best for you in the long run, based on your commitments, not based on who or what is in your face at the present moment.

For example, on Saturday night you may want to go out with your friends, even though you have a lot of work to complete by Monday morning. You can either approach this activity consciously or less-than-consciously. **Con-**

sciously, you might set some self-imposed **limit** on your party time before you go out, try to get to bed at a reasonable hour, and maybe spend a few minutes reading before you go to sleep. In the **less conscious** (or "daydream") mode, you would jump right into your party preparation routine without thinking where it fits into your larger life, and then into the party itself. It's great to be totally "in the moment" in your compartment, but if you were being introspective, you would realize when you were socially satisfied and go home. But because you aren't thinking about a bigger picture, you often end up wasting many extra hours, late at night, in an activity that no longer really interests you.

TECHNIQUES TO INCREASE CONCENTRATION

The following techniques are useful both to restore consciousness and to increase the coordination within your conscious mind. If you have trouble staying focused, prioritize activities that will help you concentrate.

Short Naps

When you start to feel tired or distracted, take a twenty- or thirty-minute nap. Remember, short naps are much more useful than any time you spend daydreaming.

Good, Regular Food

Because studying is a sedentary activity, your brain will often run out of energy before your stomach lets you know that you need to refuel. Therefore, you should keep up a regular eating schedule and try to consume foods that are high in nutrients and low in empty calories and saturated fats. Since you use your body less actively than otherwise during long periods of studying, be aware of more subtle hunger signals, and have a regular intake of small, healthy meals and *lots* of fluids, punctuated by short trips to the bathroom (good hydration really helps alertness). Don't fall into the trap of munching nacho cheese chips, gummy worms, or other empty carbo-only stuff, which often substitutes for thinking when you are at the desk (do I try to comprehend that sentence or reach for another cheese puff?). Rather than one or two very large meals, **small portions**, taken **several times a day** are another key to sustained mental performance.

Group study/group activities

Interacting with other people is a great way to keep your consciousness engaged. Though you should try to study earlier in the day, if you do have to cram until the wee hours, try to do it with a friend or study partner, who can help you stay alert, and will also keep you from staying up too late.

Take short, active breaks

Run, take a shower, wash your car, straighten up your room, wash dishes, or work on something else, just to get the circulation going again. Try to pick activities that don't take more

> **Two (of Many) Good Books on Relaxation & Meditation**
> *Meditation, Eknath Easwaran (1991).*
> *Meditation for Dummies, Stephan Bodian (1999).*

than twenty minutes (this isn't the time to organize your CD collection) unless you can leave an unfinished project until later.

Meditation

Regularly training your mind to 'be quiet' (to stop the incessant babbling of your many mindsets) for short periods can help greatly increase your focus, relaxation, and overall sense of well-being. There are several types of relaxation meditation, two of which we will discuss briefly here.

Focusing
Meditation involves drawing all your consciousness to a single, simple focal point, using that focus to gently push all other thoughts from your mind. Sit on the floor with your legs crossed or in a chair with your back straight and try it out for ten or twenty minutes whenever you find your mind seriously wandering, anxious, arguing with itself, or over-stressed. Some people focus on an object (like a candle flame) or ritual behavior (like Tai Chi) in this process, but many simply choose to focus on a mantra, a simple word or phrase that you will repeat to yourself such as *one*, *I am at peace*, or *I am letting go*. You may also choose to count slowly from one to ten. Take long, deep breaths and repeat your mantra as you inhale. As you focus on your slowly repeated mantra, gently brush all other thoughts from your mind. Don't be forceful with yourself. Just

let the thoughts go, and blank them out by gently redirecting your attention to your mantra.

Muscle Relaxation

Thoughts that will not quiet down come from mindsets that are *not* following your instructions to be quiet, and hence, at that time, they are **"not you"** because "you" want peace and quiet. Relaxation can bring these independent mindsets back into integration, so that in the future they will listen to your request to focus for long periods of time. Here is a popular relaxation technique known as **the theatre.** It also takes just twenty minutes to start having real effects:

- Set your watch alarm for twenty minutes. Find a quiet place where you can relax, but not so relaxed that you will fall asleep. A good position is sitting with your back against a wall, your legs folded, and your hands at your sides. As soon as you are seated, begin relaxing your body, from your feet on up. An easy way to do this is to tense up specific muscles, then slowly let them relax. Begin with your toes, slowly working your way up to your face (your eyes often take the longest to relax). When you've done all your muscle relaxations, keeping your eyes closed, form a mental picture of yourself walking into a darkened theatre. It is completely empty, and everything is black. Take your favorite seat in a cozy chair. Watch the drapes open, and see a blank white screen. Picture yourself climbing into the screen, and everything going blank. Whenever a thought tries to pop into your head (and many will), blot it out by focusing back on the white screen, and then climb in again, fading everything to blank. When the timer goes off, you are done.

Prayer

Spiritual life of any form, if it is part of your path, can give you deep inner serenity, strength and perspective to deal with life's challenges. If your inner reality is not easily disturbed by external reality, you'll be far more able to concentrate and get the job done, regardless of circumstances.

Concentration/alertness on test day

On test day, you need to be comfortable and alert, but not too comfortable. Wear **loose-fitting clothing**, but give the test some importance by **dressing up for it a bit**, so that just glancing at your clothes reminds you that you are taking this seriously. Don't wear sweats that you relax in at home. The important thing is to maintain a mental edge throughout the test. If you are in the excellent habit of taking your shoes off and wiggling or stamping your feet occasionally to restore circulation when you feel sleepy or tired, then you should consider wearing thicker socks, double layers of socks, or socks and sandals to the test. This arrangement leaves you free to kick off your shoes or wiggle your toes without the cold floor distracting you.

Pre-test Preparations

What should you do to prepare for test day, and what should you bring with you?

- **Drinks:** Caffeine-containing drink (such as Red Bull or other colas, a thermos of coffee, etc.)

- **Food:** *Unwrapped* pieces of energy bars (with protein are usually better) that you take into the test in an upper shirt pocket, unless food is specifically prohibited. Reach for a piece of a bar if you feel your blood sugar taking a dive or your stomach growling big-time mid-test. Some natural sugars metabolize quickly (strawberry-banana smoothies, for example) and will give you a quick boost.

- **Sleep:** If you want to sleep a few extra hours before the test to get a mental boost, don't do it the night before, but instead do it three or preferably four nights before your test day. This way you will avoid the residual sleepiness people feel the *day after* they have slept significantly longer than what they usually do.

- **Exercise:** *Very light* aerobic exercise the week of your test (breaking a sweat for a half-hour or less), followed by a quick swim or shower can increase your alertness. However, unless you have been exercising for *weeks* leading up to the test week, last-minute heavy exercise may actually *decrease* your alertness on the test, so be wary of it.

- *Extreme strategy!* **Short-term liquid diet:** Consuming only soups, juices, smoothies, water, etc. before the test is another interesting way to boost your alertness level over a two- or three-day period (try it before a practice test if you don't believe it!). Highly liquid diets are a bit like fasting because your body still feels a bit hungry even though it is getting all the nutrients it needs. Consequently your mental state will be more agitated and alert. Just be sure to use this technique no more than two or three days leading up to a test: long-term adherence to a highly liquid diet is medically unsound.

- **A quality breakfast: Food with enough protein to** keep you going through the morning (assuming the test is in the morning).

6. EMOTION (STAYING POSITIVE AND BALANCED AND AVOIDING TRAPS)

It is very difficult to maintain a positive and receptive attitude while trying to learn new and difficult information, especially if you under time constraints and stress. There are many ways in which your emotional life influences your ability to study or concentrate. Learning to recognize, acknowledge, and control your attitude is another one of our nine keys to the study process.

There are three main ways students commonly come to experience **emotionally related** study problems:
1. Trivialize the study process
2. Fall prey to fear, perfectionism, procrastination, and self-esteem problems
3. Get overly stressed and depressed

Discussion of each follows, along with some examples of the negative self-talk that can accompany the emotion. Do any of these seem familiar to you?

1. Trivializing the Study Process
"I get sick of grade-grubbing, and I don't see any immediate benefit from studying."

"What I am studying has nothing to do with real life. I doubt I will even use this information as a doctor."

"Whatever I study I seem to forget after a while. I don't see any long-term benefits to studying."

"I am wasting my life studying. I spend so much time with my nose in books that I miss out on all the other things I want to do."

These are classic sour grapes attitudes, which students often express when they are reluctant to study. However, no small critique or trivialization of the studying process can invalidate the many benefits of studying. First-of-all, studying **improves your attention span**, **concentration ability**, **memory capacity**, and **general interest in activities**, academic or otherwise. Studying focuses attention and brings the conscious mind to full speed. In that way, studying makes you more alive. Second, studying gives you a fulfilling sense of accomplishment and a feeling of mastery over your own mind. Good grades are not the only reason to study.

A need to trivialize the studying process usually stems from feelings of frustration, impotence, struggle, and stress. If you feel as though you aren't getting anywhere, you aren't likely to think that studying is a very effective use of your time, but it is. In the future, don't dwell on what you didn't do. Instead, reward yourself for every success and accomplishment, no matter how small. Don't focus on what you *should* have done by now or what other people are doing. Stay focused on what is happening right now. You just put in three hours of work, and that feels great. If you let yourself enjoy it, you'll want to do more as soon as you can.

2. Falling Prey to Fear, Perfectionism, Procrastination, and Self-Esteem Problems

"I get this totally irrational fear and anxiety as a test approaches."

"I'm a perfectionist. I can't work quickly enough because I need everything to be done well."

"I procrastinate way too much. I never feel motivated to study until the last second, when it's too late to do well."

"I sometimes have serious doubts about my own abilities to succeed."

"I am not sure if I have made the right choice of study. Maybe I am not cut out to be a doctor."

Studying is extremely difficult. Consider all the work you have to do to get through a year of biology or to prepare for the MCAT. When you really think about it, **long-term studying of a complex subject is one of the most difficult things you will ever do.** When you learn to study well, everything else will seem easy by comparison. In fact, the **strong personal qualities** that students gain from studying are the major reason that employers prefer to hire people with a college degree. In that sense, your fears are justified. What you have to do is often very hard. But that doesn't mean you can't do it.

You cannot eliminate all your fears, nor is it effective to try to ignore or repress them. Instead, try to **acknowledge and experience the emotion**. If you are feeling fear in a present situation, channel fear into action that can change the situation now. Are you worrying about your chemistry midterm? Well, pull out a book and start doing practice problems.

You can also counteract feelings of fear by recognizing the **worst-case scenario** in a situation that is worrying you, then deciding how you would deal with that situation in the (unlikely) event that the worst-case scenario occurs. Open your journal and draw three columns. Put **Fear** in column one and then write out your fear, just the way you feel it. For example: "I am afraid that I will not pass my Organic Chemistry midterm, no matter how hard I study." In the second column, write down all the **Consequences** if this fear were to be realized, such as: "I would then have to get an A on the final to do minimally well in the class. I might have to drop and take the class again. I might even fail the class." As you write these things down, think them through and don't panic. If you get only a very low pass on Organic Chemistry, would that mean that you could never get into medical school? No, it would not. Many students get into med school with below-average grades (a few Cs and even a D or F, when emergencies occur) in a few classes. Medical schools do not expect perfection. After you have a list of all the consequences, use column three, **Solutions**, to brainstorm how you will deal with the fear, and prevent or minimize the most likely unpleasant consequences. For example: "I will approach my TA or professor about extra credit work or retaking the test. I will do four to six hours of problem-solving in this class per week, between the midterm and final. I will hire a tutor if necessary. I will withdraw from Organic Chemistry. I will retake Organic Chemistry over the summer. I will take Organic Chemistry at the local junior college and rock it."

Perfectionism, procrastination and low self-esteem are fear generators that usually stem from an obsessive fear of failure. By engaging constantly, rather than very selectively, in these behaviors you are abusing yourself, making it impossible to ever satisfactorily complete the goals you have set for yourself. Even if you reach your main goal (say, an 11 on Verbal Reasoning on the MCAT or an A in Biology), you might still feel dissatisfied if minor things didn't go perfectly. Counteract your fears by honestly confronting them. Think about why you are scared, then consider all the ways you could go about making that fear less important. Consider using this affirmation:

"I care about myself enough, moment by moment, to stop procrastinating"

3. Getting Overly Stressed and Depressed

"I feel too stressed to study. I am so worried about all the things I have to do that I can't concentrate properly."

"I am completely overwhelmed by the amount of work I have to do."

"I get really sick of studying after a short while."

"I get depressed, because there's never enough time to learn anything well."

Stress is unhealthy and can make it difficult to study or absorb information. Worst of all, it drains the joy from life. Unfortunately, stress can also be **addictive**. On occasion, you may have found that stress gave you the extra kick you needed to complete a project on time or to cram for a midterm. At some point, repetitive stress can become an unwanted traveler, appearing unbidden whenever you have any project to complete, however minor. In fact, **you may start procrastinating, just to get the extra rush that stress gives you as you near a deadline**. Maybe you live with a constant feeling of anxiety, which gets in the way of your studying. You may seem to always have your nose in a book yet never get anything done, spinning your wheels as you worry about other things and wait for a crisis to motivate you again.

The Anxiety and Phobia Workbook, by Edmund Bourne, is a well-regarded resource for anyone experiencing mild to severe stress, anxiety, panic, and related depression. It offers advice on extensive relaxation techniques, diet and exercise programs, etc.

Depression, like stress, can be one of the most powerful forces that inhibit your ability to study properly. Some people also experience depression as a result of extreme stress. If you are struggling with mild depression, try implementing a **regular exercise program**. Endorphins generated during cardiovascular exercise can reliably and substantially improve your mood and focus for hours, as well as regulate all your body's stress-repairing antioxidant enzymes. Sometimes, exercise twice a day (e.g., a short run in the morning, short swim in the evening) is needed to really keep an even mood. Start off very easy (choose habit over intensity), and take a quick nap if you are sleepy afterward. Other valuable strategies include consulting friends and reading a few clinical books on depression and anxiety. If your depression or anxiety seems particularly hard to shake, see a school counselor, who can never hurt and may be quite helpful. Study the anatomy of your emotional issues, and reflect on their patterns in your life, and you can always develop healthy counterhabits to moderate their effects.

7. REPETITION AND COGNITIVE MAPS

In learning theory, retention and recall are usually considered to be two separate mental processes. **Retention** is the ability to recognize something you've seen before, or to make a "judgment of familiarity." **Recall** is the ability to remember an event or concept given only a vague or general prompt. When something is on the "tip of the tongue," it is sitting somewhere between retention and recall.

There are separate learning techniques for developing both retention and recall. When it comes to retention, one of the most important aspects is **how**

important you think the information is. Therefore, your emotion, concentration, and commitment level all play a role in your ability to retain information. Another factor that helps improve retention is **repetition**. As early as the 1870s, psychologists such as Herman Ebbinghaus found that repetition of simple information several times over the duration of your short term memory (roughly **within the last 24 hours**) increases its importance, and causes the information to transfer into long-term memory more often than when information is not repeated. But knowing you know something (retention) is only half the battle. You also have to be able to bring it up and out of your mind.

To improve recall, studies have shown that building **cognitive maps**, or **schemas** is important to help quickly access learned information. Cognitive maps create consistent relationships between various members of a set of information. Three very common types of maps are:

- **Categorical maps,** which list specific instances under a general category, concept, or label. These lists can be quite long, and may include many "subcategory" maps. Many science outlines use categorical maps to arrange data.

- **Coordinate maps,** which show a limited number of items that relate to one another in a highly specific way. A table setting, or the laws of enthalpy and entropy (represented as equation, diagram, or sample problem) are examples of coordinate structures. Any diagram or picture that represents a particular ordered thing (such as an annotated diagram of a crystal of salt), rather than a collection of unrelated things, is a kind of coordinate map.

- **Serial process maps** are a number of events that are organized as a process string, so that thinking of any one prompts you to recall the entire string. An example of a serial structure is the alphabet. Another is a short bullet point list that represents some sequence. Another is solving a homework or test problem by grinding through a series of steps. Another is a serial mnemonic (such as "Kings Play Chess On Fine Grained Sand" for taxonomy in biology) that helps you remember all the items on a list (which may be *any* type of list, category, coordinate, or serial process).

Why do we go into such detail about each map? Because **all three types of maps are highly useful for representing science information**, but the average student tends to be weak in using one or two of them. Is that true with you? If so, you can greatly improve the effectiveness of your mapmaking by looking for **category** relationships, **coordinate** relationships and **process** relationships, and by using a good mix of each in your studies.

There are two very important implications of these study techniques. First, realize that **writing and modifying your science outlines** is one of the most important creative activities you can perform in science courses. It is a powerful learning process of deciding exactly where (occasionally in multiple places) some concept will go on your "personal map." Second, understand that **actively rewriting your lecture notes within twenty-four hours** of taking them will significantly boost your learning. This is because you engage in *both* repetition and the creation of a new map within your short-term experience of the information. As you review and rewrite, you try to equally use categorizing, drawings and lists to improve your understanding of the concepts you are trying to learn.

8. TESTING THE LEARNING PROCESS

Testing provides a reality check on your learning progress. In addition, the ability to take tests and perform well on them is a learned skill, which can be particularly difficult for some people. Solving problems under timed conditions requires an **accurate and well-used cognitive map** that helps you quickly call up needed information. Test-taking also takes a certain amount of **creativity** and **intuition**, which help you choose the most feasible path to a solution.

Taking practice tests is another integral part to the study process. When it comes to MCAT prep, they are absolutely essential.

Practice Tests Help You...

Develop intuition

Intuition is gained through the accumulation of specialized knowledge over time. Test-taking intuition comes from solving large numbers of problems over time, in a specific subject area.

Hone your speed

Taking timed sample tests will develop your sense of pacing and increase your speed.

Avoid test-taking flaws

Some people who are excellent at studying have had so little experience testing that they have trouble with fundamental mental tasks, such as pacing, controlling anxiety, and maintaining concentration.

As we discussed in Chapter Six, you will need to complete as many practice tests as possible when you are preparing for the MCAT. If you struggle with test-taking in your undergraduate classes, go to your professor or TA and ask for exams from previous years. Sit down at your desk and get busy with them.

9. THE POWER OF AFFIRMATIONS OR MANTRAS

To program yourself for success, we recommend the periodic use of **affirmations** or **mantras**. The simple act of repeating carefully chosen positive statements is a powerful way to stay in touch with a vision of your own preferred future.

Affirmations are occasionally grouped into two overlapping categories: commitments (think back to the first study key) and beliefs. Your **commitments** are the descriptions both of your **current goals** and some of the **preferred methods** you try to use to work toward them. Here are some examples:

"I will ace the MCAT."

"I will visualize my medical future daily."

"I will watch no television that isn't pre-scheduled."

"I will build 'The List' of Medical Schools."

"I will live at my MCAT desk two-plus hours per day."

"After each quarter/semester, I will rethink and rewrite my commitments to myself."

"I will do small, executable projects each day—most important and urgent first."

"I will visualize to completion, complete to satisfaction."

Beliefs are important, motivating ideals and values about yourself and the world. They are statements or mindsets that you believe to be true and that you wish to remain close to. Your beliefs should help you feel **in control** of some part of your life (at the very least your attitude, and what you choose to believe) and inspire you to do better. Your master list may grow to many pages over your lifetime, but strive to keep only a few, both the **newest** and the **most powerful** ones in your mind and in front of you on a semi-regular basis. Some students' beliefs examples include:

"I respect myself enough to put time into my work."

"I value completion, not perfection."

"Errors are a sign of my humanity. As I learn, I have the right to fail."

"I should get excited, not anxious, before a performance."

After you have written out your affirmations, place them where your consciousness will be **frequently reminded** of their existence. Hang them above your computer, in the basthroom, over the coffee maker, in your car, in the front of your notebook, on a bookmark, wherever seems natural. Don't make them wordy, because they are intended to be read over and over until they are internalized.

We'll close this appendix with a few more affirmations to consider. Try any of them on for size and make your own. Any one or two of these, if internalized and regularly refreshed, might have a major positive impact on your ability to study. Such affirmations might even help you to more deeply live your life if you let them.

Think about those **special times** when you have managed to do three times your normal amount of studying in a period of time and you aren't sure why. Those times when you were **100 percent in The Zone**. Ask yourself what it was, exactly, that put you into that magical state, and turn that knowledge into an affirmation. Share your favorites with others to increase their clarity and power.

I will blow away my MCAT. I will identify and be accepted to the schools of my choice.

I am my *introspective mind*. I will learn to watch myself.

I believe our greatest limitations are the ones we place upon ourselves.

I will develop my sense of immediacy. There is no time but the present.

I should *think* of the future, but *emote* here and now.

(i.e., Think about where I am going, but keep my feelings in the present moment.)

I should let what I *say* structure what I *do*. Always.

This is my time in the sun. I will *watch* my time unfold. I will choose my actions based on my time.

(i.e., I should get in the habit [enjoy the process] of looking at my watch several times a day.)

I will set immediate goals and reap immediate rewards.

I like myself enough, moment by moment, to stop procrastinating.

A mind believes what you tell it, day by day.

Nothing is more powerful than an idea. What I can conceive and believe, I can achieve.

I will exercise, protect, and pace my energies of thought and emotion.

No one can continually resist the force of a positive individual.

When I think of a negative, I will think of all the positives that minimize or eliminate it.

Errors are a sign of my humanity. Inside each failure is a lesson in creating success.

I will make time for my mindsets but won't let them take control. I am *more* than my mindsets.

Stress must be managed in real time. I will practice "moving meditation."

Read, listen, and read again for wisdom and insight.

I will eliminate violent thoughts and inputs.

I want to succeed in my goals more than anything else in life.

Think ahead — where will I be in the next ten minutes... tomorrow... in ten years?

Video Assignments for Appendix 1:

Awakenings, Rocky, and *When We Were Kings*

APPENDIX 2
DIRECTORY OF ALLOPATHIC AND OSTEOPATHIC MEDICAL SCHOOLS IN NORTH AMERICA

ALLOPATHIC MEDICAL SCHOOLS: UNITED STATES, CANADA, PUERTO RICO

All phone numbers and addresses are for admissions offices unless otherwise indicated.

Albany Medical College
www.amc.edu/
Mail Code 34, Room MS-129
47 New Scotland Avenue
Albany, NY 12208
518-262-5521

Albert Einstein College of Medicine
of Yeshiva University
www.aecom.yu.edu/
1300 Morris Park Avenue
Bronx, NY 10461
718-430-2106

Baylor College of Medicine
http://public.bcm.tmc.edu
One Baylor Plaza
Houston, TX 77030
713-798-4842

Boston University School of
Medicine
www.bumc.bu.edu/
715 Albany Street
Boston, MA 02118
617-638-4630

Brown Medical School
http://bms.brown.edu/med/
Box G-A212, 97 Waterman Street
Providence, RI 02912-9706
401-863-2149

Case Western Reserve University
School of Medicine
http://mediswww.meds.cwru.edu
10900 Euclid Avenue
Cleveland, OH 44106-4920
216-368-3450

Columbia University College of
Physicians and Surgeons
http://cpmcnet.columbia.edu/dept/ps/
630 West 168th Street
P&S 1-416
New York, NY 10032
212-305-3595
psadmissions@columbia.edu

Cornell University Weill Medical
College
www.med.cornell.edu
445 East 69th Street, Room 104
New York, NY 10021
212-746-1067

Creighton University School of
    Medicine
http://medicine.creighton.edu/
2500 California Plaza
Omaha, NE 68178
402-280-2799
medschool@creighton.edu

Dalhousie University Faculty of
    Medicine
www.medicine.dal.ca/
CRC Building, Room C-205
5849 University Avenue
Halifax, NS
Canada B3H 4H7
902-494-1874

Dartmouth Medical School
www.dartmouth.edu/dms/
3 Rope Ferry Road
Hanover, NH 03755-1404
603-650-1505

Drexel University College of
    Medicine
www.drexel.edu/med/
2900 Queen Lane
Philadelphia, PA 19129
215-991-8202

Duke University School of Medicine
http://medschool.duke.edu/
DUMC 3710, Duke University
    Medical Center
Post Office Box 3710
Durham, NC 27710
919-684-2985

East Carolina University Brody
    School of Medicine
www.ecu.edu/med/
The Brody School of Medicine
East Carolina University
600 Moye Boulevard
Greenville, NC 27858-4354
252-744-2202

East Tennessee State University James
    H. Quillen College of Medicine
http://qcom.etsu.edu/
PO Box 70580
Johnson City, TN 37614-1708
423-439-2033

Eastern Virginia Medical School
    of the Medical College of
    Hampton Roads
www.evms.edu/
721 Fairfax Avenue
Norfolk, VA 23507-2000
757-446-5812

Emory University School of
Medicine
www.emory.edu/WHSC/MED/
med.html
Woodruff Health Sciences Center
Administration Building
1440 Clifton Road, NE, Suite 115
Atlanta, GA 30322-4510
404-727-5660

Rosalind Franklin University of
Medicine & Science
www.finchcms.edu
3333 Green Bay Road
North Chicago, IL 60064
847-578-3204

Florida State University College of
Medicine
www.med.fsu.edu/
Florida State University College of
Medicine Admissions Office
Tallahassee, FL 32306-4300
medadmissions@med.fsu.edu

George Washington University School
of Medicine and Health Sciences
www.gwumc.edu/
2300 Eye Street, N.W.
Washington, DC 20037
(school's general address)
202-994-3506

Georgetown University School of
Medicine
http://gumc.georgetown.edu
Box 571421
Washington, DC 20057-1421
202-687-1154

Harvard Medical School
www.hms.harvard.edu/
25 Shattuck Street
Boston, MA 02115-6092
617-432-1550

Howard University College of
Medicine
www.med.howard.edu/
520 W Street, N.W.
Washington, DC 20059
202-806-6279

Indiana University School of
Medicine
www.medicine.iu.edu/
Indiana University Medical Center
1120 South Drive
Fesler Hall 213
Indianapolis, IN 46202-5113
317-274-3772

Jefferson Medical College of
  Thomas Jefferson University
www.jefferson.edu/jmc/
1025 Walnut Street
Philadelphia, PA 19107-5083
215-955-6983

Johns Hopkins University
www.hopkinsmedicine.org/admissions
720 Rutland Avenue
Baltimore, MD 21205-2196
410-955-3182

Keck School of Medicine of the
  University of Southern California
www.usc.edu/schools/medicine/
1975 Zonal Avenue
KAM 100-C
Los Angeles, CA 90089-9021
323-442-2552

Laval University Faculty of Medicine
www.fmed.ulaval.ca/
Quebec City, PQ
Canada G1K 7P4
418-656-2131

Loma Linda University School of
  Medicine
www.llu.edu/llu/medicine/
Loma Linda, CA 92350
909-558-4467

Louisiana State University School
  of Medicine in New Orleans
www.medschool.lsuhsc.edu/
1901 Perdido Street, Box P3-4
New Orleans, LA 70112-1393
504-568-6262

Louisiana State University School
  of Medicine in Shreveport
www.sh.lsuhsc.edu/academics/
  admission.html
Post Office Box 33932
Shreveport, LA 71130-3932
318-675-5190

Loyola University Chicago
Stritch School of Medicine
www.meddean.luc.edu/index.cfm
2160 South First Avenue
Maywood, IL 60153
708-216-3229

Marshall University
Joan C. Edwards School of Medicine
http://musom.marshall.edu
1600 Medical Center Drive
Huntington WV, 25701
304-691-1738

Mayo Medical School
www.mayo.edu/mms
200 First Street, S.W.
Rochester, MN 55905
507-284-3671

McGill University Faculty of
    Medicine
www.med.mcgill.ca/
3655 Promenade Sir William Osler,
    Room 633
Montreal, Quebec, Canada
H3G 1Y6
514-398-3517

McMaster University School of
    Medicine
www.fhs.mcmaster.ca/
Health Sciences Centre
    (general address)
Room 1B7
1200 Main Street West
Hamilton, ON
Canada L8N 3Z5
905-525-9140
    (general phone number)

Medical College of Georgia School
    of Medicine
www.mcg.edu/SOM/Index.html
School of Medicine - AA-2040
Medical College of Georgia
Augusta, GA 30912-4760
706-721-3186

Medical College of Ohio
www.mco.edu/smed/smedmain.html
P.O. Box 10008 (general address)
Toledo, OH 43699-0008
419-383-4229
    (general phone number)

Medical College of Wisconsin
www.mcw.edu/
8701 Watertown Plank Road
Milwaukee, WI 53226
414-456-8246

Medical University of South
    Carolina College of Medicine
http://www2.musc.edu/medicine.html
96 Jonathan Lucas Street
    (general address)
P.O. Box 250617
Charleston, SC 29425
803-792-3283
    (general phone number)

Meharry Medical College School of
    Medicine
www.mmc.edu/medschool/
    Default.htm
1005 Dr. D. B. Todd, Jr. Boulevard
Nashville, TN 37208-3599
615-327-6223

Memorial University of Newfoundland
   Faculty of Medicine
www.med.mun.ca/med/
Faculty of Medicine
Memorial University of Newfoundland
Room 1751, Health Sciences Centre
St. John's, NL, Canada, A1B 3V6
709-777-6615

Mercer University School of
   Medicine
http://musm.mercer.edu/musm/
Office of Admissions
1550 College Street
Macon, GA 31207
478-301-2542

Michigan State University College
   of Human Medicine
www.chm.msu.edu/
A-239 Life Sciences Building
East Lansing, MI 48824
517-353-9620

Morehouse School of Medicine
www.msm.edu/
720 Westview Drive, S.W.
Atlanta, GA 30310
404-752-1500

Mount Sinai School of Medicine of
   New York University
www.mssm.edu/
Annenberg 5-04A, Box 1002
One Gustave L. Levy Place
New York, NY 10029-6574
212-241-6696

New York Medical College
www.nymc.edu/
Administration Building
Valhalla, NY 10595
914-594-4507

New York University School of
   Medicine
www.med.nyu.edu/
550 First Avenue
New York, NY 10016
212-263-5290

Northeastern Ohio Universities
   College of Medicine
www.neoucom.edu/
4209 State Route 44
Post Office Box 95, State Route 44
Rootstown, OH 44272-0095
330-325-6270

Northwestern University Medical School
www.nums.nwu.edu/
Morton Building 1-606
303 East Chicago Avenue
Chicago, IL 60611-3008
312-503-8206

Ohio State University College of Medicine and Public Health
www.med.ohio-state.edu/
254 Meiling Hall
370 West Ninth Avenue
Columbus, OH 43210-1238
614-292-7137

Oregon Health & Science University School of Medicine
www.ohsu.edu
3181 S.W. Sam Jackson Park Road
(general address)
Portland, OR 97239-3098
503-494-7800
(general phone number)

Pennsylvania State University College of Medicine
www.hmc.psu.edu/college/
Office of Student Affairs H060
Biomedical Research Building
Room C-1802
500 University Drive
Hershey, PA 17033
717-531-8755

Ponce School of Medicine
www.psm.edu
PO Box 7004
Ponce, PR 00732
787-840-2575 ext 2131, 2132

Queen's University Faculty of Health Sciences
http://meds.queensu.ca
Kingston, ON
Canada K7L 3N6
613-533-2542

Rush Medical College of Rush University
www.rushu.rush.edu/medcol
Suite 524-H
600 S. Paulina
Chicago, IL 60612-3832
312-942-6913

Saint Louis University School of Medicine
www.slu.edu/colleges/med/
1402 South Grand Boulevard
St. Louis, MO 63104
314-577-8205

Southern Illinois University School
of Medicine
www.siumed.edu/
801 North Rutledge
P.O. Box 19620
Springfield, IL 62794-9620
217-545-6013

Stanford University School of
Medicine
www.med.stanford.edu
251 Campus Drive, MSOB 3rd floor
Stanford, CA 94305-5404
650-723-6861

State University of New York
Downstate Medical Center
College of Medicine
www.hscbklyn.edu/
450 Clarkson Avenue, Box 97
Brooklyn, NY 11203-2098
718-270-2446

State University of New York
Upstate Medical University
www.upstate.edu
Weiskotten Hall
766 Irving Avenue
Rm 1215
Syracuse, NY 13210-2375
315-464-4570 or 800-736-2171

Stony Brook University Health
Sciences Center School of
Medicine
www.informatics.sunysb.edu/som/
Stony Brook School of Medicine
Dean's Office
Health Sciences Center Level 4
Stony Brook, NY 11794-8430
631-444-2113

Temple University School of
Medicine
www.temple.edu/medschool/
3340 N. Broad Street
SFC, Suite 305
Philadelphia, PA 19140
215-707-3656

Texas Tech University Health Sciences
Center School of Medicine
www.ttuhsc.edu/
Room 2B116
3601 4th Street, MS 6216
Lubbock, TX 79430
806-743-2297

The Texas A&M University System
Health Science Center College
of Medicine
http://medicine.tamu.edu/
Office of Student Affairs and
Admissions
159 Joe H. Reynolds Medical
Building
College Station, TX 77843-1114
979-845-7743

The University of Western Ontario
Faculty of Medicine & Dentistry
www.med.uwo.ca/
Dental Sciences Building
The University of Western Ontario
London, Ontario N6A 5C1
519-661-3744

Tufts University School of Medicine
www.tufts.edu/med/
136 Harrison Avenue
Boston, MA 02111
617-636-6571

Tulane University School of
Medicine
www.som.tulane.edu/
1430 Tulane Avenue, SL-67
New Orleans, LA 70112-2699
504-588-5187

University of Medicine and Den-
tistry of New Jersey—New
Jersey Medical School
UMDNJ—New Jersey Medical
School
185 South Orange Avenue
Newark, NJ 07103-2714
973-972-4631

University of Medicine and Dentistry of New Jersey—Robert
Wood Johnson Medical School
http://www2.umdnj.edu/rwjpweb/
675 Hoes Lane
Piscataway, NJ 08854-5635
732-235-4576

Uniformed Services University of
the Health Sciences F. Edward
Hebert School of Medicine
www.usuhs.mil/
4301 Jones Bridge Road, Room
A1041
Bethesda, MD 20814-4799
800-772-1743

Universidad Central del Caribe
School of Medicine
www.uccaribe.edu/
Call Box 60327
Bayamon, PR 00960-6032
787-798-6732

Universite de Montreal Faculty of
Medicine
http://medes3.med.umontreal.ca/
2900 boulevard Edouard-Montpetit
P.O. Box 6128, Succ. Centre-Ville
Montreal, PQ
Canada H3C 3J7
514-343-6265

Universite de Sherbrooke Faculty of
Medicine
www.usherbrooke.ca/
3001 12th Avenue North
Sherbrooke, PQ
Canada J1H 5N4
819-564-5208

University at Buffalo
(State University of New York)
School of Medicine & Biomedical
Sciences
www.wings.buffalo.edu/smbs
131 Biomedical Education Bldg.
Buffalo, NY 14214-3013
716-829-3466

University of Alabama School of
Medicine
www.uab.edu/uasom/
Medical Student Services
VH P-100
1530 3rd Avenue S
Birmingham, AL 35294-0019
205-934-2330

University of Alberta Faculty of
Medicine and Dentistry
www.med.ualberta.ca/
2-45 Medical Sciences Building
University of Alberta
Edmonton, Alberta, Canada
780-492-6350

University of Arizona College of
Medicine
www.medicine.arizona.edu/
Arizona Health Sciences Center
P.O. Box 245075
Tucson, AZ 85724-5075
520-626-6214

University of Arkansas College of
Medicine
www.uams.edu/com/
4301 West Markham Street, Slot 551
Little Rock, AR 72205
501-686-5354

University of British Columbia
Faculty of Medicine
www.med.ubc.ca/
317-2194 Health Sciences Mall
Vancouver, BC
Canada V6T 1Z3
604-822-4482

University of Calgary Faculty of
Medicine
www.med.ucalgary.ca/
G302 Health Sciences Centre
3330 Hospital Drive, N.W.
Calgary, AB
Canada T2N 4N1
403-220-4262

University of California, Davis,
School of Medicine
www-med.ucdavis.edu/
Room 126, MS1-C
One Shields Avenue
Davis, CA 95616-8661
530-752-2717

University of California, Irvine,
College of Medicine
www.com.uci.edu
Medical Education Building 802
Irvine, CA 92697-3950
949-824-5388 or 800-824-5388

University of California, Los
Angeles
David Geffen School of Medicine
www.medsch.ucla.edu/
12-105 Center for Health Sciences
Box 957035
Los Angeles, CA 90095-7035
310-825-6081

University of California, San Diego,
School of Medicine
http://medicine.ucsd.edu/
La Jolla, CA 92093
619-534-3880

University of California, San
Francisco, School of Medicine
www.som.ucsf.edu/
513 Parnassus Avenue, Room C-
200, Box 0408
San Francisco, CA 94143-0410
415-476-4044

University of Chicago Pritzker
School of Medicine
http://pritzker.bsd.uchicago.edu/
5841 South Maryland Avenue,
MC1000
Chicago, IL 60637-1470
773-834-5412

University of Cincinnati College of
Medicine
www.med.uc.edu/
P.O. Box 670555
Cincinnati, OH 45267-0555
513-558-7314

University of Colorado Health
Sciences Center School of
Medicine
www.uchsc.edu/sm/sm/offdean.htm
UCHSC 4200 East Ninth Avenue,
Box C297
Denver, CO 80262
303-315-7361

University of Connecticut School of
Medicine
www.uchc.edu/
263 Farmington Avenue
Farmington, CT 06030
860-679-4306

University of Florida College of
Medicine
www.med.ufl.edu
Box 100215
J. Hillis Miller Health Center
Gainesville, FL 32610
352-392-4569

University of Hawaii John A. Burns
School of Medicine
http://hawaiimed.hawaii.edu/
1960 East-West Road
(general address)
Honolulu, HI 96822
808-956-8300
(general phone number)

University of Illinois College of
Medicine
www.uic.edu/depts/mcam/
808 South Wood Street MC-783
Chicago, IL 60612-7302
312-996-5635

University of Iowa Roy J. and Lucille
A. Carver College of Medicine
www.medicine.uiowa.edu/
200 Medicine Administration
Building
Iowa City, IA 52242-1101
319-335-6703

University of Kansas School of
Medicine
www.kumc.edu/som/som.html
3901 Rainbow Boulevard
(general address)
Kansas City, KS 66160-7300
913-588-5200
(general phone number)

University of Kentucky College of
Medicine
www.mc.uky.edu/medicine/
800 Rose Street
MN 102 UKMC
Lexington, KY 40536-0298
859-323-6161

University of Louisville School of
Medicine
www.louisville.edu/medschool/
Abell Administration Center
323 East Chestnut Street
Louisville, KY 40202-3866
502-852-5193
or 800-334-8635 ext 5193

University of Manitoba Faculty of
Medicine
www.umanitoba.ca/faculties/
medicine/home.html
424 University Centre
Winnipeg, MB
Canada R3T 2N2
204-474-8825/8815

University of Maryland School of
Medicine
http://medschool.umaryland.edu
Bressler Research Building
655 W. Baltimore Street, 1-005
Baltimore, MD 21201
410-706-7478

University of Massachusetts
Medical School
www.umassmed.edu
55 Lake Avenue North
Worcester, MA 01655
508-856-2323

University of Miami School of
Medicine
www.med.miami.edu/
P.O. Box 016159
Miami, FL 33101
305-243-6791

University of Michigan Medical
School
www.med.umich.edu/medschool/
1301 Catherine Road
Medical Science Building I
Ann Arbor, MI 48109-0624
734-764-6317

University of Minnesota Medical
School - Twin Cities
www.med.umn.edu/
Mayo Mail Code #293
420 Delaware Street SE
Minneapolis, MN 55455
612-625-1188

University of Minnesota —Duluth
School of Medicine
http://penguin.d.umn.edu/
1035 University Drive
Duluth, MN 55812
218-726-8511
medadmis@d.umn.edu

University of Mississippi School of
Medicine
http://som.umc.edu
2500 North State Street-4505
Jackson, MS 39216
601-984-5010

University of Missouri—Columbia
School of Medicine
www.hsc.missouri.edu/~medicine/
School of Medicine
MA213-215
Columbia, MO 65212
573-882-9219

University of Missouri—Kansas
City School of Medicine
http://research.med.umkc.edu/
120 Administrative Center
5100 Rockhill Road
Kansas City, MO 64110
816-235-1111

University of Nebraska College of
Medicine
www.unmc.edu/UNCOM/
986545 Nebraska Medical Center
Omaha, NE 68198-6545
402-559-2259

University of Nevada School of
Medicine
www.unr.edu/med/
University of Nevada School of
Medicine
Pennington Medical Education
Building 357
Reno, NV 89557-0046
775-784-6063

University of New Mexico School
of Medicine
http://hsc.unm.edu/som/admissions/
Office of Admissions
The University of New Mexico
School of Medicine
Albuquerque, NM 87131-5166
505-272-4766.

University of North Carolina at
Chapel Hill School of Medicine
www.med.unc.edu/
School of Medicine, CB# 9500, Rm.
121 MacNider Bldg.
Chapel Hill, NC 27599-9500
919-962-8331

University of North Dakota School
of Medicine and Health Sciences
www.med.und.nodak.edu/
Office of Student Affairs and
Admissions
University of North Dakota
School of Medicine and Health
Sciences
P.O. Box 9037
Grand Forks, ND 58202-9037
701-777-4221

University of Oklahoma College of
Medicine
www.medicine.ouhsc.edu/
BMSB, Room 374
P.O. Box 26901
Oklahoma City, OK 73190
405-271-2331

University of Ottawa Faculty of
Medicine
www.uottawa.ca/academic/med/
451 Smyth Road, Room 2046
(general address)
Ottawa, ON
Canada K1H 8M5
613-562-5409
(general phone number)

University of Pennsylvania Health
System
www.uphs.upenn.edu/
Office of Admissions and
Financial Aid
Suite 100 Stemmler Hall
Philadelphia, PA 19104-6056
215-898-8001

University of Pittsburgh School of
Medicine
www.dean-med.pitt.edu/
University of Pittsburgh School
of Medicine
Office of Admissions and
Financial Aid
518 Scaife Hall
Pittsburgh, PA 15261
412-648-9891

University of Puerto Rico School
of Medicine
www.rcm.upr.edu/index_i.htm
Medical Sciences Campus
PO Box 365067
San Juan, PR 00936-5067
Telephone 787-758-2525
ext 5231, 5211, and 5215

University of Rochester School of
Medicine and Dentistry
www.urmc.rochester.edu/SMD/
601 Elmwood Ave, Box 601A
Rochester, NY 14642
585-275-4539

University of Saskatchewan College
of Medicine
www.usask.ca/medicine/
B103 Health Sciences Building
107 Wiggins Road
Saskatoon, SK
Canada S7N 5E5
306-966-8554

University of South Alabama
College of Medicine
www.southalabama.edu/com/
241 CSAB
Mobile, AL 36688
251-460-7176

University of South Carolina School
of Medicine
www.med.sc.edu/
School of Medicine Campus
Building 1
Columbia, SC 29208
803-733-3325

University of South Dakota School
of Medicine
www.usd.edu/med/
1400 West 22nd
Sioux Falls, SD 57105-1570
605-677-6886
usdsmsa@usd.edu

University of South Florida College
of Medicine
http://com1.med.usf.edu/med.html
12901 Bruce B. Downs Boulevard,
Box 2
Tampa, FL 33612-4799
813-974-2229

University of Southern California
School of Medicine
1975 Zonal Avenue
Los Angeles, CA 90033
213-342-2552
medadmit@hsc.usc.edu

University of Tennessee Health
Science Center College of
Medicine
www.utmem.edu
800 Madison Avenue
Memphis, TN 38163
901-448-5559

University of Texas Medical School
at San Antonio
www.uthscsa.edu/som/som_main.htm
7703 Floyd Curl Drive
San Antonio, TX 78229-3900
210-567-2665

University of Texas Southwestern
Medical Center at Dallas
Southwestern Medical School
http://www3.utsouthwestern.edu/
5323 Harry Hines Boulevard
Dallas, TX 75390
214-648-5617
admissions@utsouthwestern.edu

University of Texas Medical Branch
at Galveston
www.utmb.edu/301
University Boulevard
Galveston, TX 77555
409-771-3517

University of Texas Medical School
at Houston
www.med.uth.tmc.edu/
6431 Fannin Street
Houston, TX 77030
713-500-5116

University of Toronto Faculty of
Medicine
www.library.utoronto.ca/medicine/
1 King's College Circle
Toronto, ON
Canada M5S 1A8
416-978-2717

University of Utah School of
Medicine
www.med.utah.edu/som/
30 North 1900 East
Salt Lake City, UT 84132-2101
801-581-7498
deans.admissions@hsc.utah.edu

University of Vermont College of
Medicine
www.med.uvm.edu
E109 Given Building
Burlington, VT 05405
802-656-2154
MedAdmissions@uvm.edu

University of Virginia School of
Medicine Health System
www.med.virginia.edu/schools/
medschl.html
P.O. Box 800793-McKim Hall
Charlottesville, VA 22908
804-924-5571

University of Washington School of
Medicine
www.washington.edu/medical/som/
index.html
1959 NE Pacific
Seattle, WA 98195-6340
206-543-7212
askuwsom@u.washington.edu

University of Wisconsin Medical
School
www.medsch.wisc.edu
1300 University Avenue
Madison, WI 53706
608-262-2327

Vanderbilt University School of
Medicine
www.mc.vanderbilt.edu/medschool/
21st Avenue South at Garland Avenue
Nashville, TN 37232
615-322-2145
Medsch.Admis@mcmail.vanderbilt.edu

Virginia Commonwealth University
School of Medicine
www.medschool.vcu.edu/
P.O. Box 980565
Richmond, VA 23298-0565
804-828-1264
webmaster@www.vcu.edu

Wake Forest University School of
Medicine
www.wfubmc.edu
Medical Center Boulevard
Winston-Salem, NC 27157
336-716-4262
medadmit@wfubmc.edu

Washington University in St. Louis
School of Medicine
http://medinfo.wustl.edu/
660 South Euclid Avenue
Box 8106
St. Louis, MO 63110
314-362-6848
wumscoa@msnotes.wustl.edu

Wayne State University School of
Medicine
www.med.wayne.edu/
540 East Canfield Avenue
Detroit, MI 48201
313-577-1466
dstreet@med.wayne.edu

West Virginia University School of
Medicine
www.hsc.wvu.edu/som/
Morgantown, WV 26506
304-293-2408
medadmissions@hsc.edu

Wright State University School of
  Medicine
www.med.wright.edu/
P.O. Box 927
Dayton, OH 45401-0927
937-775-2934

Yale University School of Medicine
http://info.med.yale.edu/medical/
333 Cedar Street
P.O. Box 208055
New Haven, CT 06520-8055
203-785-2643
medicalschool.admissions
  @quickmail.yale.edu

OSTEOPATHIC MEDICAL SCHOOLS: UNITED STATES

Arizona College of Osteopathic
  Medicine
Midwestern University
www.midwestern.edu
Office of Admissions
19555 North 59th Avenue
Glendale, AZ 85308
admissaz@arizona.midwestern.edu

Chicago College of Osteopathic
  Medicine
Midwestern University
www.midwestern.edu
555 31st Street
Downers Grove IL 60515
800-458-6253

Des Moines University College of
  Osteopathic Medicine and Surgery
www.dmu.edu
3200 Grand Avenue
Des Moines IA, 50312
515-271-1578

Kirksville College of Osteopathic
  Medicine
www.kcom.edu
800 West Jefferson
Kirksville, MO 63501
660-626-2237

Lake Erie College of Osteopathic
  Medicine
www.lecom.edu
1858 West Grandview Boulevard
Erie, PA 16509
814-866-8111

Michigan State University College
  of Osteopathic Medicine
www.com.msu.edu
C110 East Fee Hall, MSUCAOM
East Lansing, MI 48824
517-353-7740
comadm@com.msu.edu

New York College of Osteopathic
  Medicine
New York Institute of Technology
www.nyit.edu/nycom
Box 179
Old Westbury, NY 11568
516-626-6947

Nova Southeastern University
http://medicine.nova.edu
3200 South University Drive
Fort Lauderdale, FL 33328
954-262-1101
com@nova.edu

Ohio University College of Osteo-
    pathic Medicine
www.oucom.ohiou.edu
102 Grosvenor Hall
Athens, OH 45701
740-593-2256
admissions@exchange.oucom.ohiou.edu

Oklahoma State University
http://osu.com.okstate.edu/index.htm
1111 West 17th Street
Tulsa, OK 74107
800-677-1972
bostb@chs.okstate.edu

Philadelphia College of Osteopathic
    Medicine
www.pcom.edu
4170 City Avenue
Philadephia, PA 19131
800-999-6998
admissions@pcom.edu

Pikeville College School of Osteo-
    pathic Medicine
http://pcsom.pc.edu/
147 Sycamore Street
Pikesville, KY 41501
606-432-9617

Touro University—California
    College of Osteopathic Medicine
www.tucom.edu
Dr. Donald Haight,
    Director of Admissions
Mare Island, CA 94952
888-880-7336

The University of Health Sciences
    College of Osteopathic Medicine
www.uhs.edu
1750 Independence Ave
Kansas City, MO 64106-1453
816-283-2000
admissions@uhs.edu

University of Medicine and Den-
    tistry of New Jersey School of
    Osteopathic Medicine
http://som.umdnj.edu/index.htm
One Medical Center Drive, Suite 162
Stratford, NJ 08084
856-566-7050
somadm@umdnj.edu

University of New England College
    of Osteopathic Medicine
www.une.edu/com
UNECOM
Hills Beach Road
Biddeford, ME 04005
207-283-0171
admissions@mailbox.une.edu

University of North Texas Health
Science Center
www.hsc.unt.edu/
Texas College of Osteopathic
Medicine
3500 Camp Bowie Blvd.
Fort Worth, TX 76107-2699
817-735-2204
studaffr@hsc.unt.edu

Virginia College of Osteopathic
Medicine
2265 Kraft Drive
Blacksburg, VA 24060
540-231-4000
admisswions@vcom.vt.edu

West Virginia School of Osteopathic Medicine
www.wvsom.edu
400 North Lee Street
Lewisburg, WV 24901
800-356-7836
admissions@wvcom.edu

Western University of Health
Sciences
www.westernu.edu
College of Osteopathic Medicine of
the Pacific
College Plaza
Pomona, CA 91766-1889
909-623-6116

Video Assignments for Appendix 2:

Patch Adams, *Rudy*, and *Remember the Titans*

APPENDIX 3
MEDICALLY RELATED
SUMMER OPPORTUNITIES

SUMMER OPPORTUNITIES BY REGION

EASTERN STATES

Albert Einstein College of Medicine of Yeshiva University

Minority Undergraduate Student Summer Research Opportunity Program (MSSROP)

Nilda I. Soto, Assistant Dean
Minority Student Summer Research Opportunity Program
Office of Minority Student Affairs
Albert Einstein College of Medicine
1300 Morris Park Avenue—Belfer 205
Bronx, NY 10461
718-430-3091
Email: soto@aecom.yu.edu

Albert Einstein College of Medicine of Yeshiva University

Summer Undergraduate Research Program (SURP)

Participants spend nine weeks in a laboratory at the Albert Einstein College of Medicine. Each student works under the direct supervision of a faculty member on an original research project. In addition, students participate in a series of special seminars and research lectures.

Summer Undergraduate Research Program
Sue Golding Graduate Division
Albert Einstein College of Medicine
Jack and Pearl Resnick Campus
1300 Morris Park Avenue, Room 201 Belfer
Bronx, NY 10461
718-430-2345
Website: www.aecom.yu.edu/sggd

Albert Einstein College of Medicine of Yeshiva University

Hispanic Center of Excellence
Summer Undergraduate Mentorship Program
Dr. Marlene Rivera, Coordinator
Summer Undergraduate Mentorship Program
Hispanic Center of Excellence
Albert Einstein College of Medicine of Yeshiva University
Jack and Pearl Resnick Campus
1300 Morris Park Avenue, Mazer Building, Room 219
Bronx, NY 10461
718-991-0605 ext. 260 or Jessie Vega at 718-430-2792

American Society for Microbiology

ASM/AAAS Mass Media Science and Engineering Fellows Program

The program is designed to strengthen the relationship between science and technology and the media.

AAAS Mass Media Science and Engineering Fellows Program
1200 New York Avenue, NW
Washington, DC 20005
202-326-6760
Email: cpatterson@asmusa.org
Website: www.asmusa.org/pcsrc/medfel.htm

Bellevue Hospital Center

Project Health Care (PHC)

The program, centered around the Department of Emergency, exposes students to a variety of experiences and knowledge about careers in health care.

Ms. Priscilla A. Daniels, Director
Department of Volunteer Services
Bellevue Hospital Center
First Avenue and 27th Street, Rm A-25
New York, NY 10016
212-562-4858

Brookhaven National Laboratory

Science Undergraduate Laboratory Internships (SULI)
Cathy Osiecki / Mel Morris
Science Education Center, Bldg. 438
Brookhaven National Laboratory
PO Box 5000, Upton, NY 11973-5000
Email: cathyo@bnl.gov; mmorris@bnl.gov
Website: www.bnl.gov/scied/programs/suli

Bridgeport Hospital

Yale University School of Medicine and Fairfield University
Research Associates Program
Department of Emergency Medicine
Bridgeport Hospital
267 Grant Street
Bridgeport, CT 06610
203-384-4610
Email: cra@raprogram.com
Website: www.raprogram.com/

Burdette Tomlin Memorial Hospital

Pre-Medical Orientation at the Shore
Ruth E. Particelli, Director
Volunteer Services Department
Burdette Tomlin Memorial Hospital
2 Stone Harbor Boulevard
Cape May Court House, NJ 08210
609-463-2367

Carnegie Mellon University

Research Internship in Clinical Psychology
Dr. Lynn Friedman, Director of Research Internship in Clinical Psychology
Warner Hall 108
Carnegie Mellon University
5000 Forbes Avenue
Pittsburgh, PA 15213-3890
412-371-9801 (leave clear, detailed messages)
Email: lf0j@andrew.cmu.edu

Chinatown Health Clinic

Project AHEAD [Asian Health Education and Development]
Jennifer Lee, Project AHEAD Coordinator
Chinatown Health Clinic
125 Walker Street
New York, NY 10013
212-379-6988
Email: JLee@cbwchc.org

Columbia University College of Physicians and Surgeons

Minority Medical Education Program (MMEP)
Hilda Hutcherson, M.D.
Richele Jordan-Davis, Ed.M.
Columbia University College of Physicians & Surgeons
630 West 168 Street,
P&S Room 3-413
New York, NY 10032
212-305-4157
Email: mmep-ps@.columbia.edu

Cornell University Graduate School of Medical Sciences

The ACCESS Summer Research Program
Ms. Francoise Freyre, M.A., Assistant Dean
Joan and Sanford Weill Graduate School of Medical Sciences of Cornell
    University
445 East 69th Street
New York, NY 10021
212-746-6120
Website: www.med.cornell.edu/gradschool

Gnyha Ventures

Summer Internship Program
Amy Kaufman, Assistant Director
Greater New York Hospital Association (GNYHA)
555 West 57th Street, 15th Floor
New York, NY 10019
212-259-0730
Email: kaufman@gnyha.org
Website: www.gnyhaventures.com

Hartford Hospital

Summer Student Fellowship Program
Department of Medical Education
Hartford Hospital
80 Seymour Street
PO Box 5037
Hartford, CT 06102-5037
860-545-2536
Website: www.harthosp.org

Howard University

Summer Health Careers Advanced Enrichment Program
Dr. Georgiana Aboko-Cole
Director, Center for Preprofessional Education
Box 473, Administrative Building
Howard University
Washington, DC 20059
202-238-2363
Email: preprofessional@howard.edu

Jackson Laboratory

Summer Student Program
Educational Office
The Jackson Laboratory
600 Main Street
Bar Harbor, ME 04609-1500
207-288-6249
Email: summerstudents@jax.org
Website: www.jax.org/education/ssp.html

Massachusetts General Hospital (MGH)

MGH Summer Research Trainee Program
Rosy Sarafoudi, Program Coordinator
Multicultural Affairs Office
MGH Summer Research Trainee Program
Massachusetts General Hospital
55 Fruit Street, BUL 123
Boston, MA 02114
617-724-3832
Email: mao@partners.org
Website: www.mgh.harvard.edu/mao/srtp.html

Massachusetts Institute of Technology

Summer Research Program
MIT Summer Research Program (MSRP)
Graduate Students Office
Room 3-138
Cambridge, MA 02139-4307
617-253-9462
Email: mit-srp@mit.edu
Website: http://web.mit.edu/gso/admissions/summer.html

Mount Sinai School of Medicine

Graduate School of Biological Sciences
Summer Undergraduate Research Program (SURP)
Mount Sinai School of Medicine
Box 1022
One Gustave L. Levy Place, Box 1022
New York, NY 10029-6574
212-241-6546
Email: grads@mssm.edu
Website: www.mssm.edu/gradschool/surp/index.shtml

National Cancer Institute at Frederick

Undergraduate Intern Program & Cancer Research Training Award (CRTA)
National Cancer Institute at Frederick
PO Box B, Building 428
Frederick, MD 21702-1201
301-846-1000
Website: web.ncifcrf.gov/careers/student_programs/internships

National Institutes of Health

Summer Internship Program in Biomedical Research (SIP)
Research and Training Opportunities at NIH
National Institutes of Health
Building 7, Room 300
Bethesda, MD 20892-0760
301-469-1409
Website: www.training.nih.gov/student/internship/internship.asp

Sloan Kettering Institute

Summer Research Internship Program
Memorial Sloan Kettering Cancer Center
1275 York Avenue
New York, NY 10021
Website: www.mskcc.org/mskcc/html/10150.cfm

Smithsonian Institution

Research Training Program
Mary Sangrey
NHB MRC 166, Room W411
PO Box 37012
Smithsonian Institution
Washington, DC 20023-7012
202-357-4548
Email: sangrey.mary@nmnh.si.edu
Website: www.nmnh.si.edu/rtp/information/infointro.html

University of Connecticut

Schools of Medicine and Dental Medicine Graduate Programs
College Summer Fellowship Program
Summer Fellowship Program
University of Connecticut School of Medicine
Student Services Center
263 Farmington Avenue
Farmington, CT 06030-1905
860-679-3971
Website: medicine.uchc.edu/programs/col_fellow/index.shtml
Email: rwalsh@nso1.uchc.edu

University of Connecticut Health Center

Undergraduate Summer Research Internships for Research in the Biological
    and Biomedical Sciences
Summer Research Internships Program
University of Connecticut Health Center
Student Affairs/Student Services Center
263 Farmington Avenue, Room AG062
Farmington, CT 06030-1905
860-679-3971
Website: http://grad.uchc.edu/internships/intern_desc.html
Email: rwalsh@nso1.uchc.edu

University of Massachusetts Medical Center

Summer Enrichment Program (SEP)
Summer Enrichment Program
Office of Outreach Programs
University of Massachusetts Medical School
55 Lake Avenue North
Worcester, MA 01655-0132
877-395-3149 (toll free)
508-856-6540
Website: www.umassmed.edu/outreach/sep.cfm

University of Medicine & Dentistry of New Jersey (UMDNJ)

Neuroscience Undergraduate Summer Research Program for New Jersey
Students
Dr. Cheryl Dreyfus
Department of Neuroscience and Cell Biology
UMDNJ-Robert Wood Johnson Medical School
675 Hoes Lane, CABM, Room 339
Piscataway, New Jersey 08854-5635
732-235-5382
Email: dreyfus@cabm.rutgers.edu
Website: www2.umdnj.edu/neuroweb/summer_prog/

UMDNJ—New Jersey Medical School

Minority Medical Education Program (MMEP)
Mr. Lonnie Wright
Director, Undergraduate and Pre-Matriculated Programs
UMDNJ—New Jersey Medical School
185 South Orange Avenue, MSB, C-646
Newark, NJ 07103
973-972-3762/63
Email: wrightlo@umdnj.edu
Website: www.umdnj.edu/njmsweb/educ/OSPprgms.html

UMDNJ—Robert Wood Johnson Medical School

Summer Clinical Internship Program
Carol Terregino, M.D., Assistant Dean for Admissions
UMDNJ-RWJMS, TC118
675 Hoes Lane
Piscataway, NJ 08854
732-235-4577
Website: http://rwjms.umdnj.edu/summint04.htm

Weill Cornell Medical College

Travelers Summer Research Fellowship Program for Premedical Minority
  Students
Bruce L. Ballard, M.D., Associate Dean
Joan and Sanford I. Weill Medical College of Cornell University
445 East 69th Street, Room 110
New York, NY 10021
212-746-1057
Website: www.med.cornell.edu/travelers

Weill Cornell Medical College

Weill Cornell / Rockefeller / Sloan-Kettering
Gateways to the Laboratory Program
Weill Cornell/Rockefeller/Sloan-Kettering
Tri-Institutional MD-PhD Program
1300 York Avenue, Room D-115
New York, NY 10021-4896
888-U2-MD-PhD (toll free)
212-746-6023
Email: mdphd@med.cornell.edu
Website: www.med.cornell.edu/mdphd/summer2.html

Yale School of Medicine

Biomedical Science Training and Enrichment Program Bio (STEP)
Office of Multicultural Affairs
Yale University School of Medicine
PO Box 208036
New Haven, CT 06520-8036
203-785-7545
Email: omca@yale.edu
Website: http://info.med.yale.edu/omca/programs/biostep.htm

WESTERN STATES

Arizona Heart Foundation

Colonel Alexander W. Gentleman Cardiovascular Summer Student Program
Arizona Heart Institute Foundation
Cardiovascular Summer Student Program
2632 N 20th Street
Phoenix, AZ 85006
602-955-2200
Email: foundation@azheart.com
Website: www.azheartfoundation.org/database.asp?id=14

American Chemical Society

Undergraduate Fellowships in Nuclear Chemistry and Radiochemistry
ACS Summer Schools in Nuclear & Radiochemistry
Dr. Sue B. Clark, Director
Department of Chemistry
Washington State University
Pullman, WA   99164-4630
509-335-1411
Email: nuclear@wsu.edu
Website: www.cofc.edu/~nuclear/nukess.html

American Heart Association

Undergraduate Student Research Program
American Heart Association, Western States Affiliate
Research Department
1710 Gilbreth Road
Burlingame, CA 94010-1317
650-259-6700

Lovelace Respiratory Research Institute

Lovelace Respiratory Research Institute
Joann Griffith
2425 Ridgecrest Drive SE
Albuquerque, NM 8710
505-348-9474
Email: jgriffit@lrri.org
Website: www.lrri.org/education.html

Northern Arizona University

National Science Foundation Funded Research Experience for Under-
graduates in Neural & Behavioral Sciences
Steven Vuturo, REU Coordinator
Department of Biological Sciences
Northern Arizona University
Box 5640
Flagstaff, AZ 86011
Email: Steven.Vuturo@NAU.EDU
Website: http://jan.ucc.nau.edu/~shuster/

San Jose State University

HCOP Summer Enrichment Program
Veronica Giles, Program Coordinator
San Jose State University
330 MacQuarrie Hall
San Jose, CA 95192-0049
408-924-2911/2936
Email: VGiles@email.sjsu.edu
Website: www2.sjsu.edu/depts/hcop/services.html

Stanford University

HCOP Summer Residential Program
Stanford Summer HCOP
Kathryn Fitzgerald, Associate Director
Stanford University School of Medicine
Center of Excellence
251 Campus Drive, Suite X347
Stanford, CA 94305-5413
650-498-4003
Email: kathrynf@stanford.edu
Website: http://hcop.stanford.edu/

University of California, Berkeley

Summer Research Opportunities Program (SROP)
University of California, Berkeley
Graduate Division
316 Sproul Hall
Berkeley, CA 94720-5900
510-643-6010
Email: gop@uclink.berkeley.edu
Website: www.grad.berkeley.edu/gop/srop.shtml

University of California, Berkeley

Summer Undergraduate Program for Engineering Research at Berkeley
(SUPERB)
Beatriz Lopez-Flores
312 McLaughlin Hall, College of Engineering
Center for Underrepresented Engineering Students (CUES)
University of California, Berkeley
Berkeley, CA 94720-1702
510-642-6443
Email: cblf@coe.berkeley.edu
Website: www.coe.berkeley.edu/cues/superb

University of California, Davis

Summer NIEHS Training Program in Environmental Toxicology
Department of Environmental Toxicology
University of California, Davis
One Shields Avenue
Davis, CA 95616-8588
530-752-4521
Email: mflee@ucdavis.edu
Website: www.envtox.ucdavis.edu/niehs_summer

University of Colorado Health Sciences Center

Biomedical Sciences Program/GEMS
Sonia Flores, PhD, Director
GEMS Program
University of Colorado Health Sciences Center
Box C-304, 4200 E. Ninth Ave., Denver, CO 80262
303-315-0055
Email: Sonia.Flores@uchsc.edu
Website: www.uchsc.edu/gs/gs/

University of North Dakota School of Medicine and Health Sciences

Indians into Medicine Program (INMED)
INMED Program
University of North Dakota School of Medicine and Health Sciences
501 North Columbia Road
Grand Forks, ND 58202-9037
701-777-3037
Website: www.med.und.nodak.edu/depts/inmed/summer.htm

SOUTHERN STATES

Duke University School of Medicine

Summer Biomedical Science Institute
Minority Medical Education Program (MMEP)
Maureen D. Cullins
Duke University School of Medicine
3625 DUMC
Durham, NC 27710
866-277-3453 (toll free)
Email: mmep@mc.duke.edu

East Carolina University School of Medicine

Summer Program for Future Doctors
Mrs. Christy Lopez
Academic Support and Enrichment Center
Brody School of Medicine
2N64 Brody Medical Sciences Building
Greenville, NC 27858-4354
252-744-2500
Email: ascc@mail.ecu.edu
Website: www.ecu.edu/ascc/SummerProgram.htm

Georgia Institute of Technology

Undergraduate Summer Research
Program Director
HHMI Undergraduate Summer Research
School of Biology
Atlanta, GA 30332-0230
Email: susan.longuepee@biology.gatech.edu
Website: www.biology.gatech.edu/howard/hhfly.html

Medical College of Georgia

Student Educational Enrichment Program
Undergraduate Research Apprentice Program
Wilma A. Sykes-Brown, M.A.
Medical College of Georgia
Office of Special Academic Programs
School of Medicine Suite CB-1801
Student Educational Enrichment Programs
Augusta, GA 30912-1900
706-721-2522
Email: wsykes@mail.mcg.edu
Website: www.mcg.edu/careers/specop/Apply.htm

University of South Alabama

Undergraduate Research Programs Molecular and Cellular Pharmacology
Alma Platt
University of South Alabama
MSB 3370
Mobile, AL 36688
251-460-6497
Email: aplatt@usouthal.edu
Website: www.southalabama.edu/com/pharmacology/surf.html

University of Miami School of Medicine

Health Careers Motivation Program
Astrid K. Mack, Ph.D.
Minority Students
Health Careers Motivation Program
University of Miami School of Medicine
PO Box 016960 R 128
Miami, FL 33101
305-243-5998
Email: AMack@med.miami.edu

University of Oklahoma Health Sciences Center

Headlands Indian Health Careers Summer Academic Enrichment Program
Tom Hardy
Headlands Indian Health Careers
BSE-200
PO Box 26901
Oklahoma City, OK 73190
405-271-2250
Email: Tom-Hardy@ouhsc.edu
Website: www.headlands.ouhsc.edu

University of Texas Medical Center

Summer Undergraduate Research Program
The Graduate School of Biomedical Sciences
The University of Texas Medical Branch
301 University Blvd.
Galveston, Texas 77555-1050
409-772-2665
Email: lcteed@utmb.edu
Website: http://gsbs.utmb.edu/surp/

MIDWESTERN STATES

Argonne National Laboratory

Science Undergraduate Laboratory Internships (SULI)
Summer Research Participation (SRP) Programs
DOE Science Undergraduate Laboratory Internships Program
Division of Educational Programs
Argonne National Laboratory
Argonne, IL 60439-4845
Website: www.dep.anl.gov/p_undergrad/summer.htm
Email: Lreed@dep.anl.gov

Creighton University

Summer Research Institute for Underrepresented Students
Channing Bunch, Recruitment and Retention Coordinator
Multicultural and Community Affairs
Creighton University
2500 California Plaza
Omaha, NE 68178
877-857-2854 (toll free)
Email: minorityaffairs@creighton.edu
Website: www.creighton.edu/hsmaca/summer_research.htm

Case Western Reserve University

Summer Undergraduate Research Program (SURP)
Department of Physiology and Biophysics
SURP Coordinator
School of Medicine
Case Western Reserve University
Cleveland, OH 44106-4970
216-368-2084
Email: PHOL-INFO@case.edu
Website: http://physiology.cwru.edu/surp.html

Case Western Reserve University

Summer Program in Undergraduate Research (SPUR)
Julia Brown
Department of Biology
Case Western Reserve University
10900 Euclid Ave.
Cleveland, OH 44106-7080
216-368-3556
Email: jab12@po.cwru.edu%20
Website: www.cwru.edu/artsci/biol/hhmi/spur.htm

Case Western Reserve University

Health Careers Enhancement Program for Minorities (HCEM)
Minority Medical Education Program (MMEP)
Nivo Hanson
Assistant to the Director of the Office of Minority Programs Medicine
216-368-1914
Email: nah8@po.cwru.edu
Website: www.aamc.org/meded/minority/mmep/

Drexel University College of Medicine

Summer Undergraduate Research Fellowship
Michele Morales
Academic Coordinator
Drexel University College of Medicine
Biomedical Graduate Studies
2900 Queen Lane, Ste 239
Philadelphia, PA 19129
215-991-8571
Email: SURF@drexel.edu
Website: www.drexel.edu/med/biograd/surf.asp

Illinois Institute of Technology

Chicago Area Health and Medical Careers Program (CAHMCP)
Joan Krueger, Preceptorship Director
3424 S. State, Suite 4000
Chicago IL 60616-3793
312-567-3092
Email: krueger@iit.edu
Website: cahmcp.iit.edu/index.html

Herman B. Wells Center for Pediatric Research

Summer Research Program
702 Barnhill Drive and 1044 W. Walnut
Indianapolis, IN 46202
317-274-8900
Website: www.iupui.edu/%7Ewellsctr/wellsctrimg/int.html

Indiana University Cancer Center

Summer Research Program
Eardie Curry, PharmD, BCOP
Indiana University Cancer Center
Summer Research Program
Program Administrator
W7567A Myers Building, WHS
1001 West 10th Street
Indianapolis, IN 46202
317-613-2315 ext 318
Website: http://iucc.iu.edu/srp/

Mayo Graduate School

Summer Undergraduate Research Fellowship (SURF)
Glenda Mueller
Student Recruitment Programs Coordinator
Mayo Graduate School
200 First Street SW
Rochester, MN 55905
507-284-3862
Email: gmueller@mayo.edu
Website: www.mayo.edu/mgs/surf.html

The Metrohealth Foundation, Inc.

Edward M. Chester, M.D. Summer Scholars Program
Amy Dwyer-Shute
The MetroHealth System
Division of Neonatology
Bell Greve 2nd Floor
2500 MetroHealth Drive
Cleveland, OH 44109-1998
216-778-5637
Email: ashute@aol.com
Website: www.metrohealth.org

Ohio College of Podiatric Medicine

Pre-Professional Internship Program
Aaron Berger, Student Recruiter
The Office of Student Affairs and Admission
Ohio College of Podiatric Medicine
10515 Carnegie Avenue
Cleveland, OH 44106
800-821-6562 (toll free in Ohio)
800-238-7903 (toll free outside of Ohio)
Email: aberger@ocpm.edu
Website: www.ocpm.edu/departments/student_affairs/admissions/
    internship.asp

Ohio University College of Osteopathic Medicine

Summer Scholars Program
Ohio University College of Osteopathic Medicine
Center of Excellence for Multicultural Medicine
030 Grosvenor Hall
Athens, OH 45701
740-593-0898
Email: scotts1@ohio.edu
Website: www.oucom.ohiou.edu/COE%20Excel/COEScholars.htm

Ohio University College of Osteopathic Medicine

Summer Undergraduate Research Fellowship (SURF)
John Schriner, M.Ed.
Director of Admissions
102B Grosvenor Hall
Ohio University
College of Osteopathic Medicine
Athens, Ohio 45701
740-593-4313 or 800-345-1560
Email: Admissions@exchange.oucom.ohiou.edu%20
Website: www.oucom.ohiou.edu/surfprog.htm

Summer Research Program

Mallinckrodt Institute of Radiology, Washington University School of Medicine
Mallinckrodt Institute of Radiology
Washington University School of Medicine
510 S. Kingshighway Boulevard Campus Box 8225
St. Louis, MO 63110
314-362-4696
Email: lewisjas@mir.wustl.edu (Jason S. Lewis, Ph.D.)
    or andersoncj@mir.wustl.edu (Carolyn J. Anderson, Ph.D.)
Website: www.mir.wustl.edu/graphics/assets/media/
    Summer%20Research%20Program/APPL2004.doc

The Siteman Cancer Center

Summer Opportunities at Barnes-Jewish Hospital and Washington
University School of Medicine

The program is designed for premedical and medical students interested in
working on cancer research projects.

Theresa Waldhoff
The Alvin J. Siteman Cancer Center
Box 8100
660 S. Euclid Ave.
St. Louis, MO 63110
314-4454-8943
Email: brian.springer@wustl.edu (Brian C. Springer)
Website: www.siteman.wustl.edu/physician/prof_education/summer.shtml

Temple University School of Podiatric Medicine

Summer Internship Program (SIP)
Temple University School of Podiatric Medicine.
Office of Student Affairs
8th at Race Streets
Philadelphia, PA 19107
215-625-5451 or (800-220-FEET)
Website: podiatry.temple.edu/admissions/admissions.html#internship

University of Iowa College of Medicine

Medical Scientist Training Program
Summer Undergraduate MSTP Research Program (SUMR)
Robin Davisson, Ph.D., and Neal Weintraub, M.D.
Program Directors
The University of Iowa
1186 Medical Laboratories
Iowa City, IA 52242-1811
800-551-6787 or 319-335-8303
Email: mstp@uiowa.edu
Website: www.medicine.uiowa.edu/mstp/sumr

University of Kansas Medical Center

Health Careers Pathways Program (HCPP)
Ms. Amber Regan-Kendrick
Health Careers Pathway Program
University of Kansas Medical Center
3007 Student Center Building
3901 Rainbow Boulevard
Kansas City, Kansas 66160-7120
913-588-1236
Email: akendrick@kumc.edu
Websites: www2.kumc.edu/oced/hcpp.htm

University of Michigan School of Public Health

Department of Health Management and Policy

Health Management Summer Enrichment Program (SEP)

Dr. Richard Lichtenstein, Director or Carmen Harrison, Program Administrator

Department of Health Management and Policy

M3226 School of Public Health II

The University of Michigan

109 Observatory

Ann Arbor, MI 48109-2029

734-936-3296

Email: UM_SEP@umich.edu

Website: www.sph.umich.edu/hmp/sep_hmp.html

University of Minnesota

Life Sciences Summer Undergraduate Research Programs (LSSURP)

Summer Undergraduate Research Programs

University of Minnesota—Twin Cities

College of Biological Sciences—LSSURP

124 Snyder Hall Del Code 6174

1475 Gortner Ave.

St. Paul, MN 55108-1095

612-625-2275

Email: summer_research@cbs.umn.edu

Website: www.cbs.umn.edu/main/summer_research/

University of Cincinnati College of Medicine

Summer Premedical Enrichment Program (SPEP)
Pathways to Health Careers
University of Cincinnati College of Medicine
231 Albert Sabin Way
PO Box 670552
Cincinnati, OH 45267-0552
513-558-7212 or 513-558-7334
Email: Roberta.Handwerger@UC.edu
Website: www.med.uc.edu/admissions/summerenrich.cfm

University of Cincinnati College of Medicine

Summer Research Scholars Program formerly (MARC/MBRS)
Pathways to Health Careers
University of Cincinnati College of Medicine
231 Albert Sabin Way
PO Box 670552
Cincinnati, OH 45267-0552
513-558-7212 or 513-558-7334
Email: Roberta.Handwerger@UC.edu
Website: www.med.uc.edu/admissions/summerenrich.cfm

Washington University in St. Louis

Biomedical Research Apprenticeship Program (BiomedRAP)
Washington University
BioMedRAP-Box 8226
660 South Euclid Avenue
St. Louis, MO 63110-1093
Email: biomedrap@dbbs.wustl.edu (Taya Scott)
Website: http://biomedrap.wustl.edu/

University of Pittsburgh/Carnegie Mellon

Summer Undergraduate Program for Minority Students
University of Pittsburgh MSTP
526 Scaife Hall
3550 Terrace Street
Pittsburgh, PA 15261
412-648-2324
Email: mdphd2@medschool.pitt.edu
Website: www.mdphd.pitt.edu/sprogram_brochure.asp

University of Pittsburgh School of Medicine

Summer Premedical Academic Enrichment Program (SPAEP)
The University of Pittsburgh School of Medicine
Office of Student Affairs/Minority Programs
M-247 Scaife Hall
Pittsburgh, PA 15261
412-648-8987
Email: minorityaffairs@medschool.pitt.edu
Website: www.dean-med.pitt.edu

NATIONAL (MULTI-STATE) PROGRAMS

Association of American Medical Colleges (AAMC)

Summer Medical Education Program (SMEP)

Six-week enrichment program for talented underrepresented minority students interested in medicine. The program, located at eleven different sites, is designed to assist students by providing clinical/laboratory exposure and academic enrichment in areas such as the biological and physical sciences, strategies for solving verbal reasoning exercises, and MCAT preparation.

Website: www.aamc.org/students/considering/smep/start.htm

National Institutes of Health

Summer Internships in Biomedical Research

Labs accept students in Baltimore, Bethesda, and Frederick, MD, Research Triangle Park Raleigh/Durham, NC, Hamilton, MT, and Phoenix, AZ

Website: www.training.nih.gov/student/internship/internship.asp

Video Assignments for Appendix 3:

Beyond Rangoon, *Bull Durham*, and *The Natural*

APPENDIX 4
WEB RESOURCES

GENERAL REFERENCE & RESOURCES

Association of American Medical Colleges

www.aamc.org

The grand dame of your medical training. You will get to know her well.

The Student Doctor Network (SDN)

www.studentdoctor.net

An independent, volunteer organization, SDN seeks to provide prospective and current medical students with unbiased information about the field. Contains a chat room, medical school diaries, and financial aid advice. The site also contains an extensive interview feedback section, in which applicants rate their interview experience at different medical schools, including information such as closed or open file format, sample questions, and length of interview.

American Medical Students Association

www.amsa.org

National medical student association, focused on the needs of the medically underserved and inequities in the health care system, both nationally and internationally, as well as promoting active improvement in medical education. Since 1968, AMSA has been a fully independent student organization. Site includes membership info and news.

Stanford's MedWorld

www.med.stanford.edu/medworld/home/

Contains doctor diaries, doctor radio, and feature articles about medical research.

All Allied Health Schools

www.allalliedhealthschools.com

Browse or search for programs in all allied health fields, including and physician's assistant and pharmacy programs.

The Princeton Review

www.PrincetonReview.com

We're obviously a little biased, but we do collect a ton of data (like admissions statistics) from all American allopathic and osteopathic medical schools, and it's all searchable for free on our site.

OSTEOPATHIC MEDICINE

American Association of Colleges of Osteopathic Medicine (AACOM)

www.aacom.org

Student Osteopathic Medical Association (SOMA)

www.studentdo.com

PREMED

Med School Chat

www.medschoolchat.com

Chat with counselors and med students about medical school. Also includes essay and exam tips and medical school reviews written by students.

MEDICAL NEWS

MedConnect

www.medconnect.com

News and information about the health care industry.

CNN Health

www.cnn.com/HEALTH/

Health Hippo

http://hippo.findlaw.com/hippohome.html
FindLaw's extensive collection of policy and regulatory materials related to health care.

MEDICAL JOURNALS

British Medical Journal

www.tecc.co.uk/bmj

Journal of the American Medical Association

http://jama.ama-assn.org/

Journal of Biological Chemistry

www.jbc.org

Nature

www.nature.com

New England Journal of Medicine

www.nejm.org

Science

www.sciencemag.org

FINANCIAL AID & SCHOLARSHIPS

FAFSA [Free Application for Student Assistance]

www.fafsa.ed.gov

Official site of the FAFSA, the mandatory form for financial aid awards.

National Health Service Corps

www.bphc.hrsa.gov/nhsc

eStudentLoan

www.estudentloan.com

Get loan advice or use the Loan Finder to find a loan appropriate to your circumstance and needs.

Grad Loans

www.gradloans.com

Site contains an introduction to financial aid, grad loan information, and a loan finder. You can apply for loans online through this site.

MINORITY STUDENTS

Minorities in Medicine

www.aamc.org/students/minorities/start.htm

Student National Medical Association

www.snma.org

Association of minority medical students.

Bristol-Myers Squibb

Minority Fellowships in Academic Medicine
www.bms.com/sr/philanthropy/data/public.html

Congressional Black Caucus Foundation

Public Health Fellowships
http://cbcfinc.org/index.html

WOMEN

American Medical Women's Association

www.amwa-doc.org
Nationwide association of women physicians.

MomMD

www.mommd.com
Online community of female physicians, med students, and premeds who are mothers.

GAY AND LESBIAN STUDENTS

Gay and Lesbian Medical Association

www.glma.org

Lesbian, Gay, and Bisexual People in Medicine

www.amsa.org/adv/lgbpm/

STUDENTS WITH DISABILITIES

AbilityInfo

www.abilityinfo.com

RECAP OF YOUR VIDEO ASSIGNMENTS

FORTY-FIVE INSPIRATIONAL MOVIES TO HELP WITH YOUR PATH

Medicine is like a sport in many ways. It is both competitive and cooperative, it requires great performance and endurance, and it is a very social and humanizing enterprise. For each assignment, we have combined an inspiring medical movie with two inspiring sports movies to get you thinking about how you are walking (or running!) your own path to becoming a passionate future physician. Enjoy!

MD: The Making of a Doctor, *Breaking Away*, and *American Flyers*

Vital Signs, *Vision Quest*, and *The Karate Kid*

Lorenzo's Oil, *Hoosiers*, and *Hoop Dreams*

Gross Anatomy, *Without Limits*, and *Prefontaine*

The Doctor, *American Anthem*, and *The Princess Bride*

Ciderhouse Rules, *Youngblood*, and *Slap Shot*

ER, *Real Genius*, and *Searching for Bobby Fisher*

And the Band Played On, *Gandhi*, and *Field of Dreams*

City of Joy, *Endurance*, and *Running Brave*

Cancer Warrior, *Dead Poet's Society*, and *Chariots of Fire*

Survivor M.D., *Stand and Deliver*, and *Days of Thunder*

Awakenings, *Rocky*, and *When We Were Kings*

Patch Adams, *Rudy*, and *Remember the Titans*

Beyond Rangoon, *Bull Durham*, and *The Natural*

Philadelphia, *Victory*, and *Phorpa (the Cup)*

Video Assignments for Appendix 4:

Philadelphia, *Victory* and *Phorpa (the Cup)*

ABOUT THE AUTHORS

JOHN SMART, M.S.

Co-founder and CEO of Hyperlearning and co-creator of the Hyperlearning MCAT program, John was Hyperlearning's medical school admissions director, responsible for counseling approximately 3,000 premedical students at five University of California schools from 1990-1998. Through this program his materials, advice, and educational seminars have been widely used within the California premedical community. In 1996, he interviewed at twelve and was accepted to four U.S. medical schools (U.C.S.D., Dartmouth, U.S.C. and New York Medical College). He completed the first two years of medical school (M.S. equivalent in Human Physiology and Medicine) at U.C.S.D. School of Medicine, and is now completing an M.S. program in Future Studies at the U. of Houston. He is president of an educational nonprofit (Acceleration Studies Foundation) that helps executives better understand and manage accelerating technological change (http://accelerating.org). John continues to teach and counsel premedical students through the Princeton Review.

STEPHEN L. NELSON JR., M.D. PH.D.

Stephen obtained his Ph.D. in 1996 from University of California, Riverside, in Biomedical Sciences with emphasis on radiation-induced mutations. He subsequently earned his M.D. from University of California, San Diego in 2000, funded by the Health Professions Scholarship Program, United States Air Force. He completed his pediatrics residency in San Antonio, Texas. After working as a board certified Pediatrician in Los Angeles, he then transferred to Stanford University to undergo his child neurology fellowship. During the past ten years he has taught MCAT preparation courses for Hyperlearning and the Princeton Review as a Senior Biology Instructor, and co-authored the biology review notes for Hyperlearning's acclaimed MCAT preparation system. Many of the students he has taught and assisted are now attending medical schools throughout the country. He continues to be involved in educating premedical students through The Princeton Review. At the same time, he still works as a pediatrician, and is involved in teaching residents and medical students the art of pediatric medicine. His greatest joy comes from his children and lovely wife, Mona.

JULIE DOHERTY, PRINCETON REVIEW WRITER

Julie Doherty graduated from Stanford University in 1998 with a degree in English. She went on to work as a writer and editor for various high tech companies in San Francisco, then spent several years in Mexico. South of the border, she worked as a preschool teacher, traveled extensively, and wrote for a variety of publications on a freelance basis, including *The Best Colleges* series produced by The Princeton Review. Currently, Julie works in the radiology department of a hospital in Marin County, California. In the evenings, she studies biology and art, and continues to write in her spare time.

CRIS DORNAUS, ILLUSTRATOR

Cris is an artist and illustrator in Los Angeles, California. She has worked in many interesting fields, including comics, fantasy art, film and children's media. Cris shares her studio with a kleptomaniac white weasel and a small collection of bizarre succulent plants she calls her "Martian Garden." When she's not busy creating with pencil, pen, brush or mouse, she enjoys hiking, dancing, sushi (or any kind of good food!), live music, costume events and taking advantage of the Los Angeles Public Library's huge selection of books. Her website is www.FunkyFantaLiscious.com.

NOTES

NOTES

NOTES

NOTES

NOTES

NOTES

NOTES

More expert advice from
The Princeton Review

If you want to give yourself the best chance for getting into the medical school of your choice, we can help you get the highest test scores, make the most informed choices, and make the most of your experience once you get there. Whether you want to be an M.D., a nurse, or any other kind of health care professional, we can even help you ace the tests and make a career move that will let you use your skills and education to their best advantage.

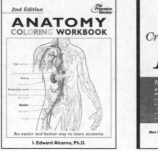

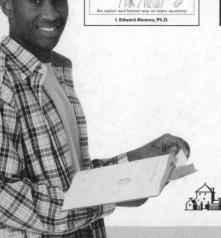

Cracking the MCAT with
Practice Questions on CD-ROM
0-375-76352-X • $59.95

Practice MCATs
0-375-76456-9 • $22.95

Best 162 Medical Schools
0-375-76420-8 • $22.95

Cracking the NCLEX-RN
7th edition
0-375-76316-3 • $25.00

Cracking the NCLEX-RN with
Sample Tests on CD-ROM
7th edition
0-375-76302-3 • $34.95
WIN/MAC compatible

Anatomy Coloring Workbook
2nd edition
0-375-76342-2 • $19.95

Biology Coloring Workbook
0-679-77884-5 • $18.00

Human Brain Coloring Workbook
0-679-77885-3 • $17.00

PhysiologyColoring Workbook
0-679-77850-0 • $18.00

Available at Bookstores Everywhere
PrincetonReview.com